THE ETERNAL ARMY

THE TERRACOTTA SOLDIERS OF THE FIRST CHINESE EMPEROR

EDITED BY
ROBERTO CIARLA

WHITE STAR PUBLISHERS

TEXT
ROBERTO CIARLA
LIONELLO LANCIOTTI
MAURIZIO SCARPARI
ALEXANDRA WETZEL

PHOTOGRAPHS
ARALDO DE LUCA

editorial project
VALERIA MANFERTO DE FABIANIS

editorial coordination
LAURA ACCOMAZZO
FEDERICA ROMAGNOLI

graphic design
PATRIZIA BALOCCO LOVISETTI

graphic layout
PATRIZIA BALOCCO LOVISETTI
PAOLA PIACCO

© 2005 White Star S.p.A.
Via Candido Sassone, 22/24
13100 Vercelli
www.whitestar.it

TRANSLATION: Timothy Stroud and Sarah Ponting

ISBN 88-544-0082-3

Reprints:
1 2 3 4 5 6   09 08 07 06 05

Printed in China
Color separation by Fotomec, Turin

❖

2 The head of this horseman is protected by a sort of cap,
which was probably made of leather.

❖

4-5 One of the functionaries of Pit K0006 still has traces
of pigment, which give his face a pinkish complexion.

❖

6-7 This front view of Chariot No. 1 shows the great attention to
detail lavished on both the chariot and the horses and their harnesses.

❖

8 The serene composure and extraordinary delicacy of the facial
features of young functionary 9 are very striking.

"Burning books and constructing buildings is the habitual task of princes; the only remarkable thing about Shih Huang Ti is the scale on which he worked."

Jorge Luis Borges

The school trip for the Spring Festival in 1975, organized by the Language Institute of Peking where I was studying Chinese, did not plan to stop at Xi'an. The city was a little off the beaten track and, after all, did not have much to offer. However, during the next five years, shortly after China opened its doors to mass tourism, Xi'an was to become the country's most visited city. In fact it was during the year of my school trip that talk began to circulate of a curious find made in March 1974 a few miles from Xi'an, close to the burial mound of the First Emperor of China. While digging a well, some peasants from the People's Commune of Yanzhai – near the small town of Lintong, the county administrative center – had unearthed a head, then an arm, then another arm, then the many fragments of the entire body of a terracotta statue. Chinese archaeologists had continued the excavation, uncovering other fragments of the arms, hands and heads of thousands of soldiers from a Terracotta Army that never seemed to end.

The Chinese archaeologists very quickly realized that this 'chance' discovery was a historic event. The discovery had taken place just one mile to the east of the burial mound of Emperor Qin Shi Huangdi, the man who in 221 BC had unified the 'Warring States' and conquered new lands, from the borders of the steppes to the northern edges of what is today Vietnam, to create a single state destined to last until modern times. If we consider that to the peoples of the West that empire has always been China, though for the inhabitants the name of the state is Zhong Guo (Middle Kingdom), the First Emperor's historical importance is clear.

The name China, which was passed to the West via India (where it appeared in several passages in Book II of the *Arthashastra* treatise, dated to ca. 150 BC) is derived directly from Qin — in another transcription Ch'in. What was surprising about the discovery was not the fact in itself. It was known that the burial mound area was surrounded by sacrificial pits, and some had even been excavated, though they were found to contain only small statues of a kneeling figure. Several aspects of the find were truly astonishing: the cyclopic size of the 'monument,' the fact that the statues were life-size, their huge number and the care taken over the details of the uniforms and faces, no two of which were alike. Also intriguing was the fortuitousness of the discovery at a particular moment in recent Chinese politics. Specifically, the last glimmers of the Cultural Revolution were dying away in a sterile political rather than philosophic debate over the centuries-old struggle between Confucianism (in 1975 considered an expression of reactionary social forces) and the philosophy of the Legalist school, and therefore Qin Shi Huangdi who had implemented it (an expression of progressive, people-based ideas). The debate masked a white-hot topical issue: in the political struggle in China at the start of the 1970s, the Confucians were the symbol of the moderates and their champion was Zhou Enlai (the Prime Minister). The Legalists, by contrast, symbolized the radicals, the 'Band of Four' and their champion, the aging Chairman Mao, then close to death. We suspect that the discovery that year was not really accidental. But that is of little importance; to the east of Xi'an, Chinese archae-

ologists had made one of the most significant discoveries in the history of the discipline, uncovering just a tiny fraction of one of the great monuments of antiquity: the Mausoleum of Qin Shi Huangdi. The discovery surprised everyone – historians, archaeologists and the public – because it was thought that everything was known about the emperor and his tomb. We were unaware, however, that he had wished to be accompanied by an army of mute soldiers. Our limited knowledge came, above all, from ancient China's greatest and most respected historian, Sima Qian. In the 2nd century BC, in his capacity as Great Historian in the archives of the Han dynasty, this scholar had written exhaustively of the First August Sovereign in his unequalled work *Shi Ji* (Historical Records). The work covered the history of China from its mythical beginnings until Sima Qian's own day. It was a generally held opinion by historians, in part resulting from the underrating of Sima Qian's information, that Qin Shi Huangdi's only merit was to have reunified China under one of the more ephemeral dynasties (it lasted just fifteen years). It was almost a dogma to assert that his only achievement was the 'reunification' but, as we shall see, reunification is the wrong term: creation or unification would be the right one, as before him China did not exist.

On the other hand, Sima Qian, who clearly stated that he had had access to the original Qin documents and who had got wind of the approach to be taken by less objective historians, said in the foreword to the 'Chronological Tables of the Six States': '... After the Qin had achieved unification, every copy of the Classic of Poetry and the Classic of History was burned throughout the

empire, together with the historical documents of the various feudal lords, all that there were, because they severely criticized Qin. The Classic of Poetry and Classic of History reappeared because copies had been hidden in the houses of the people, but the historical documents were only stored in the Zhou archives, and therefore they were all destroyed. How terrible! How terrible! All that remained are the documents of the Qin historians and these do not include the Annals, and the texts are summarized and incomplete.

'Nonetheless, there are remarkable things also in the changes of power of the Warring States. Why should we learn only from early antiquity? The seizure of power by Qin was accompanied by so much violence, yet with time Qin too was able to change and the results were great.… Scholars, influenced by what they have heard, see only that Qin held the empire for a short period and they do not analyze the beginning and end of the thing. And so they make Qin an object of ridicule and say no more. This is indeed ridiculous, like trying to eat with your ear, and truly regrettable.'

I have learned this lesson of history and will attempt to clarify the 'beginning and end of the thing,' making use of archaeological data and the inexhaustible source of information provided by Sima Qian for just this purpose, for, when bringing the foreword to the 'Chronological Tables of the Six States' to an end, he wrote, 'I hope that in the future there will be gentlemen who will read my work carefully.' That I should be considered a gentleman in the sense that Sima Qian intended would be too great an honor, but a careful reader – that yes.

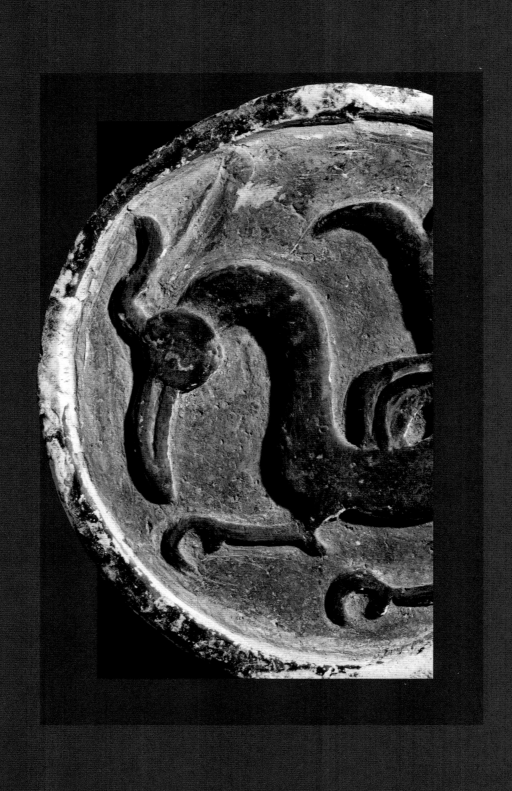

HISTORY,
PHILOSOPHY
AND LAW

INTRODUCTION

THE ANCIENT CULTURES OF CHINA

At the end of the 3rd millennium BC, eastern Asia – from the sub-Siberian regions to the sub-tropical regions of southeastern continental Asia, and from the deserts of Central Asia to the Japanese archipelagoes – appeared like a multi-colored mosaic of different cultures. In fact, the more that archaeological studies are carried out, the more these cultures appear to have been well-defined and complete in themselves. Consequently, the tiles in the mosaic were particularly numerous in the Japanese islands, southern Korea, along the Liao river valley in China, in the middle and lower valley of the Huanghe (Yellow River), and along the valleys of this river's tributaries, in particular that of the Wei and, west of that, in the river valleys of what is termed the Gansu 'Corridor.'

To the south there were also many tiles that covered the coastal regions and middle–lower valley of the Changjiang or Yangzi kiang (Blue River), the island of Taiwan, the valley of the Songkoi (Red River) in Vietnam, various coastal zones around the mouth of the Mekong River, and several areas in central and northeast Thailand. Those zones where the tiles of the mosaic are not so numerous and clearly defined represent less densely inhabited areas or zones where archaeological investigations are either just beginning or have not yet begun.

We know that in the 7th millennium BC millet and the cauliflower were cultivated as food crops in the loess regions of the Wei valley and middle Huanghe valley, and that this was accompanied by breeding sheep, pigs and fowls, while soy beans seems to have been grown in the river plains of northeast China. At least from the 6th or 5th millennium BC, rice growing was undoubtedly the principal agricultural activity of small communities in the Yangzi basin, to which was added the breeding of buffaloes, dogs and pigs. In southeastern continental Asia, at the end of the 3rd millennium BC, the practice of rice-growing had hardly begun, while on the islands of Japan cultivation techniques were only 'imported' around the 4th century BC, together with the use of metal.

We also know that along the band of grassy steppes that runs in an uninterrupted arc from northern Korea, across modern northern China to central Asia and beyond, the local late-Neolithic cultures had begun a 'reconversion' of the economy, giving way to different, mixed forms of production, probably as a result of a general climate change in the 2nd millennium BC, accompanied by less rainfall and colder temperatures. Depending on the altitude and the rainfall, these mixed economies ranged from seasonal agriculture with settled or seasonal migration livestock-breeding, to the specialized breeding of sheep, cattle and horses supported by the cultivation of a very limited number of vegetables or plants.

Archaeological data show how in the 3rd millennium BC the many cultures in the immense area described above entered into stable contact with one another and how, following expansion routes provided by the river valleys, grassy highlands and coastal plains, they created regional circuits of contact and spheres of interaction. These enabled goods, innovations and ideas to be exchanged, thus creating a general cultural and technological matrix even for groups separated by great distances. This is the case, for example, of certain types of earthenware, like the cooking pots with three legs (generically referred to as *ding*), cooking pots (*fu*), bowls on a high pedestal (*dou*), and a type of 'knife-like sickle.' This could be shaped like a trapezoid, crescent or rectangle and, when bound to the hand through holes on the back or around grooves at the sides, was used to cut the ears of the cereal crops. The common use of certain types of pots reflects common culinary customs (for example, boiling and steam cooking) and the diffusion of tools such as the knife-sickle suggest the establishment of agricultural practices based on substantially similar techniques.

❖

21 left This bottle with a painted spiral motif is a typical artifact of the Majiayao culture (ca. 3200-2000 BC), which flourished, in various stages of development, in the highlands of the modern provinces of Gansu and Qinghai. This bottle dates back to the transitional period between the Majiayao phase and the Banshan phase, around 2700 BC. (Musée Guimet, Paris)

❖

21 center Prehistoric Chinese potters discovered that a certain type of clay, (kaolin, from Chinese gaoling tu) available along the Yangzi and Yellow River valleys was suitable for modeling and firing at high temperatures. After firing, the clay assumed a whitish color, as in the case of this ewer or gui, with three conical feet that were perhaps derived from the form of an animal's udders, typical of the late period (ca. 2800-2500 BC) of the Dawenkou culture (4200-2500 BC), which flourished in the river and lake habitats of the Shandong peninsula. (Musée Guimet, Paris)

❖

21 right The two ring handles beneath the center of gravity of this pot-bellied oval jar, dating back to the Machang phase (2300-2000 BC) of the Majiayao culture, must have assisted the pouring of its contents — perhaps millet — with the aid of the anthropomorphic grip beneath the rim. The usually geometric decoration that occupies three quarters of the body of such vases, characteristic of the Majiayao culture, has led many scholars to believe that they were generally placed on the ground and thus chiefly visible from above. (Musée Guimet, Paris)

In addition, elements more closely connected to the ideological sphere seem to have been shared in several cultural areas, for instance, the use of jade for non-utilitarian tools (probably ritual or status symbols), the use of pots that represented certain forms, and zoomorphic decorative motifs in which the animal was either decomposed or deformed; this may have been to emphasize its sacred or supernatural nature. Within this framework of sociocultural processes, contacts and technological and ideological exchanges, the possible migratory movements of people across various regions of eastern Asia in the prehistoric and protohistoric times must not be underestimated. This was the case from the 3rd millennium BC with flows of peoples speaking Austronesian/Austroasiatic languages from southern China and Taiwan toward southeastern continental Asia and Indo-Pacific archipelagoes; also of peoples speaking Indo-European languages that began to penetrate the northwest of modern China, perhaps in the 3rd or 2nd millennia BC.

The area that is of major interest to us lies between the Huanghe valley to the north and the Yangzi valley to the south, and between the Sichuan basin in the west and the Pacific coastal regions to the east. This was where original elements of various cultures were exchanged, shared and amalgamated to create a 'Chinese sphere of interaction.' It was within this region that many of the cultural elements developed to form the material and ideological base from which civilization started to develop in China. Archaeological finds show how many of the groups in that area still maintained village-based social structures at the start of the 3rd millennium BC. Within these communities achievement of positions of status — as funerary rituals, above all, tend to suggest — seems to have been ephemeral, perhaps determined by the virtues or abilities demonstrated by the individual in life. It is interesting to note, however, that at the end of that millennium, some of those cultures had already developed strongly hierarchical social structures no longer based on the solidarity of the village, but on regional systems of territorial control. Within these more extensive systems political structures began to develop in which leadership rested in the hands of a particular lineage, possibly distributed between various villages. By this time the villages were defended by pressed earth walls, a technique of construction, known as *hangtu*, that was retained in classical Chinese masonry.

For example, the settlement pattern from the Longshan Culture in Shandong and Henan (ca. 3000–2000 BC) had a clear hierarchy in which groups of villages gravitated around a larger and probably dominant center. Equally, funerary models seen in the necropolis of the Taosi site (representative of a local Longshan facies in the southern part of Shanxi province) suggest the presence of three main levels of status (and wealth) that may have been related to a segmented lineage arrangement.

Graves from the Liangzhu Culture (ca. 3200–2200 BC) have been found in the lower Yangzi valley, in which the existence of strongly hierarchical social structures is clear, though, in this case, the sacred sphere carried more weight than wealth. Examination of the grave goods has revealed that 'specialists' in the sphere of the sacred, ritual or spiritual were rewarded with a position of pre-eminence, even after death. This is evidenced by the segregation in the grave-furniture of precious objects (principally jade ritual objects) that were not available to the rest of the community, even to the individuals that had produced them.

In the westernmost regions of the Chinese sphere of interaction (i.e., in the loess areas of Gansu and the Wei valley where the Qin state was to develop in the 1st millennium BC) archaeology has also revealed — though less dramatically than in the middle Huanghe and lower Yangzi valleys — the development of clear social hierarchies. In this area the break with the substitution of Neolithic economic traditions is also evident with the increasing prevalence of sheep breeding over the raising of pigs. In particular, in the Qijia Culture (ca. 2200–1600 BC) in Gansu, the production of small tools made of copper/bronze (this copper/bronze 'formula' is used when doubt exists as to the real nature of the metal, which makes a great difference in terms of technology), some made by forging, others with the use of molds, signals the break with the Neolithic traditions. Various scholars have attempted to recognize Qijia metallurgy as the bridge across which the smelting of copper alloys was transmitted from central Asia to the Huanghe valley. However, the archaeological evidence is still fragmented and controversial, and does not exclude the autonomous invention of metallurgy in the valley of the Yellow River.

❖

22 *This strangely shaped jade amulet depicts a larva with a vaguely pig-like face, which according to some scholars is associated with the symbolism of rebirth, typical of the Hongshan culture, which was centered on the Liao river valley (northwest China) between 4500 and 2900 BC and was probably the first civilization to cultivate soybeans. (Musée Guimet, Paris)*

❖

23 *This jade figure, with lobes adorned with ear disks, was probably an amulet or the depiction of a "spirit" and belongs to the late Neolithic period. (Smithsonian Institution, Freer/Sackler, Washington)*

MYTHICAL EMPERORS AND THREE DYNASTIES

This short description of the period from East Asia's prehistory until the formation of the centralized Qin Empire must concentrate on a single small area. This is the middle Huanghe valley; it lies between the Wei valley, the northwest region of modern Henan province, and the southwest region of Shanxi province. This area has always been recognized, both by historiographers and popular tradition, as the crucible of the Chinese civilization. Historiography and folklore have believed that the deeds of the mythical heroes took place here, first and foremost, the *San Huang* (The Three Noblemen); these were followed by the *Wu Di* (the Five Emperors) and the Three Wise Sovereigns: Yao, Shun and Yu. It was Yu who founded the first of the consecutive Three Dynasties (*San Dai*): Xia, Shang and Zhou. The existence of the Xia dynasty – which, according to traditional historiography, reigned between the 21st and 16th centuries BC – remains controversial, despite the enthusiasm of some experts, particularly Chinese, for their historical veracity. As things stand, there is no archaeological or textual evidence to prove their existence irrefutably.

However, the distribution of the Erlitou Culture in a small region between the southwest corner of Shanxi province and the Luo river in Henan province coincides with the region traditionally assigned to the Xia dynasty. Furthermore, the dating of the Erlitou Culture to 1900–1350 BC partially corresponds to that of the Xia. On the site of Erlitou (Yanshi county, Henan province), the many archaeological finds confirm a mature phase of development of a complex 'early state' social structure. The finds include palatial buildings and tombs that vary in their degrees of richness, status symbols made from jade, turquoise and lacquer decorated with zoomorphic motifs. The presence of a mature bronze-working tradition as demonstrated by a foundry, and a wide range of tools and ritual vessels of the *jue*, *ding* and *jia* types confirm in the same time the presence of specialized craftsman and of a sophisticated religious system. On the other hand, scholars have always been convinced that Xia, Shang and Zhou were three of many regional polities (of which the *Wan Guo*, the 'Ten Thousand Kingdoms,' referred to in the sources as belonging to the period of the mythical sovereigns, may be an echo) that followed a parallel and contemporary evolution. All of them, in the 2nd millennium BC, gained and lost dominance over one another. The fact that different polities with comparable levels of social and technological complexity co-existed with those of the Erlitou/Xia and, above all, the Shang and Zhou is of fundamental importance to understanding the development of Chinese culture. In fact, the Erlitou/Xia, Shang and Zhou were not isolated phenomena, but were part of a varied process of interaction between cultures and groups of linguistic and ethnic diversity. The last phase of this process of interaction was the cultural aggregation and political centralization carried out by the First August Sovereign of the Qin dynasty in the 3rd century BC.

The reason why there is no more than a distant echo in ancient Chinese historical texts of the political and territorial entities other than those of the Xia, Shang and Zhou is due to a concomitance of factors; the most important of these was the developed use of writing. This technique of communication and record keeping was responsible for the transmission of knowledge in all its forms and present in the middle Huanghe valley uninterruptedly from the late Shang period onwards. The first historical dynasty in China was the Shang (16 century–1045 BC). This is one of the most engaging chapters in the archaeology of east Asia and occurred in two main phases of development: the first (16th–13th centuries BC) is known as the Erligang phase, named after the site in the city of Zhengzhou (Henan province). It was a period of expansion of the Shang culture, as is confirmed by sporadic settlements found between the Central Plain and the Yangzi valley. The second phase (13th century–1045 BC) is called the Yin phase after the name of the last Shang capital near Anyang (Henan province); in this, Shang political activity seems to have been concentrated in the territory that probably corresponded to the state of Shang. This lay along the middle valley of the Yellow River between the south part of modern Hebei province and the north part of Henan province.

❖

Many scholars believe that the most ancient cultural heroes, San Huang, Wu Di and the three Wise Sovereigns, are the "personification" of technological or social innovations. Equally mythical are the oldest rulers of the first Xia, Shang and Zhou dynasties, such as Yang, of the Zi family, the legendary founder of the Shang dynasty, who lived for 100 years according to tradition (British Library, London).

During the Erligang phase, the technique of bronze casting achieved its full development. An alloy of copper, tin and lead was poured into elaborate clay molds for the manufacture of ritual vases and weapons. Control of the production cycle and, in particular, exclusive ownership of bronze products – which were charged with various symbolic and ideological meanings expressed by the form and decoration of ritual paraphernalia – became a major aspect of the manifestation of aristocratic power. It is also probable that the use of the more archaic form of 'Chinese' writing

matured during the Erligang phase but archaeological evidence of this fundamental cultural innovation currently only dates to the era of King Wu Ding of Yin around 1200 BC. Although it is of extraordinary importance, the evidence is somewhat limited, consisting of annotations written on the shoulder blades of animals and plastrons (a plastron is the lower plate of a tortoise). They related to the divinatory practices for which the bones and plastron were used. Besides providing the names and sequence of Shang kings of Yin (not very different to the one listed by the

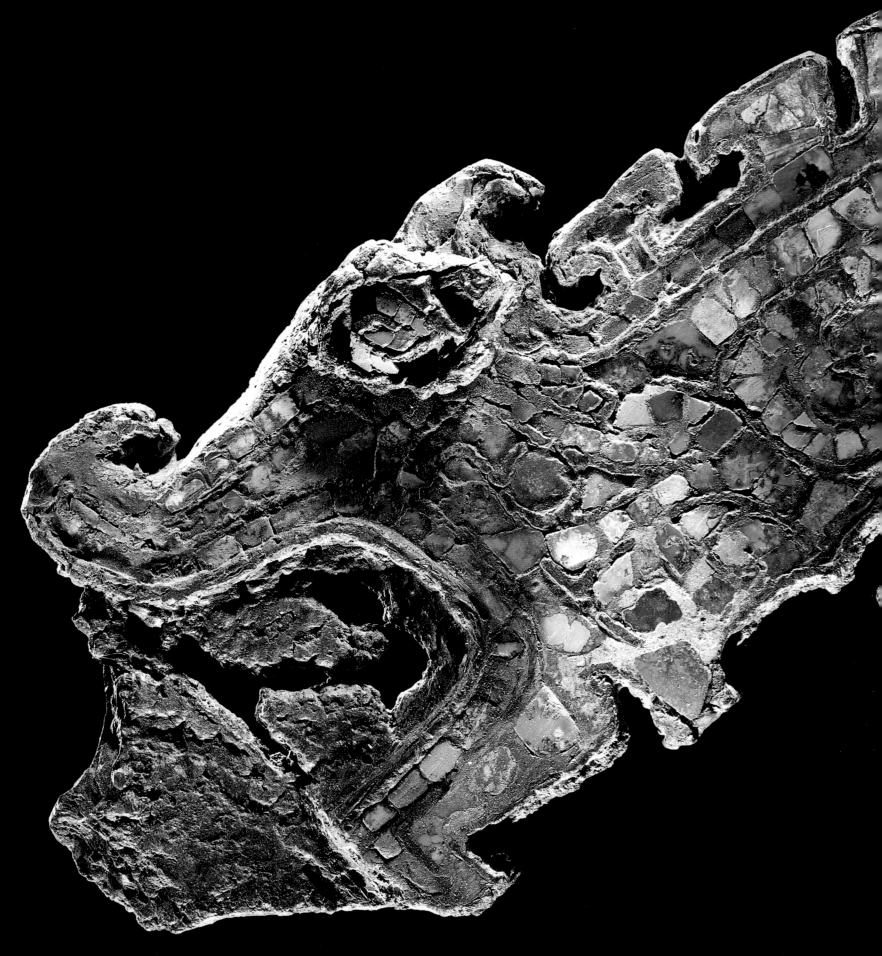

Han historian, Sima Qian, in his work *Shi Ji*), the inscriptions provide information of unique historical importance, despite their purpose and still being not completely deciphered. For example, the divinatory inscriptions report the names of peoples thought to be extraneous to the cultural world of the Shang, like the various 'barbarian' peoples Di, Rong and Qiang, and peoples closer to the Shang culture like the Zhou. The oracular inscriptions do not mention the Qin, however, though it was only a few centuries later that they aggressively pushed their way onto the stage of Chinese history.

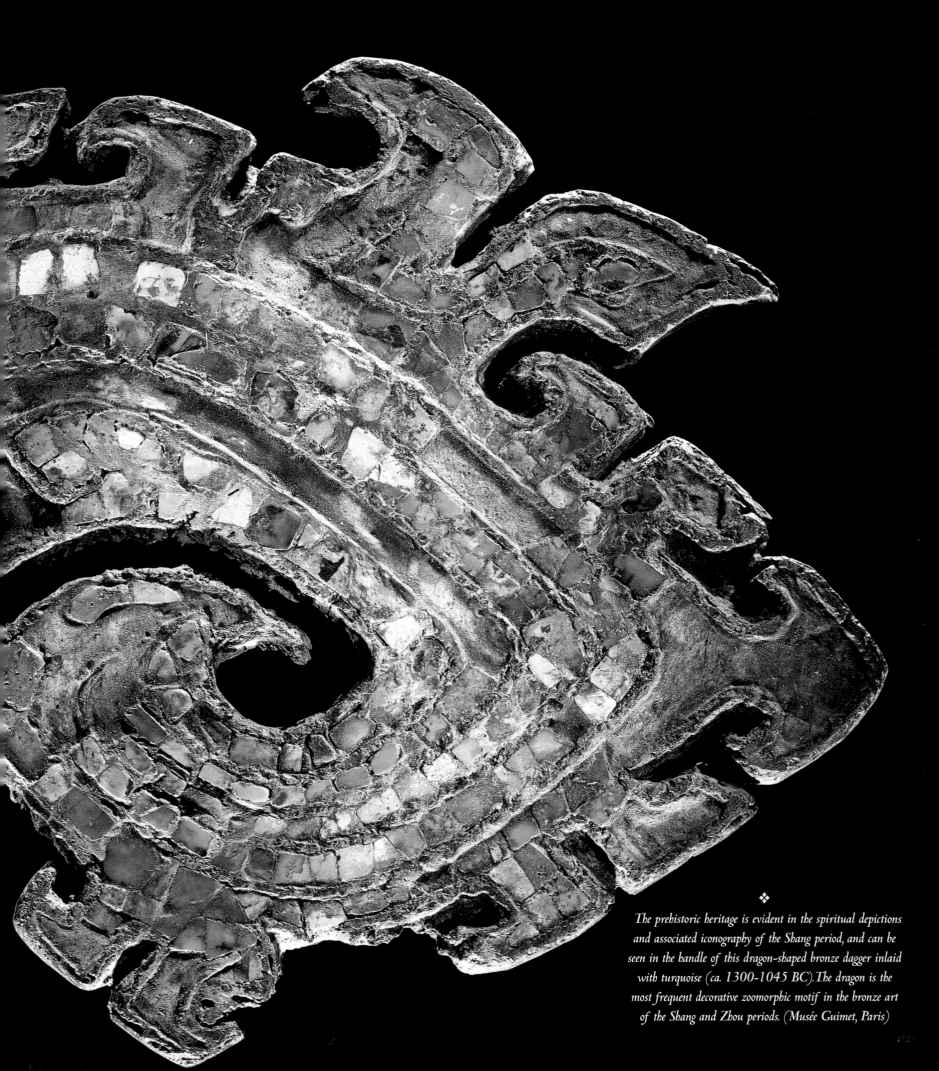

❖

The prehistoric heritage is evident in the spiritual depictions and associated iconography of the Shang period, and can be seen in the handle of this dragon-shaped bronze dagger inlaid with turquoise (ca. 1300-1045 BC). The dragon is the most frequent decorative zoomorphic motif in the bronze art of the Shang and Zhou periods. (Musée Guimet, Paris)

As far as the Zhou are concerned, they are mentioned in inscriptions of the Shang kings Wu Ding (?–1189 BC) and Zu Geng (1188–1178 BC), first as allies, then as enemies, then once again as allies. After Zu Geng, no more references to the Zhou were given. It is worth dwelling a moment on the events that led the Zhou to conquer the Shang. In fact, as we shall see, there are many similarities with the events that later took the Qin rulers to the conquest of regions to the east, south and north of their lands in the Wei valley. It is held by some that the Zhou were originally from the valley of the Fen, a left-hand tributary of the Huanghe in Shanxi province. From here, perhaps during the rule of Zu Geng, they migrated west to the Wei valley where, at the foot of Qishan (Mount Qi) on the left bank of the Wei, they dominated the flat terraces of the area later known as Zhou Yuan (Zhou Plain). Other scholars, however, believe the Zhou arrived at Qishan from a little farther north. The debate is still in progress, particularly as archaeological data have not resolved the issue. Archaeological evidence, in fact, shows that throughout the 2nd millennium BC the Wei valley was open to contact with the steppes, the Yangzi valley, the Sichuan basin and the middle Huanghe valley. This fact raises the possibility that the founders of the new dynasty emerged as leaders of a group of peoples, rather assorted from the cultural point of view, determined to conquer the Shang civilization. Though archaeology does not support fully the historical and literary tradition, it is reasonable to think that the Zhou were not originally from the Wei valley. Probably they were formed by a small group of clans (of which the

Ji was dominant) that constantly interacted with other cultural entities in their movement toward Qishan. From the Shang the Zhou acquired the knowledge of writing and bronze-working while contacts with pastoral peoples on the steppes may have underlain the origin of several types of bronze weapons and animalistic decorations. The Zhou established relationships of co-existence with the Qiang peoples from the grasslands of the northwest, and it seems that many of the consorts of the Zhou kings came from Qiang clans.

Meanwhile, the agricultural peoples of the Wei valley (the successors of the Longshan Culture of Shanxi) were slowly absorbed. Zhou culture and society were therefore assimilative by nature, as was to be the case with the Qin, and it allowed them to grow in terms of quality, quantity and territory. From their settlements on the slopes of Qishan, where in recent times temples dedicated to the cult of their ancestors have been uncovered, the Zhou extended their dominion across the entire Wei valley. This latter is a region so well defended by natural barriers that it is called Guanzhong ('inside the passes', i.e., mountain passes). From Qishan, the Zhou moved their political and ritual center to the east, where they founded the city of Feng on the left bank of the Feng river, a tributary of the Wei near modern Xi'an. Then, in 1053 BC, they made their move toward the Shang territories. They crossed the Huanghe and conquered the fortified settlements of the Fen valley, then those in the Qin valley so as to have access to the central plain where they took the Shang capital – Yin – in 1045 BC after the battle of Muye, just 32 miles south of the city.

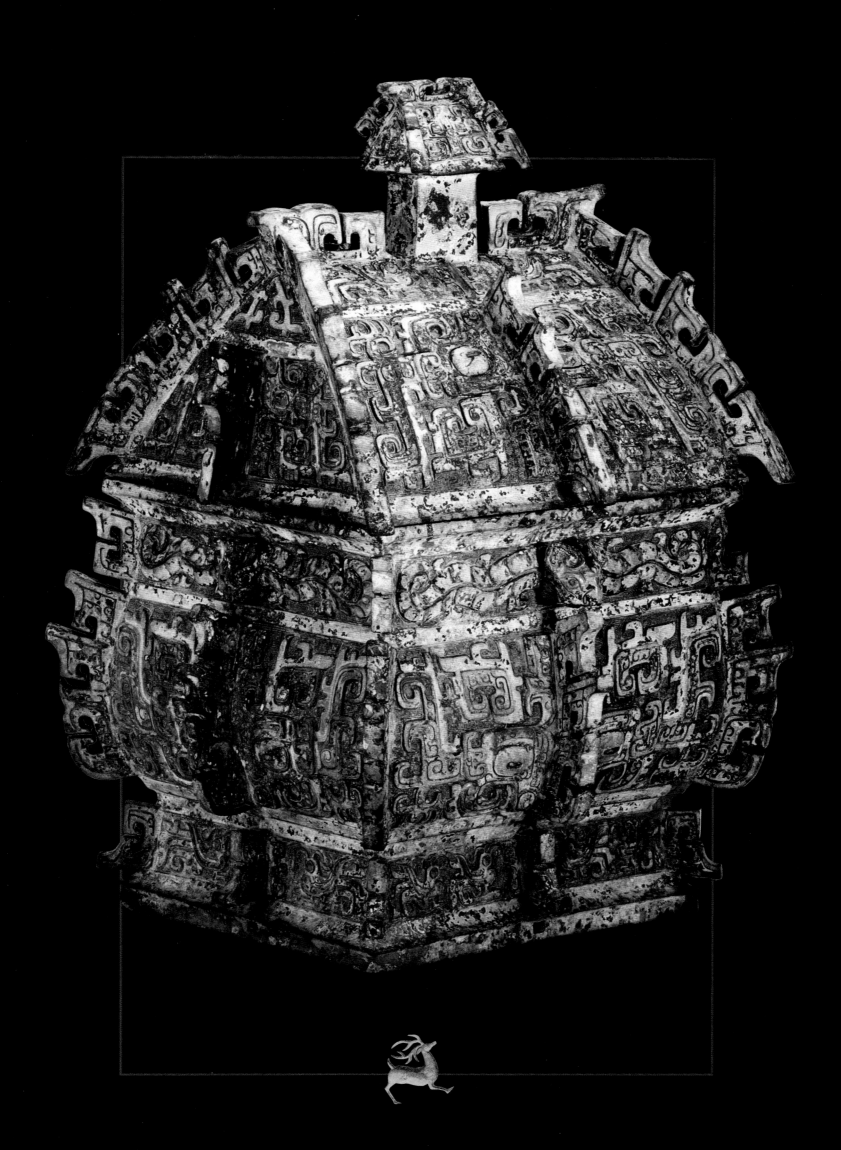

Before moving on to a brief description of the period of the Zhou dynasty, an epoch in which the Qin began to take their own first steps in history, it is as well to clarify some concepts. Without an awareness of the concepts, the long path that led to the creation of the centralized state of the First August Sovereign would appear unfocused and devoid of interest, as though it were simply a mere sequence of aggressive territorial acquisitions. On the contrary, that path, on which the Qin were one of the last to set out, represents one of the greatest and most innovative creations in the history of political and social institutions in East Asia.

It must be borne in mind that at the time of the Shang dynasty, the political and administrative structure was still substantially family-based (a sort of patrimonial state), though spread through various hierarchical levels for the management of both territory and population. Only in the late Shang period does evidence of extra-patrimonial territories become convincing, when the rulers began to delegate control of bits of territory to members of the royal family in return for goods and services. The term given in the oracular inscriptions to these bits of territory is *guo*, a graphical transposition of a property physically bound-ed by walls and defended with weapons. The Shang 'state' consisted of the uneven series of differently sized *guo* that grew up around the ceremonial center of Yin (referred to in inscriptions as *Da Yi Shang*, Shang the Large City), though it had no stable or defined borders. Inside and around the state were different ethnic and cultural groups, some on the same level of cultural, social and technological development. Marvelous examples of these centers of cultural diversity are, for instance, the Wucheng-Xin'gan Culture on the lower Yangzi, the Sanxingdui Culture in the Sichuan basin, and the culture or cultures, still hardly supported by archaeology, of the middle Yangzi where bronze *nao* bells were produced, like the Ningxiang bell in north Hunan that weighs 485 pounds. Most of the other societies were at a pre-state social level, for example, those on the steppes. From this area the knowledge and use of the chariot, a bronze device in the shape of a figure 3 to tie the horses' bridles around the charioteer's waist, a knife with a curved edge, and mirrors made from bronze were very probably transmitted to the Shang around 1200 BC. Other societies, located in more remote areas, were at a level that did not even produce bronze.

The decisive step toward a system of govern-

❖

30 top Ji Chang, better known as King Wen, was the first sovereign of the Zhou dynasty.

❖

30 bottom During the Shang and Western Zhou periods, it is conjectured that battles were fought between teams aboard chariots. In such situations, the ge — a long wooden shaft fitted with an orthogonal blade — constituted an essential weapon.

ment capable of tightening the links of the network of *guo* was taken by the first Zhou rulers, who conquered all the Shang territories and their satellites as far as the Shandong peninsula between 1045 and 1042 BC. They were obliged to take that step as the territories that they now had to govern were immensely larger than the Wei river valley, and were also socially diverse as they incorporated peoples and cultures very different to the traditional Zhou society. The Zhou era is divided into two main periods by Chinese historiographers based on the location of the Zhou 'capital,' i.e., the political and ritual center and residence of the Zhou ruler. The first one was the period of the Western Zhou (1045–770 BC), when the dynastic residence was based in Hao founded on the bank opposite Feng at the time of the conquest of the Shang. The second period was called the period of the Eastern Zhou (770–256 BC) as the Zhou rulers established themselves in the fortified settlement of Chengzhou near the modern Luoyang (Henan province). This was founded by Dan, the duke of Zhou (*Zhou Gong Dan*), soon after the defeat of the Shang in fighting for control of the important ford across the Huanghe at Mengjin and the pass of Tongguan, which was the entrance proper to the Wei valley.

❖

31 top right This oval instrument is a zhong *bell and dates back to the period between the 9th and 8th centuries BC.*

❖

31 bottom During the Spring and Autumn period, a new system of exchange was developed, based on the use of bronze standards that took relatively different forms in different states, such as that shown here that exemplifies the "knife" type used in the reign of Qi during the Warring States period, as attested by the inscription.

The two kings and the duke of Zhou who conquered Shang – Wen Wang (ruled 1099/1056–1050 BC), Wu Wang (ruled 1049/45–1043 BC) and his brother Zhou Gong Dan (1042–1036 BC), a regent in place of Wu's son, Cheng (ruled 1035–1066 BC), though it is not clear why – are recorded in Chinese historiography as the models par excellence of virtues from which good government follows: wisdom, rectitude, filial piety, pride, and justice. This fame was well deserved as these three were the principal authors of the political and administrative reconstruction at the base of the events that led, almost a thousand years later, to the creation of the Qin empire. The Zhou, however, did not destroyed the lineage, the state, the culture or the ancestral temples of the Shang; instead they absorbed them to create a new and original culture. For example, Shang craftsmen (first and foremost the casters of bronze ritual vessels), as well as 'specialists' in ritual matters and administration, were all taken to Hao or sent to work in the service of members of the

Zhou lineage. These latter, displaced in the old and new territories, ensured the control of the kingdom. Tradition also attributes many important innovations to these leaders, most importantly, the Shang concept of sovereignty, which was based on the complex relationship between the living ruler and the spirits of those past, was supplanted by the concept that was to hold the Chinese empire stable until the early 20th century. This fundamental concept was the legitimization of royalty by the mandate (*ming*) of the highest divinity, *Tian* (Heaven), who was a god unknown to the Shang. Since the Zhou king's relationship with Heaven was like that between a son and his father (from which was derived the title *Tian Zi*, Son of Heaven), and since he was king and head of the royal lineage by heavenly mandate (*tian ming*), he was invested with an aura of absolute sacredness and religiosity. From this was to follow, then and forever, that in the world (*Tian Xia* ('[what lies] beneath Heaven')) it was impossible for two kings to coexist. Only the loss of favor of Heaven, the heavenly mandate,

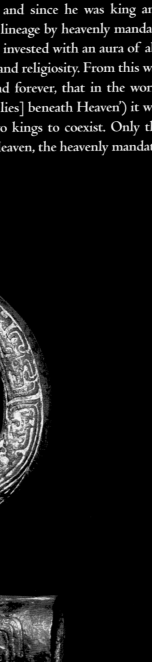

32 The coiled dragon shown in this photograph forms part of a chariot harness from the period of the Western Zhou dynasty (1045-771 BC). The end section was fastened to the wooden shaft through a pin in the hole on the grip or, as one of a pair, to the highest points of the horses' yoke.

33 The ritual vases of the early period of the Western Zhou dynasty, such as this large two-handled bowl, or gui, from the 11th-10th century BC that was used to present the sacred dishes during ceremonial banquets, convey a sensation of heaviness and austerity. Note the perfect symmetry of the two sides of the vase, in terms of both shape and decoration.

This terrifying bronze mask can be dated to the beginning of the Western Zhou period and is of the same kind found
in the sacrificial graves containing war chariots and horses. These discoveries have enabled us to conjecture that such
masks were used as both decorative and symbolic ornaments for the chariot bodies. (Musée Guimet, Paris)

and the manifestation of suitable signs would permit the end of one dynasty and the ascent of a new Son of Heaven, whoever he might be.

Supported by this powerful ideological basis, the Zhou sovereigns began the creation of an administration founded on a hierarchy of clearly defined functions. This allowed the practice of the system of government in which the ruler personally delegated limited rights of sovereignty over portions of his territory (and newly conquered territories) to members of the collateral branches of the lineage. The closer to the royal branch of the lineage, the more hierarchically elevated the individuals were. This typically Zhou system, known as *Zong Fa* (Norms of the Lineage) can be considered a genuine feudal system regulated by relationships of ritual dependence between the king and his 'vassals.' These relationships were continually renewed by ceremonial visits and exchanges of gifts, of which ritual bronze vases with celebratory inscriptions are one of the most evident forms. The *Zong Fa* system used by the Zhou kings to control the territories conquered from the Shang was further reinforced during the conquest of other regions. In practice, the system consisted of the subjection as a vassal (clearly expressed by the term *feng* on the ritual bronze vases) of a member of the Zhou house with the presentation of a *guo* (a term that only later came to signify a 'state,' 'princedom' or 'kingdom'). The *guo* consisted of a fortified city that provided the feudal lord with his residence, an ancestral temple, the seat of his clan (whose members were the core of the army), his administrative staff (functionaries, scribes, priests and officials) and a population. Whether autochthonous, deported or immigrated, the economic activities of this population were based on crafts and agriculture. In this organization there were two principal social categories: the *guoren* (the residents who lived within the city walls) and the *yeren* (the 'men of the open fields'), i.e., those who did not enjoy the protection offered by the walls and the civilizing effect of an urban environment.

In turn the lord of the *guo*, who was usually referred to with the title *gong* or *hou* (translatable as duke and marquis), could assign to collateral branches of his clan the title of one or more satellite settlements (*yi*). The *yi* at times only differed from the *guo* by their prohibition of being the site of the ancestral temple of the main lineage that ruled the *guo*.

❖

This little bronze box shaped like a small cart was part of the rich grave goods of Tomb 87M7, dating from the late Western Zhou period, that was discovered at Shangguo in Shanxi province. The region gave rise to original local artistic styles, as can be seen in this artifact, which combines stylistic elements of Zhou art with others closer to the "verism" of the art of the steppes: small full-relief figures of birds, tigers, a monkey and a nude man, with a mutilated left foot. The victims of this type of mutilation were entrusted with the task of guard.

36-37 The eight percussion instruments shown here are bian zhongs *(or flat zhongs) belonging to the late Spring and Autumn period. They resembled bells without a clapper and were usually hung in groups and beaten like a gong. Each zhong of this set produced a distinct note when hit with the hammer. The tone and timbre of the note could vary according to the point in which the instrument was struck. The music produced by these* zhongs *accompanied the ceremonies of the aristocracy and was considered a distinctive feature of the Zhou civilization. (Musée Guimet, Paris)*

Structured in this manner, the *guo* were a powerful base for the conquest of new territories and for the diffusion of the Shang/Zhou cultural mix. At the time of King Wu and Zhou Gong Dan, territorial expansion took place to the north and south, into the Taihang mountains, and east-west down the Huanghe valley. Zhou Gong was assigned the strategic command of the walled city of Chengzhou, and two young brothers of the future king Cheng were given the *guo* of Jin, near Houma in the lower Fen valley (Shanxi province), and Ying, near Pingdingshan (central Henan province). A brother of King Wu received Wey in northeast Henan to control the area of the old Shang capital, and the eldest son of Zhou Gong was given Lu, in the western zone of the Shandong peninsula. Tai Gong Wang, the general of the army that defeated the Shang, was assigned Qi near the mouth of the Huanghe just north of the Shandong peninsula. Lastly, the half brother of King Cheng was rewarded with the *guo* of Yan in the extreme north of the Central Plain to control the Bohai Gulf and access through the Taihang mountains.

These were the principal *guo* at the start of the Western Zhou dynasty and, with time, progressively became the settings for the merger of the Shang/Zhou amalgam with the autochthonous cultural substrate of the conquered lands. The result was a new cultural, social and even linguistic sphere, referred to as Hua Xia, with which all the citizens identified and which represented the clear distinction between 'civilization' and 'barbarism.' Growth through feudal segmentation within each *guo* was only possible through the progressive conquest of lands and peoples that existed between one *guo* and another. Furthermore, whereas on the one hand this development permitted the creation of a homogeneous political and cultural framework that covered all of the central plain, the middle and lower Huanghe valley, the Wei valley, Shandong, the Huai valley and the upper Han valley, on the other hand it contained within itself the limits of its own efficiency.

In fact, during the late period of the Western Zhou (ca. 865–771 BC), the exponential growth of the feudal households caused the progressive weakening of the sacred aura of the Zhou king. Meanwhile the territorial, cultural and economic

37 top This ritual bronze vase (16.5 inches tall) is known as the Kang Hou gui *(Marquis of Kang's gui) due to the inscription inside, which reveals that it was commissioned by a certain* si tu *(Supervisor of the Lands) called Mei (Mei Situ) to celebrate the ceremony in which King Wu assigned the territory of Wey (or Wey guo) to the Marquis of Kang, his own brother, as a reward for having quelled the rebellion of the recently conquered Shang. (British Museum, London)*

expansion of the *guo* in 'peripheral' regions to the south, east, north and northeast (far from the Hua Xia in terms of ethnic type, language, culture and economy) was to produce a destabilizing effect that was to reverberate at the heart of the kingdom and result later in the disappearance of the Zhou from history.

Xuan died in 782 BC, the most able of the last Zhou kings, who had resisted the raids of the nomadic Xianyun in the west (the Rong in historic sources) and those of the Yi in the east. He had also brought prestige back to royal authority by intervening in the struggles of succession in the *guo* of Wey, Qi and Lu. Xuan Wang was succeeded by his son, You (ruled 781–771 BC), whose second year as king was marked by ominous signs from Heaven: an earthquake destroyed the area of the capital city and there were eclipses of both the sun and moon. At this point the king destroyed one of the pillars of the *Zong Fa* system, i.e., the dynastic succession from father to eldest son, and brought permanent discredit to the vacillating moral power of the Son of Heaven. The king disinherited, in fact, Yi Jiu, his son by his legitimate consort who came from the small *guo* of Shen, and designated his son by his concubine Bao Si as his heir. In retaliation, the lord of Shen, who was one of those responsible for the victory of Xuan Wang against the Yi 'barbarians,' allied himself with the 'barbarians of the west,' the Quan Rong (Rong Dogs). These Rong Dogs were the same Xianyun driven back by Xuan Wang, and they invaded the Wei valley, destroying the capital city Hao. Everything seemed lost for the aristocracy and kingdom of the Zhou but the Qin entered into the history. The duke of the ancient *guo* of Jin, who had expanded in the Fen valley, and the head of the small fief of Qin in the extreme west of the Wei valley, provided protection to Yi Jiu, the legitimate heir, and his court by escorting them to the eastern capital, Chengzhou. Here Yi Jiu received the insignia of Zhou regality and reigned with the name Ping Wang from 770 to 720 BC, and in doing so founded the dynasty of the Eastern Zhou. Grateful for services rendered, Ping Wang rewarded the lord of Qin with the title *gong* (duke) and assigned him the entire ancestral territory of the Zhou – the Wei valley – so that he could defend it from the attacks of the 'barbarians.' In this manner, the duke of Qin, himself a 'barbarian' rather than Hua Xia, was elevated to one of the noblest households of the Zhou.

Who were the Qin? What was their origin? What archaeological traces of them have been found and what references to them exist in the most ancient historical texts in China?

38 top This small jar housed in the British Museum is a fine example of a rare type of terracotta vase from the Warring States period (475-221 BC). The reddish clay body was fired at a low temperature after having been coated with white slip, and was further decorated with colored pigments and glass paste. Such products were probably produced only for funerary purposes and appear to imitate bronze prototypes with rich inserts of gold, silver and colored semiprecious stones.

38 bottom The form of this steamer, known as a he in
Chinese, is immediately recognizable as belonging to the type of
bronze vases produced at the beginning of the Warring States period
(475-221 BC). However, in this case, it is a pottery imitation
made for funerary purposes only. This custom was featured in the
funeral rituals of several states from at least the middle phase of
the Spring and Autumn period and often led to potters to create
original vase forms using a material — clay — that was obviously
more malleable than metal.

38-39 Chinese art always requires a second look. Indeed at first
glance we would all be tempted to say that the bronze end section
shown in this picture depicts a real animal. However, a closer look
reveals that it is one of those fantastic tusked hybrids that populate the
art of the Warring States period (475-221 BC). The exceptional
quality of the artifact, which was probably a chariot decoration, in
terms of both harmony of form and technical skill, indicates that it
was made for use by one of the refined noble households of the period.
(Nelson Gallery of Art, Kansans City)

The Mythical Origins of the Qin

Our knowledge of the history of the Qin is based on two main sources. The first is *Zuo Zhuan* (The Tradition of Zuo) perhaps compiled by Zuo Qiuming in the state of Lu in the Warring States period (475–221 BC) and later added as a commentary to the *Chunqiu* (Spring and Autumn [of the state of Lu]). The second source is several chapters in the most important historical work of ancient China, the *Shi Ji* (Historical Records), drawn up by Sima Qian (145–89 BC), the Court Historian to the Western Han dynasty (206 BC–23 AD). Particularly relevant sections of this work are the chapter *Qin Ben Ji* (Basic Annals of Qin), the chapter *Qin Shi Huang Ben Ji* (Basic Annals of the First Qin Emperor), and a dozen or so *Liezhuan* (Biographies) of politicians, generals, philosophers, famous assassins and strolling players who worked in Qin or who were closely connected with the events in Qin. More recently these sources have received excellent though sectarian support directly from Qin in the later Warring States period, with the *Bian Nian Ji* (Chronicle of the Years) and a series of legal texts found in Yunmeng necropolis, which will be discussed in the coming pages. No less important is the *Shang Jun Shu* (Book of the Lord of Shang), a work sadly incomplete and mostly limited to the reforms made in Qin by Shang Yang around the middle of the 4th century.

Archaeologically, our main source of information, particularly regarding the earliest period, is a thousand or so tombs datable from the start of the Spring and Autumn period (770 or 722 BC). These fall into two types: those along the Wei valley in the state of Qin and those in territories progressively conquered during the period of the Warring States (475–221 BC) and in the Qin dynasty (221–206 BC). The latter type (found in the modern provinces of Henan, Shanxi, Inner Mongolia, Hubei, Sichuan, Guangdong and Guangxi) indicate the directions followed in the expansion of the kingdom of Qin and often reveal a combination of Qin cultural elements with autochthonous features of the regions conquered. The former provide important information for our understanding of the process of absorption of the culture and, above all, of the Zhou ideology followed by the early Qin leaders. But they also tell us about the links that the Qin maintained with the sphere of nomadic herders of the north, and that of the more diverse agricultural and pastoral economies of the western regions (Gansu and Sichuan). These latter are particularly important: they were open on the one hand to the chain of central Asiatic oases, and, on the other, to the corridors through the mountains that led to the upper Yangzi and the southwest regions of modern China.

As stated, the move to the middle Huanghe valley by the Zhou king, Ping, marked the start of the Eastern Zhou dynasty, an epoch that is generally split into two periods: the Spring and Autumn period, named after the accounts of the state of Lu that cover events from 771–475 BC, the year that the Chen clan usurped power in the state of Qi, and the period of Warring States that concluded with the unification of the empire by Qin Shi Huangdi in 221 BC. Its name is derived from the *Zhangguo Ce* (Stratagems of the Warring States), a text written by the 'Diplomats' School' or 'Persuaders.'

❖

The Court Historian to the Western Han dynasty, Sima Qian (145?-89? BC) was the author of the Shi ji *(Historical Records), the most important historical outline of China, which stretches from antiquity across the Three Dynasties (Xia, Shang and Zhou), followed by the Qin dynasty, up until the establishment of the Han Empire.*

As far as the Qin are concerned, the enfeoffment of the first duke of Qin – Xiang – in 770 BC marked the start of the rise of a line and people from obscure origins. At the start of his 'Basic Annals of Qin,' Sima Qian dates their ancient origins from what to us is the mythical period, *Wu Di* (Five Emperors), though it was not so to the Great Han Historian. According to Sima Qian, Nüxiu, the great granddaughter of Zhuan Zu, the second of the *Wu Di*, was sewing when a swallow dropped an egg into her mouth, leaving her pregnant, and the pregnancy resulted in the birth of Daye. Clearly Sima Qian is retelling the Qin tradition and it is one that resembles that of the first Shang ancestor.

In his chapter *Qin Ben Ji* (Basic Annals of Yin), Sima Qian refers to a certain Jian Di who, while bathing with two other women, saw a black bird lay an egg, grabbed and swallowed it, and was consequently made pregnant with Xie. The story continues that Xie ably aided the Wise Sovereign Yu to control the waters and was rewarded with a territory called Shang and with the name Zi for his clan.

The first ancestor of the Zhou was also born portentously, not from an egg but from Jiang Yuan (Progenitor of the Jiang). This young lady had unwittingly stepped on the print of the big toe of *Di*, the most powerful of the Supernatural Beings in the Shang pantheon, and consequently became pregnant with *Hou Ji* (the Lord of Millet). Hou Ji became an expert on plants, farming and harvesting and taught the art of agriculture to the people. In recompense, the mythical emperor Yao bestowed the name Ji on him, which defined the royal clan of Zhou from that time on.

Aside from their curiosity value, it is clear that the myths of origins were important to social and political cohesion (Yu, the founder of the Si royal clan of the Xia dynasty also had a portentous and non-sexual birth from a jujube tree or a stone). By claiming descent from a common ancestor, the various lineages of each clan were part of a community and were able to govern the hierarchical relationships within the clan.

Returning to the myth of origin of the Qin, who are believed by some scholars to have been coastal in origin, it is interesting to note how Dafei, the son of Daye, did not devote himself to agriculture after helping the Wise Sovereign Yu to  harness the waters. Daye devoted himself to the domestication and breeding of birds and animals, but not without having been awarded a black flag and the clan name of Ying by the Wise Sovereign Shun. Dafei had two sons: the first, Dalian, was the founder of the *Niao si* family (Custom of the Bird) from which a certain Zhongyan was descended; Zhongyan had the body of a bird but spoke like a man and was a skilled charioteer. The other son, Ruomu, was the head of the Fei family, whose descendants partly lived in the Middle Kingdom (*Zhongguo*, a term that is still used today in China) and partly between Yi and Di.

Apart from the evident clan branching with the birth of the *Niao si*, which may have harked back to the first ancestor born from the bird's egg in a totemic animal form, in this part of the Qin myth of origin we see how the descendants of the Fei branch lived partly in the Middle Kingdom (the Symbol of Civilization) and partly between the Yi and Di who were considered uncivilized people, i.e., barbarians. This aspect will be returned to.

❖

The Shi ji *(Historical Records) represents the authentic foundation stone of the entire Southeast Asian historiographic tradition. The photograph shows the title page of a Tongrentang edition of 1806. The work compiled by Sima Quan, Court Historian to the Western Han dynasty, constitutes one of the main sources of information on the history of the Qin line. (British Library, London)*

When considering myths, chronology plays no significant role, however, there are some clues that suggest a cultural development that may have taken place at the time of the Longshan late-Neolithic cultures. The most significant is the insistence on the help offered to the Wise Sovereign Yu in harnessing the waters, but which waters are being referred to? The Flood perhaps? The 'mystery' is a little lightened by one of the best preserved works from the period of Warring States: the *Mengzi* (i.e., written by 'Master Meng' or, in English terminology, Mencius). The work is in seven parts and contains the teachings of the most important philosopher of the Confucian school from the 4th century BC. In 'Book' III (III, ii, 9), discussing the moral decadence of society that followed the era of the Three Wise Sovereigns, Mencius says:

'… ever since there has been human life under Heaven [*Tian Xia means the civilized world*], order and disorder have alternated. At the time of Yao [*the first of the Wise Sovereigns*] the waters that came out of the river beds flooded the Middle Kingdom, there were serpents and dragons and the people had nowhere to live: in the low lands they built 'nests' [*the term may refer to shelters built on pillars*] and in the high lands they dug caves. The Book of Historical Annals says, "the leaking waters were a warning for us." These leaking waters were the [*great*] Flood ….'

In Mencius' account, Yu had drainage work carried out and chased the dragons and serpents back into the marshes; meanwhile the largest rivers in China found their courses and people were able to settle and live in the plains. Next, violent and oppressive rulers made their appearance.

The account seems to sum up many events indicated by archaeological study: in the first half of the 3rd millennium BC the climate phase of greatest rainfall in which the highest temperatures ranged between 2°C and 4°C came to an end. Only the western portion of the Great Central Plain beneath the Taihang mountains was formed, the rest was an immense bog that merged into the salt waters of the Bohai Gulf. This damp, marshy environment could have inspired the theme of the 'great flood.' The Longshan farmers of the 3rd millennium BC had to deal with this situation and unquestionably the taming of the plains must have been accompanied by techniques of canalization and drainage, for otherwise there could not have been any increase in agricultural production. We know indirectly that such an increase occurred thanks to the growth in the size of settlements, and the enlargement of storage pits without an increase in the quantity of farming implements. The discovery of certain skeletons from the Longshan Cultures from the end of the 3rd millennium BC indicates a rise in tension resolved with violence, in other words 'institutionalized' violence came into being; a factor which experts believe was one of the variables that accompanied the formation of the complex proto-state societies. A correspondence between archaeology and myth is, of course, just a hypothesis, although an intriguing one.

Returning to the Fei family, some lived in the civilized agricultural world of the Middle Kingdom and some among the Yi and Di barbarians. Other sources from the period of Warring States describe the Yi as tattooed, their hair worn loose, and as eaters of uncooked food, and the Di from the north as wearing skins and feathers, living in caves and not eating cereals. The choice between such irreconcilable ways of life is not isolated in the myths of origin referred to; in fact Bugu, the son of Hou Ji (the agricultural founder of the Zhou), lived among the Rong (the 'barbarians' of the west) and the Di at the end of the Xia dynasty and only two generations later the Zhou returned to farming.

Once again the myth echoes the archaeological data. It has been mentioned that in the belt of steppes and highlands in the north

The followers of Confucius included Master Meng Ke — who was better known with the Latinized name of Mencius
and is shown here in an 18th-century ideal portrait — who lived in the 4th century BC, during the Warring States
period. One of the central aspects of his work as an itinerant philosopher at various courts, was his advice to rulers to
cultivate the human virtues (ʀᴇɴ) in order to alleviate the heavy toll of human lives paid by the people due to the
constant wars based on armies of conscripted peasants.

As far as the Qin are concerned, the enfeoffment of the first duke of Qin – Xiang – in 770 BC marked the start of the rise of a line and people from obscure origins. At the start of his 'Basic Annals of Qin,' Sima Qian dates their ancient origins from what to us is the mythical period, *Wu Di* (Five Emperors), though it was not so to the Great Han Historian. According to Sima Qian, Nüxiu, the great granddaughter of Zhuan Zu, the second of the *Wu Di*, was sewing when a swallow dropped an egg into her mouth, leaving her pregnant, and the pregnancy resulted in the birth of Daye. Clearly Sima Qian is retelling the Qin tradition and it is one that resembles that of the first Shang ancestor.

In his chapter *Qin Ben Ji* (Basic Annals of Yin), Sima Qian refers to a certain Jian Di who, while bathing with two other women, saw a black bird lay an egg, grabbed and swallowed it, and was consequently made pregnant with Xie. The story continues that Xie ably aided the Wise Sovereign Yu to control the waters and was rewarded with a territory called Shang and with the name Zi for his clan.

The first ancestor of the Zhou was also born portentously, not from an egg but from Jiang Yuan (Progenitor of the Jiang). This young lady had unwittingly stepped on the print of the big toe of *Di*, the most powerful of the Supernatural Beings in the Shang pantheon, and consequently became pregnant with *Hou Ji* (the Lord of Millet). Hou Ji became an expert on plants, farming and harvesting and taught the art of agriculture to the people. In recompense, the mythical emperor Yao bestowed the name Ji on him, which defined the royal clan of Zhou from that time on.

Aside from their curiosity value, it is clear that

the myths of origins were important to social and political cohesion (Yu, the founder of the Si royal clan of the Xia dynasty also had a portentous and non-sexual birth from a jujube tree or a stone). By claiming descent from a common ancestor, the various lineages of each clan were part of a community and were able to govern the hierarchical relationships within the clan.

Returning to the myth of origin of the Qin, who are believed by some scholars to have been coastal in origin, it is interesting to note how Dafei, the son of Daye, did not devote himself to agriculture after helping the Wise Sovereign Yu to harness the waters. Daye devoted himself to the domestication and breeding of birds and animals, but not without having been awarded a black flag and the clan name of Ying by the Wise Sovereign Shun. Dafei had two sons: the first, Dalian, was the founder of the *Naio si* family (Custom of the Bird) from which a certain Zhongyan was descended; Zhongyan had the body of a bird but spoke like a man and was a skilled charioteer. The other son, Ruomu, was the head of the Fei family, whose descendants partly lived in the Middle Kingdom (*Zhongguo*, a term that is still used today in China) and partly between Yi and Di.

Apart from the evident clan branching with the birth of the *Naio si*, which may have harked back to the first ancestor born from the bird's egg in a totemic animal form, in this part of the Qin myth of origin we see how the descendants of the Fei branch lived partly in the Middle Kingdom (the Symbol of Civilization) and partly between the Yi and Di who were considered uncivilized people, i.e., barbarians. This aspect will be returned to.

❖

The Shi ji *(Historical Records) represents the authentic foundation stone of the entire Southeast Asian historiographic tradition. The photograph shows the title page of a Tongrentang edition of 1806. The work compiled by Sima Quan, Court Historian to the Western Han dynasty, constitutes one of the main sources of information on the history of the Qin line. (British Library, London)*

and northwest the late-Neolithic farming cultures began a 'reconversion' of the economy from the 2nd millennium BC, with a slow changeover to animal breeding, sometimes supported by limited agriculture. It can be hypothesized that for a long period, above all in the regions nearest the farming valleys, there was a fluctuation between agricultural and pastoral lifestyles, and that pastoral groups, especially during the 1st millennium BC, may have been attracted back to the civilization of the farmers. This is the case, for example, with the Bai Di, who were probably members of the Xianyu referred to earlier who founded the *guo* of Zhongshan (Between the Mountains) in the 5th century BC in the Taihang valleys in modern Hebei and Shanxi provinces. Archaeological discoveries in the territory of the Zhongshan have revealed a refined culture and art modeled on that of larger and more ancient Zhou *guo*. And yet in the literature the Lords of Zhongshan are treated with the ethnocentric disdain that the Hua Xia reserved for 'barbarians'; had it not been for the evidence provided by archaeology, this opinion would have been the prevalent one today.

What may have lain behind the separation of the descendants of Ruomu, among whom prevailed a pastoral vocation and a continuous association with the Rong peoples of the West (this itself is an indication that the Ying clan could have had its ancestral territories in the West), is as follows. Throughout the Shang epoch and during the period of the early Western Zhou, the Ying clan were closely related to herding and breeding (they skillfully trained horses to pull the warchariots that formed the core of the armies of the late Shang and Western Zhou rulers). Sima Qian mentions many of Ruomu's descendants, either because they drove back the Rong or were skilled

charioteers. One of these was Zaofu, the grandson of Zhai Black Wolf (here mentioned only to point out another possible link with a totemic animal), that King Mu of the Zhou (ruled 956–918 BC) chose to drive his four chargers during a hunt in the western territories. During this hunt, the 'state' of Xu, in the extreme east of the Huanghe valley, rebelled against the Zhou; consequently, Zaofu drove his four steeds with such ability that in a single day he covered 'one thousand *li*' to return the king to the capital. There are three important facts linked to this part of the oldest history of the Qin: the first does not directly involve Zaofu, the second places him in the background, and the third brings him out gloriously into the spotlight. The first is that the revolt of Xu marked the start of the decline of the Western Zhou, though it seems that effectively they had already lost control of the eastern Yi regions (which more or less correspond to the modern province of Jiangsu). Confirmation of this is suggested by the kingdom of Mu where, from this time on, no more bronze vases were cast with inscriptions dedicated to the Zhou kings.

The second fact is that Zaofu's drive is mostly remembered for the horses, so much so that – increased by four – 'the Eight Chargers of King Mu' much later became one of the favorite themes of Chinese art. And the third is that, in recognition of his achievement, Zaofu was rewarded by Mu Wang with a fief and the surname Zhao, thus giving rise to the collateral branch of the Ying clan. Zhao Cui, a minister of Duke Wen of Jin, was head of the family that founded the state of Zhao on the division of Jin at the start of the Warring States period. The territory of this state stretched from modern northern Shanxi to southern Hebei and included part of Henan.

❖

This picture of a page from a 17th-century watercolor album shows a chariot pulled by eight steeds: they are the "Eight horses of Mu Wang," a traditional motif of Chinese art that is associated with the origins of the house of Qin. Sima Qian recounts that King Mu (r. 956-918 BC) of the Zhou chose a certain Zaofu of the Ying clan, from which Qin Shi Huangdi was later descended, as the charioteer to drive his four (and later eight) fiery steeds. Zaofu was so skilled that he managed to carry King Mu back to court in a single day, covering an amazing distance, and thus allowing him to put down a rebellion. (Bibliothèque Nationale, Paris)

However, to find the Qin it is necessary to leave the collateral branch of the Zhao and jump to the era of King Xiao of the Zhou (ruled 872?–866 BC) when, according to Sima Qian, it seems that he gave Feizi, a descendant of the brother of Zhao Zaofu, the right to use (*fu yong*) a small area of land where he could graze the royal horses. King Xiao was so satisfied with Feizi's abilities as a horse-breeder that he also gave him a small fief – the *yi* (city) of Qin – on the border of the Gansu and Shanxi provinces and the title of Qin Ying, i.e., the Ying household of Qin. During the era of Qin Ying's great-grandson, Qin Zhong, the dynasty of the Western Zhou suffered its first incontrovertible sign of loss of the Heavenly Mandate. It happened, in fact, that not only the western Rong, but also the feudal lords rebelled against Li Wang (ruled 857/853–842/828 BC), who abruptly left the scene, perhaps violently. After an interregnum on which neither historical sources nor archaeological data shed much light, the Zhou throne was taken by Xuan (ruled 827/825–782 BC). Once Xuan had elevated Qin Ying to the level of *Tai Fu* (the court functionaries' level in the state hierarchy), the king sent him to repress the western Rong, but he was killed while performing this task.

At this point Sima Qian relates, '[*Qin Ying*] had five sons, of whom the eldest was called Zhuang Gong [*duke Zhuang*]'. The fact that the Great Historian does not stop to explain how Zhuang, the son of a simple *Tai Fu*, could suddenly boast the title of *gong*, inferior only to the *wang* (king) speaks volumes on the laxity of the feudal order of the last Western Zhou. In short, Zhuang had appointed himself duke of Qin. Three possibilities exist: Xuan did not know, he had nothing to say on the matter, or Zhuang was mistakenly recorded with this title by posterity. Another of Sima Qian's stories is that King Xuan entrusted 7,000 soldiers to Zhuang and his four brothers and invited them to fight the western Rong, with successful results. In consequence, Xuan not only rewarded Zhuang with the title of *yi* of Qin (which suggests that the land belonged to the Zhou king, at least theoretically) and appointed him *Xi Chui Tai Fu* (Tai Fu charged with the West), but he also awarded him the territories that the Rong had conquered from the descendants of Daluo during the era of the revolt against the wicked King Li.

The real progress made by the Qin in terms of nobility and land acquisition occurred a few years later when Zhuang's successor, Xiang, was rewarded for escorting King Ping to the eastern capital. The passage in the *Qin Ben Ji* (Basic Annals of Qin) relating to this episode describes the fief-granting ceremony so well it is worth relating in full.

'King Ping appointed Duke Xiang one of the feudal lords, bestowing upon him the lands of Mount Qi toward the West. [*The king*] said, "The Rong have not followed the Way [*of correct behavior*], they attacked and invaded our Lands of Qin and Feng, Qin successfully attacked and drove the Rong back, and so it has those lands," then [*there was*] the ritual oath and conferral of the title. Then, for the first time, Duke Xiang had a fief and as prescribed by the rite exchanged ambassadors and ceremonial gifts. He then sacrificed a black horse, a yellow ox and a goat to Shangdi on the Western Altar. In the twelfth year he attacked the Rong and advanced as far as Mount Qi where he died. [*He*] was succeeded by Duke Wen.'

This was Sima Qian's version and we can rely on him from the point of view that he had access to documents and literary sources at first hand; however, is there any archaeological evidence to confirm his story of the enfeoffment of Xiang Gong? Sadly, direct proof has not yet been found, yet certain inscriptions on bronze ritual vases from the late Western Zhou period confirms the existence of the Ying clan and give perhaps an even more accurate view of society than that described in Sima Qian's story. During recent decades, various hoards of bronze ritual vases have been found; their owners had hidden them during the turbulent events of the 8th century that culminated in the Rong invasion and removal of the Zhou household eastward. It should be remembered that ritual vessels were usually kept in the temples of the aristocratic families to be used in ceremonies that honored the ancestors and as an indication of wealth and rank. They were therefore jealously conserved and passed down from generation to generation as a commemoration of the family itself.

In one of these hoards the vases cast by at least four generations of the Wei family were found, beginning with a certain Qiu Wei who was not an aristocrat but a low-ranking skin trader, who probably supplied the court with skins and furs. The inscriptions document both the social rise of the Wei and the decline of the Zhou aristocracy; for example, the inscriptions on some vases commemorate the exchange of goods for land between Qiu Wei and high-ranking nobles. In one case a certain Ju Bo ('count' Ju, as *bo* is the third most senior title in the Zhou aristocratic hierarchy) was obliged to turn to Qiu Wei as he did not have the means to purchase the ritual jade ornaments and finishings for a chariot that were prescribed for a court ceremony. Qiu Wei supplied jade for a value of eight double strings of cowrie shells in exchange for four lots of land. Two years later, four lots were the object of a transaction of the same kind between Qiu Wei and Li, a chief of a *yi* (a city or low-level fief). Four years later, Qiu Wei supplied the same Ju Bo with gold, leather and fur trimmings for a chariot plus three bolts of fine silk for the count's wife. In exchange Qiu Wei received a wood though this also cost him two horses and various articles made from leather and fur which he gave to the woodmen and the officers who looked after the wood.

Besides recording the social mobility of the era, the fact that property still belonged to the king (Qiu Wei and Ju Bo only possessed the assets of the land, not the land itself), and the increasing importance of commerce, the significance of these inscriptions lies in the fact that the Wei family belonged to the Ying clan (which Sima Qian reports at length) and that these Ying were first and foremost livestock breeders and dealers who were in some manner employed by the Zhou court.

The Dukedom of Qin in Legend and History

A further instance of Qin culture in the late period of the Western Zhou and the early years of the Eastern Zhou is given by a series of graves in the eastern part of Gansu province. There, traditionally, the Qin lived as nomads before beginning their slow advance eastwards down the Wei valley.

The graves clearly demonstrate a distinctive characteristic of the Qin cultural milieu, quite different from the Zhou burial methods: the deceased is placed crouched along an east-west axis. In many of the graves datable to the mid-8th and mid-7th centuries BC, the fact that the deceased lies supine, following a Zhou custom, reveals the tendency of the Qin aristocracy to adhere as much as possible to the Zhou etiquette. Most probably this was a way to demonstrate their right to be part of the same cultural world (oecumene) as the Hua Xia feudal lords, even though they no longer used the Zhou sumptuary norms.

Following the Zhou rituals, the hierarchic level of the deceased in the Qin tombs was displayed through the canonic placement of an uneven number of *ding* (tripods), an even number of *gui* (large cups) (the number of *ding* minus one), a pair of tall *hu* (small jars or bottles), items for ablutions composed of a *pan* (hand basin) and *yi* (a jug to pour water over the hands), sometimes substituted with a *he* (pitcher), and a boiler with a four-footed *yan* (steamer) that might be a one-piece object or composed of two pieces.

The Qin graves, in which bodies were laid face up, were all either large or at least medium-sized, and were oriented north-south (another Zhou characteristic) and were recognizable as aristocrats' tombs. However, people below the aristocratic elite continued to be buried in accordance with the traditional Qin custom.

After the middle of the 7th century BC, even the highest levels of the aristocracy abandoned the Zhou customs and returned to their ancestral procedures. This occurred when the Qin dukedom had already launched itself on a policy of independent expansion in the Wei valley and maybe no longer needed to 'legitimatize itself' by adhering to Zhou burial customs. In all Qin burial grounds, however, one aspect is repeated: the tombs are arranged in relatively uniform groups which suggests that the members of different lineages were buried in lots for each generation.

Sima Qian states that it was only in 753 BC (the thirteenth year of the rule of Duke Wen and shortly after the start of the Eastern Zhou dynasty) that the Qin court began to keep written records. This is more or less the same period from which we have incontestable proof, in the form of archaeological finds, of their presence in the extreme west of the Wei valley.

Graves belonging to members of Qin elite have been discovered in the area between the passes of the Longshan mountains that lead from Gansu to western Shaanxi, and the city of Baoji (middle Wei valley), in which both the *Shi Ji* and place names demonstrate the presence of the Qin at the time of Duke Wen (ruled 765–716 BC). According to some scholars, these graves are pertinent to the settlement of Qian (the first 'capital' established by Wen in the modern county of Longxian) or Pingyang near Baoji (the Qin 'capital' from 714 to 618 BC). But no substantial evidence exists of either of these 'capitals,' and the chronological relationship between the necropolises and settlement is debatable in that Qian, Pingyang and Yong were not completely abandoned with the movement of the 'court' to another site.

❖

These two iron daggers – about 1.4 inches long – were discovered in 1992 in Grave 2 at Yimen, near the city of Baoji, and have golden handles set with turquoise and glass. They were part of a rich collection of grave goods: in addition to a third iron dagger, 1,138 gold artifacts were also found, along with 19 iron knives, 91 jade pieces, a necklace of 108 cornelian and 2 jade beads, a necklace of 40 turquoise beads, a necklace of 84 glass paste beads and a necklace of 1,615 small glass beads. This tomb, which dates back to the end of the Spring and Autumn period, is significant for its number of gold artifacts, which are rare in Shang and Zhou graves, and the use of iron, which testifies to the Qin smiths' mastery of metallurgy. However, it is also equally important as evidence of the presence of members of the Qin aristocracy in the region of Baoji.

Various tombs have been excavated in the mountain passes near Bianjiazhuang, datable to the early Spring and Autumn period. Graves M1 and M5 are of particular importance, which, due to the number of bronze ritual vases in the grave goods (5 *ding* tripods, 4 *gui* cups, 2 *hu* 'bottles', 1 *yan* steamer, 1 *he* pitcher and 1 *pan* hand basin), have been recognized as tombs of the nobility, perhaps of *Tai Fu*, a title previously mentioned but of which, for this period, the exact meaning and function is obscure. We do know, however, that in Qin in the late Warring States period and in the imperial era, the title *Tai Fu* was used from the fifth to ninth levels on a hierarchic scale divided into twenty levels.

The vertical rectangular shaft in the M5 grave at Bianjiazhuang containing the *guan* (inner sarcophagus) was covered by a larger area paved with wooden planks; this area was a *guo* (burial chamber) where the grave goods were placed. The goods included bronze ritual vessels, 375 lithophones (blunt-ended stone chimes used as musical instruments) copied in clay, and a wooden chariot with bronze finishings drawn by two anthropomorphic figures made of painted wood. The lithophones, war chariot and ritual vases were typical paraphernalia of the nobility. However, in this tomb the distribution of the spaces and the type of chariot were unusual: the chariot is a funerary replica of a type never found archaeologically, and is known as a *lian* (or in modern transcription, *nian*). It was pulled by men and was only used by certain levels of the nobility, beginning with the *Tai Fu*, as is shown by this grave. The *lian* provides the earliest example in the Zhou period of the use of the human figure in a funerary context and also the earliest reproduction of a man-drawn chariot; in other words, it is the forerunner of the rickshaw.

More or less from the same period as the graves at Bianjiazhuang are those excavated farther west in Yuandingshan in the valleys of eastern Gansu; two in particular are of interest. The first (98LDM1) was the tomb of a person of high rank, who was buried at a depth of 23 feet in a wooden sarcophagus inside a burial chamber (*guo*). His (or her, according to Chinese archaeologists) rank is confirmed by the many ornaments, ritual jade objects, and an almost canonical set of ritual vases. This set was composed of five *ding* tripods, two *gui* cups, three *hu* jars (two of which are four-sided), a *yi* pitcher with *pan* hand basin, and a *he* pitcher. To these were added vases that were not prescribed types: a large, deep, rounded bowl, two *hu* boxes and a sort of rough cooking pot with a lid that does not appear to have been made to fit. The most curious aspect of these vases is that they are all related to models from the late Western Zhou period. Stylistically they are unusual, as though, with the exception of the pair of *hu* boxes, each one had been made by a different workshop. The decorative motifs of some are similar but they are combined in different ways, even where, like in the set of *ding*, one would expect to find the same decoration on each vase. In some cases, the motifs are in very low relief, in others more pronounced, and in yet others are almost in full relief, for example, the crouching tigers by the foot of the two *hu* that have the heads and upper torsos of wild beasts, with large, 'square spiral' ears. Another example of decoration in almost full relief is the train of tigers, dragons and hens that runs from the handle to the lip on the *he* pitcher; the pitcher as a whole rests on four anthropomorphic feet.

The two boxes are also rather curious: one is formed by two jointed parallelepipeds and is adorned with motifs of interwoven snakes; the other is also four-sided but in the form of a small pushcart, and is formed by a series of small statues of tigers and birds at the corners and along the edges, and of a bird and a figure (a gatekeeper) that form the knobs of the sides

of the cart. It seems almost as if the elements in this set of grave goods were put together at random, having been collected from different places at slightly different times, and the assortment contrasts strongly with the stylistic uniformity of the vases in the grave goods of the Zhou aristocracy.

Another unusual feature in this tomb is the presence of sacrificial victims. The remains of three individuals — who owned many jade beads, almost all those in the grave — were found in three niches cut in the walls of the shaft a little over seven feet from the bottom. Here, beneath the skeleton of the deceased noble, a small sacrificial trench (*yao keng*) had been dug to hold the remains of a dog that wore a bronze bell round its neck.

The other tomb in Yuandingshan (98LDM3) is also of interest though less rich in its contents: there is only one niche with a sacrificial victim (over seven feet from the bottom of the shaft), only two bronze vases (a *ding* and a *zun* vase), and few jade ritual objects. However, there was the blade of a *ge* (halberd) and a short bronze dagger, both of which are unmistakably Qin.

Taken together, the vases in these tombs clearly exemplify the conservatism that the Qin maintained in the art of metal casting, at least until the 4th century BC. Both the forms of the vases and the style of the decorations are derivatives of Western Zhou models. In some cases, as in Tomb 1 at Xigaoquan near Baoji, the vases might even have been from the end of the period of the Western Zhou, and somehow came into the possession of an aristocratic Qin family, where they remained for several generations before being used as grave goods.

It is known for certain that, from the early 7th century BC, perhaps using Zhou metal casters who did not follow the court eastward, the Qin were in a position to control the entire process of casting bronze vases. Just a century later, even exported objects made in the styles of their local markets, for example, were dominant

❖

51 left This little bronze box shaped like a small cart and dating back to the early decades of the 7th century BC (beginning of the Spring and Autumn period) was found in Tomb 1 in the Qin necropolis at the foot of Mount Yuanding, in the eastern part of Gansu province, where the ancestral lands of the Qin were presumably situated.

in the northern steppes and Sichuan basin.

The Qin also made political and ritual use of metal casting, employing it as a means of demonstrating their authority and independence from the court of the Son of Heaven. The ritual bronzes that bear dedicatory inscriptions of the dukes of Qin show such use. Those seen on the eight large bells found in 1978 in the Taigongmiao (Temple of Taigong) site in Baoji are a declaration of the political program of one of the first dukes of Qin, perhaps Duke Wu (ruled 697–678 BC). It was this duke who first defined himself as 'I, the child' (hinting an Heavenly paternity) as the Zhou kings did, and in no uncertain terms claimed his sovereignty over the four corners of the earth inhabited by the 'barbarians.' His justification was that his ancestorshad received the Heavenly Mandate for this purpose, just like the Zhou kings had a century or so before. A few decades later this political design was made even more ambitious and clear by Duke Cheng (ruled 663–660 BC)

or one of his late-7th-century successors in the inscriptions on a *gui* bowl (found in 1919) and a bell (found during the Song dynasty, 960–1279 AD). The inscriptions threatened not only the 'barbarians' but also the Hua Xia nobles who dared not to present themselves at his court to render him due homage. By appropriating this rituality from the Zhou kings, the Qin dukes demonstrated their conviction that they were able to take their place, and from this standpoint Qin ritual took on the aspect of a conscious design.

Strict observance of Western Zhou rituality did not impede the Qin from displaying their own rites and beliefs. This is exemplified by their burial shafts. These, though vertical like the Zhou model, often had variations in the arrangement of the inner sarcophagus (*guan*), funerary chamber (*guo*), and, at a later date, in the addition of service areas used to express autochthonous rituals: for example, the niches that contained sacrificial victims.

51 right This large four-sided hu *jar with tapered body was also found in Tomb 1. The most curious aspect of the vases of the grave goods of this tomb is that they are stylistically unique, although all related to late Western Zhou models, as though each were manufactured by a different workshop and put together at random, having been collected from different places and at different times. This variety contrasts with the stylistic uniformity of the vases in the grave goods of the Zhou aristocracy, but could be testimony of a random collection of goods, such as booty from the forays of the Qin armies into the surrounding lands.*

Funerary Rituals and Sacrificial Victims

The question of sacrificial victims in the Qin tombs is one of the more curious and evident examples of 'disinformation' put out by Confucian historiographers to denigrate the house of the First August Sovereign of the Qin dynasty. Sad to say, planting disinformation started with Sima Qian, who was usually so objective in his judgments. It is known that human sacrifice was widely practiced by the Shang and Western Zhou aristocracies. It is also attested in many of the Zhou's feudal states up until almost the mid-Warring States period, at which time clay or wooden figures were gradually substituted for the victims. A 5th-century BC grave of a man found in Langjiazhuang, near Linzi (the capital of the state of Qi in Shandong) was found to contain the bodies of seventeen young women, each buried in her own sarcophagus around the main burial chamber. They all had their own jewels and other grave goods, and, in fact, two of the young women were accompanied by their own sacrificial victims and six by anthropomorphic figurines. The same tomb was also found to contain nine other victims of both sexes. From the position of their skeletons it was clear that some were buried alive, others killed. This tomb demonstrates that the practice of sacrifice was diffuse among the aristocracies of the era of the Eastern Zhou, and that the victims belonged to two categories: those that 'accompanied' the deceased and those who were cruelly sacrificed. Il also appears that in the 5th century BC small statues began to take the place of human victims.

In Qin the practice was officially suppressed by Duke Xian in the first year of his reign (384 BC), however, the ritual killing of concubines, particularly in the case of the emperor, was not only confirmed on the death of the First Emperor, but continued until the Ming dynasty (1368-1644 AD). The custom was then abolished with a decree issued by Emperor Xian Zong (ruled 1465–1487 AD).

It is possible to imagine that the first abolition (384 BC) of this cruel ritual occurred as a result of the changing nature of war – in which large masses of infantry were used – and of agriculture, even though we cannot exclude humanitarian considerations. The curious fact, however, is that Sima Qian attributed only to Qin the responsibility for this abhorrent practice. Describing Wu's death in 698 BC, he says,

'Duke Wu of Qin died in the twentieth year of his reign and was buried in Pingyang ... For the first time men accompanied the deceased, sixty-six people were sacrificed.'

When narrating the death of Duke Mu in 621 BC, Sima Qian added,

'... he was buried in Yong and was accompanied in death by one hundred and seventy-seven people. Three honorable Qin functionaries of the Ziyu family – Yanxi, Zhonghang and Zhenhu – were among the sacrificial victims. The Qin people knew great sorrow, and the poem 'Yellow Birds' in the Classic of Poetry was composed.'

The Great Historian's scorn led him to express clearly his negative opinion of Duke Mu although in the lines previous he spoke almost with admiration of the duke's skills of oratory, his respect for the fallen in battle, and his military successes against the Rong and dukedom of Jin. Nonetheless, he did not hesitate to say:

'... he never became the leader of the alliance, quite rightly. When he died no care was taken of the people, on the contrary, honorable functionaries were buried. When kings of the past died, they left behind them virtues and laws to be handed on, how could they have sacrificed excellent men and honorable functionaries, causing the people pain? For this we know that Qin will never be able to march victoriously east.'

In truth, this passage causes certain problems: Sima Qian well knew that the victorious march east took place and even if he had taken this judgment – as some scholars claim – from the work *Zuo Zhuan*, written when the Qin had still not conquered all of China, the incongruity remains. Could therefore it be a later addition to the *Shi Ji* made simply to denigrate the Qin, as in other cases? It is possible. And then, to what alliance was the Great Historian referring, or who was doing it for him?

An Ancient Qin Poem

The poem is named after the onomatopeic opening rhyme:

" Jiao Jiao Huang Niao . . .

The yellow birds come and go,
they perch on the jujube tree
Who will follow in the tomb of Duke Mu?
Yanshi of the Ziju
This Yanshi
is a man above a hundred
When he arrives at the pit
he looks terrified and trembles
Oh you Blue Heaven
you kill our best men
If he could be saved
we would give one hundred lives for his.

The yellow birds come and go
they perch on the mulberry tree
Who will follow in the tomb of Duke Mu?
Zhonghang of the Ziju
This Zhonghang
Is a match for a hundred
When he arrives at the pit
He looks terrified and trembles
Oh you Blue Heaven
you kill our best men
If he could be saved
we would give one hundred lives for his.

The yellow birds come and go
they perch on the brambles
Who will follow in the tomb of Duke Mu?
Zhenhu of the Ziju
This Zhenhu
who can face up a hundred valiant men
When he arrives at the pit
He looks terrified and trembles
Oh you Blue Heaven
you kill our best men
If he could be saved
we would give one hundred lives for his.

A New Political Balance: the Ba

It should be remembered that the Zhou feudal system had produced, both directly and indirectly, a proliferation of *guo* 'states' and that at the start of the Spring and Autumn period (770–475 BC) these numbered around 150, of which 15 were prominent.

At the start of the Eastern Zhou era certain events took place that should be briefly mentioned. Ping Wang of the Zhou was confined to a territory surrounded by feudal states and peoples that did not belong to the Hua Xia group, and the duke of the Zheng *guo*, which lay immediately to the east of Zhou, initially took up Ping's cause and acted as his prime minister. However, the duke of Zheng's enormous power convinced Ping and his successor Huan to create a parallel position to which the duke of Guo was appointed (this name has the same sound as the word for 'state'). Guo was a small feudal state to the west of Zhou. The duke of Zheng was offended by the favor shown to Guo and led a raid on the Zhou territories. King Huan replied with a punitive expedition against Zheng with the united armies of Wey, Chen and Cai, but not only was Huan defeated, he was personally injured. This was a real shock to the stability of the system of Zhou values and was a clear sign of the break in relations between the Son and Father of Heaven. Only the power of their sacred aura allowed the Zhou to maintain a symbolic, though not political, role as head of the feudal system. Zheng was recognized as the leader of the feudal states and maintained this role until 701 BC. This episode was the forerunner of a political change of enormous historical importance.

In the decades that followed this event, the dukedom of Qi, which controlled the strategically located plains of western Shandong, became the largest economic and military power in the Huanghe valley. Duke Huan of Qi launched a series of reforms that can be considered the spark that set off the process of administrative 'inventions' that were to lead to the 'modern' state of Qin. Deciding the Zhou feudal system of control of land and resources was outmoded, the duke of Qi divided his dominion into fifteen territorial units (called *xian*, a term that is still used) and placed them under the direct control of himself and his two 'elder ministers.' In the same way the population (both *guoren*, city-dwellers, and *yeren*, country-dwellers) were divided into administrative levels placed under the control of a hierarchy of functionaries accountable to their superiors for their actions. They were either rewarded or punished as a function of what actions they took. In short, the idea and structure had been defined of an administrative system not based on family ties, and the seed of a modern state had been sown.

In foreign policy, however, the duke of Qi was a strenuous supporter of the Zhou feudal system and intervened repeatedly and successfully in the north against various non-Hua Xia populations (mostly Di and Rong) which had endangered and actually invaded some of the less powerful feudal states. In the south Qi resisted the state of Chu, which had expanded from its base in the middle Yangzi valley to threaten the feudal states of the middle Huanghe valley. Chu was one of the most powerful non-Hua Xia cultural and political organizations and the cradle of a highly sophisticated and rich civilization born from a unique combination of different cultural elements; the nature of their culture was unquestionably 'Chinese' although it was considered distant and 'barbarian' by the states in the Huanghe valley. Chu was so detached from the Zhou feudal values that in 706 BC its ruler had adopted the title *Wang* (king) to which only the Son of Heaven was entitled in the north. It was a Zhou king, Hui (ruled 676–652 BC), who recognized the political and diplomatic skills of the duke of Qi and in 667 consecrated him as leader of the feudal states with the title of *Ba* (the Elder), perhaps created expressly for the occasion. The authority of the *Ba* was principally based on the consensus expressed at interstate meetings between the leaders of the different feudal states on the political policy proposed by Qi, a line that did not preclude the use of force. Agreement with this arrangement was expressed by physical presence at the meetings and its confirmation was expressed through solemn oaths. The vivid description of the outcome of one such meeting, held in Kuiqiu in 651 – a tool of political co-existence of unusual modernity that can be compared to a sort of 'League of Nations' – is recorded in the *Meng Zi*. It is worth

---

55 left This decorative stone element, found among the grave goods of a tomb, depicts a highly stylized horse's head and is typical of the Qin artistic style of the Warring States period. The holes at the base of the neck housed the small pins that fastened the head to the body. (Xi'an, Historical Museum)

❖

55 center and right Bronze bells from the Western Zhou period: the type in the center (from Xinzheng, Henan province) is known as a bo, *whereas that right is a* chunyu, *a musical instrument that appeared during the Spring and Autumn period. Bells and drums were used as attack or withdrawal signals during battle and accompanied the rites in temples.*

quoting in full as it clearly expresses the destabilizing elements that existed during the Spring and Autumn period.

'The first rule of their agreement was "to kill those who do not show filial devotion; not to substitute the legal heir; not to elevate a concubine to first wife." The second was "honor the deserving, support the capable, give prominence to the virtuous." The third was "respect the elderly, be gentle with the young, treat strangers and travelers well." The fourth was "functions are not hereditary, functionaries can only perform one office, in the selection of functionaries let the purpose of the office be the criterion used, do not let execution of the Tai Fu be arbitrary." The fifth was "keep embankments straight, do not impose limitations on the sale of grain, do not mark boundaries without giving notice." Then it was declared that "we who have made this agreement will maintain relationships of friendship from now on."' This resolution was established under the aegis of the *Ba*, Duke Huan of Qi, by the dukes of Jin, Song and Qin, and the king of Chu. This is the alliance to which that suspect passage in *Shi Ji* refers.

But, as always, the promise of peaceful co-existence was not kept. Political and military leadership passed to the dukedom of Jin, in modern Shanxi, at the end of the 7th century BC. Then in the first decades of the following century, the title of *Ba* passed back and forth between Chu and Jin. The sphere of political interaction in the 6th century was no longer limited to the Zhou feudal states which had either swallowed up vast non-Zhou territories and populations (various Rong, Yi and Di) or had been swallowed up by political and cultural entities not of Hua Xia origin, such as Qin and Chu. The result of this process of expansion was, on the one hand, the flourishing in the 6th and 5th centuries BC of an unprecedentedly large cultural civilization and the foundation of classical Chinese culture, and, on the other, the creation of a

system of territorial states in which the role of the *Ba* changed slowly from the defender of the feudal order and Zhou regality to the guarantor of a new pluralistic political, social and cultural entity. This entity included not just the Zhou feudal states but new and different political and ethnic entities such as Qin, Chu, and the non-Hua Xia states of the lower Yangzi valley: Wu and Yue. So influential was the entry of Wu and Yue in the political struggle of the Middle Kingdom of the era that a lord of Wu was made *Ba* in 482 BC, following the construction of a strategic canal (the first in a long series that was concluded a thousand years later with the Great Imperial Canal that joined the Yangzi and the Huanghe) that allowed the troops of Wu to be transported quickly from the Yangzi to the Central Plain.

The growth of Qin from a small dukedom to creator of the Chinese Empire has its roots in this new political, economic and ideological set-up.

Before returning to the material evidence that archaeology provides about Qin culture and growth, it would be well to dwell briefly on the poem (according to Sima Qian) composed to express grief for the bitter end of the three members of the Ziyu family sacrificed with Duke Mu: 'Yellow Birds.'

THE NECROPOLISES OF THE NOBILITY

Although the consideration in which the Qin were held by the nobles of the feudal states of Hua Xia culture was that of an unsophisticated and wild people, poetry of this type cheered the members of the Qin aristocracy, like the *Shi* (warriors) and *Tai Fu* hierarchies, to which categories perhaps the unfortunate three members of the Ziyu family belonged. What has reached us of this world, their beliefs, their wealth and their understanding of death? Many necropolises and a few palatial residences.

The tombs found in different sites of the Yong ducal necropolises (in the county of Fengxiang, Shaanxi province) are certainly of nobles. Yong was the capital of Qin from 677 to 424 BC.

The graves with a deep rectangular pit at Baqidun, from the earliest phase (ca. 714–424 BC), clearly demonstrate the hierarchical divisions typical of Qin society. The grave goods, for example in tombs BM27 and CM2, suggest the different roles (and perhaps rank) the two deceased held in life. The high rank of the dead man in BM27, who lies supine with his arms folded on his chest as was customary for the Zhou, is clear from the use of an inner sarcophagus (*guan*), two outer sarcophagi (*guo*) surrounded by an earth platform, and the grave goods of three *ding* tripods, a *yan* steamer and a *yu* hand basin. In addition to these were various clay vases, a bronze spear tip (the wooden shaft almost thirteen feet long has rotted away), six arrows, two *ge* (halberds), a bronze knife and the decomposed remains of a shield and bow. The goods placed in the grave also included twelve small ceramic lithophones, four jade ritual insignia, some cowries, a jade earring, seven

decomposed lacquer vases, three shield bosses and four bronze bells.

In tomb CM2 the deceased lay in a sarcophagus inside two *guo*. His grave goods consisted of three *ding* tripods, a large *gui* bowl, a *pan* hand basin and *yi* pitcher, a *yan* steamer and many other items of different use. However, his higher rank is revealed by the presence of two sacrificial victims placed inside niches dug on either side of the pit.

The first grave may have been that of a warrior but the second, without weapons of any sort, suggests that of a civil functionary, though this is purely conjecture. We know from historical sources that the separation of roles was not so clear cut; in the *Qin Ben Ji* many references are made to ministers and counselors who were also important generals and warriors.

From the middle of the 7th century BC, a change began to take place in the funeral ritual of Qin nobles: emphasis was placed on autochthonous ritual and cult objects though the grave goods also reflected the cultures of neighboring areas. This change also influenced the forms of the graves at least until the middle of the period of Warring States (475–221 BC).

From the middle phase of the Spring and Autumn period, one of the major aspects of Qin funerary ritual is the almost sudden replacement of bronze ritual vases with copies made expressly to be placed in tombs. These substitutes were either bronze or ceramic copies, these latter painted with red and white motifs, or, to a lesser degree, made by lacquer. In the case of pottery vases, made of course from a material that is more malleable than metal, the potters created less angular shapes of

the bronze prototypes. Such specialized new shapes often result in bizarre, extended profiles with hypertrophic, funnel-shaped necks, disproportionately large handles recalling the 'square spiral' form of ears seen in the animal decorations on bronze vases, and equally outsize bases compared to the volume of the body of the vase.

The non-utilitarian function of bronze funeral vases is so evident that at times the lid cannot be removed from the body as the object was created in a single cast. Others suffer from large flaws resulting in defects in the casting process. In the graves of this period in Zaomiao necropolis near Tongchuan (eastern Shaanxi), as in contemporary graves in Xicun and Baqidun, there appear for the first time *mingqi* (objects for the soul) that are miniature representations of the assets the deceased owned in life. Initially, these *mingqi* were formed of small clay granaries, clay carts pulled by oxen, or stone or terracotta statuettes of human figures in which the hair was gathered up on the right side of the head. This phenomenon is almost unknown, or at least is very rare, among the more eastern aristocrats, with the single exception of Chu; but Chu was a region considered by the feudal lords of the Huanghe valley to be barbarous and totally extraneous to the Hua Xia cultural tradition, even more so than Qin.

❖

57 top left The body and cover of this miniature bronze replica (ca. 4-6 inches) of a ritual hu *from the Spring and Autumn period cannot be separated, as they were cast in a single mold. The two "dragon-head" handles are set in holes made beneath the rim of the container, which was discovered in Tomb 10 of the Gaozhuang necropolis, near ancient Yong, and dates back to the 5th century BC. (Xi'an, Archeological Institute of Shaanxi Province)*

❖

57 bottom left This gray clay vase with three-footed lenticular body is a model of a fu *(steamer or cauldron) for funerary purposes. The polychrome decoration, painted on the vase before firing, is composed of two "S"-shaped motifs separated from two squares by a cross similar to the* tian *ideogram (cultivated field). (Xi'an, Archeological Institute of Shaanxi Province)*

57 *right* This ceramic hu *from Tomb 10 at Gaozhuang is typical of Qin production for solely funerary use of the late Spring and Autumn period or the beginning of the subsequent one. The desire to imitate bronze prototypes can clearly be seen in the molding of the handles and the decoration emphasized by the red pigment filling the narrow incisions on the body of the vase. (Xi'an, Archeological Institute of Shaanxi Province)*

SACRIFICIAL PITS WITH CHARIOTS AND HORSES

The presence of sacrificial pits containing war chariots pulled by two horses, often accompanied by the charioteer, was common to many of the necropolises in the feudal states during the Warring States and Spring and Autumn periods. We do not yet fully understand this aspect of feudal rituality as, in many cases, we are unable to establish exactly to which of the noble tombs in a certain necropolis the pits with chariot and horses were dedicated. We know that the offering of a variable number of war chariots and horses was a feature of royal tombs in the late Shang dynasty, we also know that the use of chariots in life was inherited by the Western Zhou as an important means to display royalty, as a symbol of military power, and as an element of high value in the gifts made to feudal lords. Consequently, a chariot and horses became a symbol of rank and power in the graves of the high Zhou aristocracy.

War chariots in the age of the Eastern Zhou were particularly important as status symbols as well as providing the shock wave in attacks by feudal armies. As the *Zhangguo Ce* (Accounts of the Warring States) testifies, the size and power of the feudal states was mainly calculated by the number of war chariots they had. Powerful kingdoms like Qin, Chu, Qi and Zhao had 1000 apiece, Yan and Wei had 700 and 600 respectively, whilst Zhongshan had 'only' 400.

The sumptuary value of war chariots is fairly clearly conveyed in sacrificial pits of this type in Qin necropolises. For example, in Shangmengcun necropolis in western Shaanxi, the chariot placed in a sacrificial pit with two horses and a dog was totally without bronze fittings except for the horses' bits and a collar bell worn by the dog that 'crouched' by the chariot's left wheel. The pit was probably related to grave M27, which seems to have been the last resting place of a low-ranking aristocrat from the Spring and Autumn period to judge by the two bronze ritual vases (a *ding* tripod and a *yan* burner).

A pit of this type, also from the Spring and Autumn period, has been found in the necropolis of lower ranking aristocrats near Yuandingshan, not far from grave 98LDM3, though it had partly been violated when it was discovered. About 70 feet long, it contained three chariots to which four horses were harnessed, and two chariots drawn by pairs of horses. Beneath the body on the first chariot lay the skeleton of the charioteer. The rich ornamentation of the chariots and the horses' harness are of the same type in vogue in the Hua Xia feudal states, but the form of the chariot bodies are different. They do not have the light, almost semi-circular body decorated with entwined plants and leather, but a heavy, rectangular body made from planks of wood. They are closer to central Asian models than to those of the Middle Kingdom, and, as such, provide a clear indication of the close relationships maintained by Qin with the peoples of the steppes.

An example of later sacrificial pits with horses and chariots is the ones in the Qin necropolis in Xincun, near the city of Fengxiang. Of the four pits found, only two have been investigated to date. They were found to contain the remains of five wooden chariots that were decomposed but still recognizable owing to the coat of hazel lacquer that originally covered all their parts. The first of the two pits — almost completely

❖

58 Two splendid Qin graves have been unearthed at the site of Yuandingshan, in the valleys of eastern Gansu. In the vicinity of one of them a partially violated pit (22 yards long) from the Spring and Autumn period was discovered. It contained three chariots harnessed to four horses and two chariots drawn by pairs of horses. The skeleton of the charioteer was discovered beneath the body of the first chariot.

❖

59 top A hundred or so noble graves belonging to small peripheral lords, dating back to the Shang and Zhou dynasties, have been excavated at Qianjiangda in the Shandong peninsula. Most unusually, the graves and accompanying pits with chariots and horses — such as that shown here — had never been pillaged.

59 bottom This gold harness decoration depicting a therimorphous mask was found in Pit S2 containing chariots and horses in the Xicun necropolis near Fengxian, a Qin tomb dating to the years between the end of the Spring and Autumn period and beginning of the Warring States period. (Xi'an, Archeological Institute of Shaanxi Province)

destroyed by treasure hunters – contained the remains of three chariots and four horses. The second grave had a chariot drawn by a pair of horses, with a wooden parasol decorated with red lacquer on a base of hazel lacquer, with the charioteer occupying a pit beneath the body of the chariot. Among the objects left by the tomb robbers were many bronze ornaments, a gold stud for the bridle, different types of weapons, bronze tools, a wooden bow (decomposed) that rested on the edge of the chariot rail. In the pit containing the remains of the charioteer, an exceptional find was made: several small accessories and gold and bronze jewels.

Despite the losses due to recent and ancient robberies, the level of opulence in the two pits is clearly much higher than that in the pit at Shangmengcun. Furthermore, as it lies in the area of the necropolises of the Yong capital, the necropolis at Xincun could have been part of the graveyard of an aristocratic clan near the center of power.

In this area, the investigations carried out since the 1980s have resulted in the necropolis being recognized as that of the clan of the Qin duke. The site has groups of graves and sacrificial pits containing chariots and horses which, judging by their size, could contain between five and ten times the quantity of objects discovered at Xincun. Unfortunately, most of the ducal graves and accompanying pits seem to have been largely pillaged and to date only one large grave has been excavated.

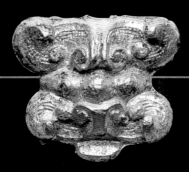

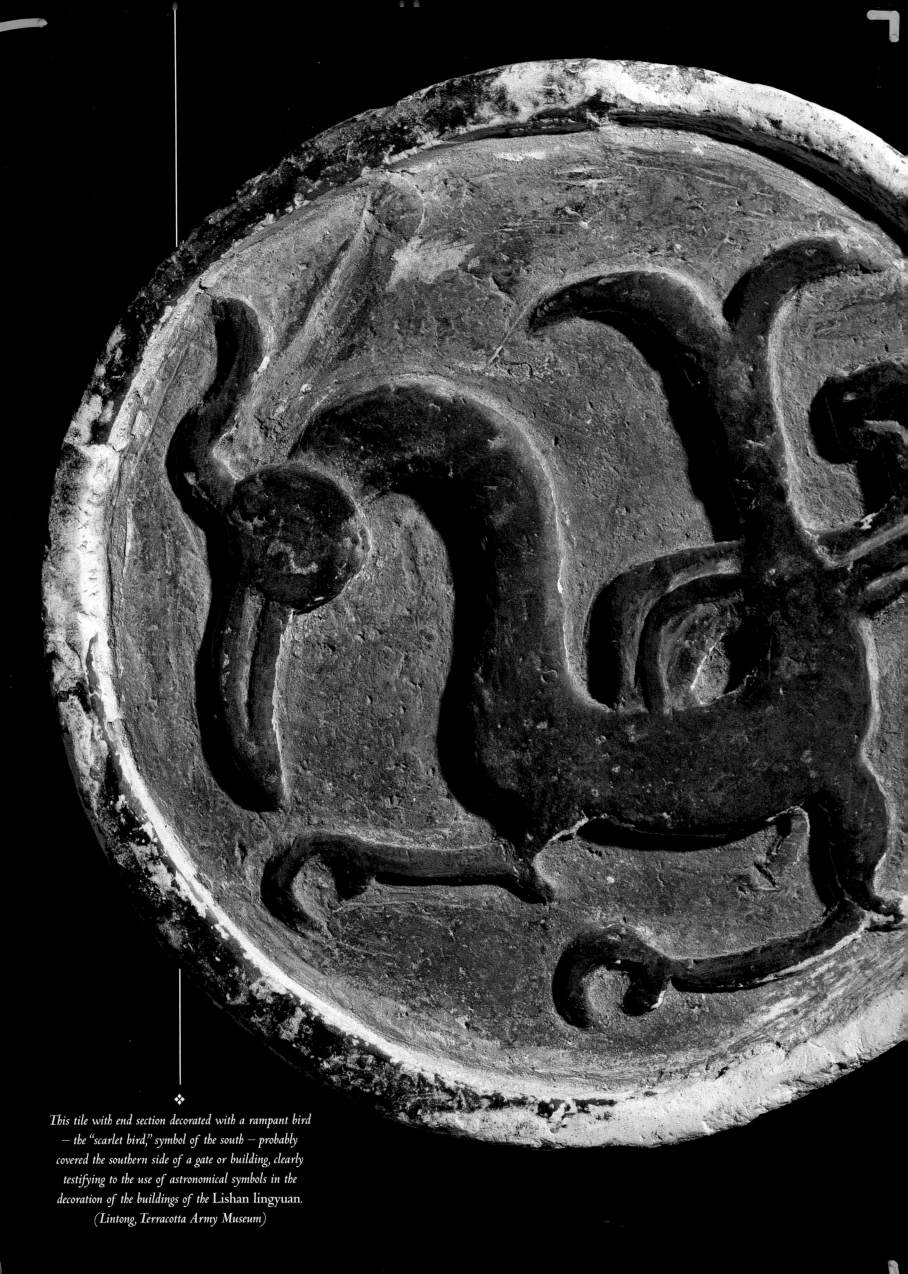

❖
*This tile with end section decorated with a rampant bird
— the "scarlet bird," symbol of the south — probably
covered the southern side of a gate or building, clearly
testifying to the use of astronomical symbols in the
decoration of the buildings of the Lishan lingyuan.
(Lintong, Terracotta Army Museum)*

YONG, THE QIN CAPITAL

The remains of Yong, a city ringed by pressed earth walls, lie south of the modern city of Fengxiang, which partly covers the ancient city. Yong was the seat of the dukes and later kings of Qin from 677 BC to the period of the Warring States. To the north lay the residential area, and to the south the necropolises, most of which were dedicated to the nobility.

The necropolis of the Qin ducal lineage covers an area of 6 square miles and is surrounded by a dike up to 23 feet deep. Inside there are forty-three large burial pits divided into thirteen groups, ten of which are surrounded by dikes. These have been measured but only slightly investigated using probes; the structure of the dikes has been subjected to limited excavation that has discovered the traces of architectural structures that originally stood over some of the larger pits and were covered with roof tiles. These structures were used to contain temples for worship of the deceased.

Five types of underground structures have been identified, based on the presence or absence of ramps that lead down to the rectangular burial pits:

18 pits with an access ramp on the two short sides (maximum total length 328 yards);

3 pits with a central access ramp on one side only (maximum total length 112 yards);

6 pits with a very short central access ramp on one long side (maximum total length 121 yards);

1 pit with a very narrow access ramp off-center on one of the short sides (total length 37 yards);

15 pits without access ramps (maximum length 116 yards).

These types of plan were not new in Qin, having been used in the royal necropolises since the Shang dynasty era (16th–11th centuries BC), but what is remarkable is the huge scale, above all in the pits with two ramps, which indicates how the dukes of Qin had adopted the forms of burial that had until then been reserved for the Son of Heaven. The eighteen monumental graves could only belong to the dukes who reigned at Yong, from Wu Gong to Xian Gong. The latter, the nineteenth duke, moved the capital eastwards in 338 BC to Yueyang and was not buried at Yong.

Of the large ducal graves, only one (MI in enclosure I) has been investigated stratigraphically. The pit is in a pyramidal shape with three large steps down to the bottom. It was 80 feet deep with two long access ramps on the east (512 feet long) and west sides (steeper and roughly 277 feet long).

❖

This gutter tile with a decorative running stag on the end section demonstrates that the buildings of the Lishan lingyuan were not only decorated with motifs associated with funerary symbology. Indeed, similar tiles have been discovered among the ruins of the palaces in the Qin capitals of Yong and Xianyang, which can be dated to the third century BC, between the Warring States period and the imperial era. (Lintong, Terracotta Army Museum)

The magnificent burial chamber (*guo*) lay at the bottom, built of huge trunks of rare wood, and standing 13 feet high and between 13 and 20 feet long. The grave itself had been entered: the few objects left were made from gold, bronze, iron, bone, stone, clay and lacquer, including thirty lithophones, many of which were inscribed. The importance of the grave (thought to be that of Duke Jing, ruled 576–537 BC) became evident when 'graves of accompaniment' (graves of those buried close to their lord as a mark of honor) were discovered around the burial chamber. These were in two groups and contained wooden sarcophagi: one group contained 72 individuals, the other 94. To these can be added 6 sacrificial victims who lay hunched up on the access ramp at a depth of approximately 17 feet, and another 14 in different points of the pit, making a total of 186 people who were to serve the duke in the tomb: 9 servants more than had accompanied Duke Mu in the afterlife 84 years earlier.

Archaeological research into the city of Yong began in the 1950s and so far has found and partly revealed the remains of large buildings which, like all ancient Chinese architectural structures, were made of a wooden framework and hard layers of pressed earth. Consequently, they cannot compare in architectural impressiveness with the palaces left by other civilizations despite being of immense historical and archaeological interest.

At this point it is important to remember that the layout of the city in archaic China followed completely different models to those we are accustomed to in the West, which were the heirs of urban concepts that evolved between the Euphrates and the Tiber. While Greek colonization in the Mediterranean was trying out new principles of city planning that were to lead to the Classical *polis*, as exemplified by 4th-century BC Athens, the cities in the Middle Kingdom at the start of the 7th century BC were developing a city plan that had been laid down by the Shang dynasty. They entered a new phase of development that was to mature fully in the period of the Warring States.

From the middle of the Spring and Autumn period, in response to the need for solid defense structures as a result of the frequent clashes and wars between states, the cities lost the prevalent-ly sacred character they had possessed in the Shang and Western Zhou periods and acquired a structure based on social and economic aggregation. In particular, though the capitals maintained their symbolic and ritual character with elaborate palaces and temples, they were ringed by defensive walls, and, while in previous periods the presence of workshops, trading areas and commoners' housing districts was unusual, it increasingly became a feature of the new model. The development of the city around a palace or temple (also walled) created a concentric model of the city known as *gong cheng*, that remained substantially unaltered right up until the early 20th century. It was only during the period of Warring States that different models were experimented with – often by modifying older settlements – that often exploited the strategic possibilities offered by water courses. The result was 'polygonal' city layouts dominated by palatial buildings built on high pressed earth platforms with a walled perimeter of different sizes and functions.

Yong was, therefore, a concentric rather than polygonal city. Investigation has been made of much of the city's south section, and of 3500 yards of the defensive walls in the western section where the remains of pressed earth ramparts (between 14 and 50 feet thick and up to 7 feet tall) still exist. Inside the city, work in the 1980s unearthed service structures like a building of 240 cubic yards used to conserve snow and ice, and many palaces and temples with clay tile roofs, drainage systems and wells. The drains used clay pipes of different type and section tied together. Although ordinary houses have not been found in the habitation area, stone plowshares, stone mortars and bronze axes confirm the existence of forms of common production. Excavation has uncovered a large number of potsherds and unbroken ceramic pots of great importance. This material has made it possible to establish a sequence of types that cover the Spring and Autumn and Warring States periods, the epoch of the Qin dynasty and much of the era of the Western Han (206 BC–23 AD). Moreover, this has demonstrated that the settlement was not abandoned after the capital was transferred, and that its use by the Qin as a cultural and production center was continued long after the fall of the Qin dynasty in 206 BC.

Complex 1 at Yong is probably the most important of the ceremonial buildings from the Spring and Autumn period discovered in all of northern China. Three buildings connected by a small pebbled avenue that face onto a central courtyard form the ceremonial complex. Behind the main hall on the north side of the courtyard stood a smaller building, while a fifth building stood on the south side slightly separate from the others and functioned as the entrance to the entire block. Each building was surrounded by a wooden arcade and was divided internally into U-shaped symmetrical sections by pressed earth walls in a plan that prefigured the traditional 'courtyard' layout (*siheyuan*) of Classical China. The complex has been recognized as the Ancestral Temple of the ducal clan. The sacredness of this area is underscored by the 181 aligned sacrificial pits: 86 of these contained an ox, 55 a goat, 1 an ox and a goat, 8 a human victim, 1 a man and a goat, and 2 contained a chariot; 28 were empty. The pouring of blood into an empty pit, it should be noted, is referred to widely in historical sources.

The heart of Qin power very probably resided in Complex 2, which is formed by a series of five communicating courtyards, circled by walls, that lay on a north-south axis 357 yards long. The courtyard at the south end, with a gate on the south side protected by an external curtain-wall, was used as an entrance, while the one at the north end was used for official receptions and ceremonies. The 'chain' of courtyards, which each contained constructions positioned symmetrically, was also to become a standard feature of the architecture of Chinese power right up until the modern age.

During the early excavations made of the Yong palatial area at the start of the 1970s, a find was made that demonstrated the importance and original beauty of the complex. A storage area was found to contain 64 bronze accessories that had a functional and decorative value: some were reinforcers of the 'cross-shaped' joints where the beams and pillars met, and others were 90° and 180° connectors designed to strengthen the beam joints. The bronze pieces are decorated with interweaving serpent motifs (*pan she*) that originated from the severe decorations of the Zhou. They are one of the best examples of the Qin art of casting from the late Spring and Autumn period.

In the light of these finds, a passage from the *Qin Ben Ji* (Basic Annals of Qin) that relates to the reign of Duke Mu (for whom 177 people were sacrificed on his burial in 621 BC) clearly mentions the beauty of the Yong palaces. At the same time, that passage is perhaps the one that best describes the political and cultural climate of the period.

Sima Qian writes that a certain You Yu, a descendant of the people of the dukedom of Jin who had settled among the Rong but who was able to speak the Rong language, was sent by the Rong on a 'diplomatic mission' to Duke Mu. It is clear that even at the end of the 7th century, the 'barbaric' world of the Rong (who were herders and farmers) was very different to that of the farmers of the feudal states of the Middle Kingdom, and that the Rong spoke a different language to the one shared by many of the feudal states, including Qin.

When he arrived at Yong, You Yu, having visited the palace and been shown its magnificence, is said to have exclaimed, 'If the demons made it, then the spirits must be exhausted; if men made it, what bitter toil for the people!'

63 left and top right These gray clay end sections of tiles are decorated with the "Green Dragon" and four quadrants, each of which contains an ideogram, composing the inscription Qi Nian Gong Dan, or "Tile of the Qinian Palace," a building constructed by the Qin Duke Hui (r. 399-387 BC). (Lintong, Terracotta Army Museum)

63 bottom This bronze connector was used to reinforce a beam joint and is decorated with "interweaving serpent" motifs (pan she). It was discovered in a pit near the Qin ducal palaces at Yong, along with 64 other bronze beam elements with the same decoration. (Xi'an, Historical Museum)

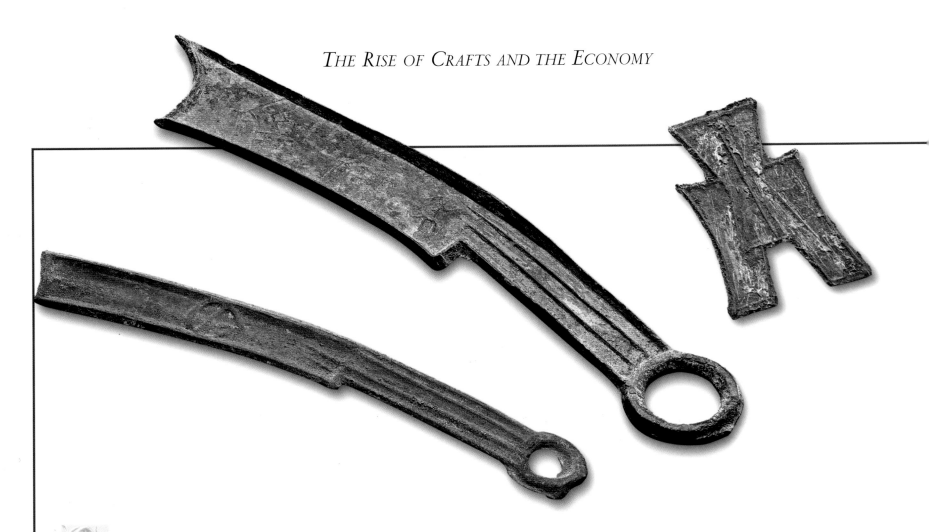

W e can suppose that one of the marvels seen by You Yu was bronze vases that were no longer (or not only) produced using the ancient method in which an elaborate mold could be used only once. A new technique had been developed, probably in Jin, based on the use of sectional pieces that could be used over and over again. He may also have seen polychrome lacquers and bronzes with rich, visible decorations made in the kingdom of Chu, where it is thought the new lost-wax casting technique may have been developed. Also, perhaps imported from the east, bronze vases with inlaid copper decorations. You Yu perhaps did not see the first objects made from a new metal – iron – for two reasons; first, because only bronze was considered *jijin*, i.e., a metal the equal of gold, and second because the first iron objects, at the start of the 6th century BC, were still rare. It was only the following century that the metal was commonly employed.

Unlike in the West, iron was not only used in forging but also casting. In both cases carbon could be added to the metal to obtain carburized iron for the production of steel weapons; on the other hand, cast iron was used to produce tools. Qin was not one of the first large iron manufacturers, even though, when the kingdom did get around to it, the results were excellent. In the Spring and Autumn period, it was Chu, Wu and Yue – the states in the Yangzi valley – that produced the best cast iron. The reasons for this were that they had large mineral deposits which they mined using remarkably modern techniques. In the meantime, they had perfected pyrotechnology (the art of manipulating heat) to the benefit of the bronze sword forgers of Yue and Wu (the swords were so good that they did not oxidize), the casters of iron weapons and vases in Chu, and the potters in Wu and Yue. The potters fired glazed pottery in long kilns at 1300°C that was so hard and shiny that the pieces could rightly be considered the forerunners of porcelain, though porcelain did not appear until nearly a thousand years later.

Historical texts and archaeological data reveal that during this same period there was a general growth in the production of handcrafts, textiles and lacquer, as well as in mining, for instance, salt extraction. These surprising innovations were no less matched by the progress made in agricultural production.

During the Spring and Autumn period, there was a gradual administrative integration of *guoren* (inhabitants that dwelt inside the city limits, which included large areas of cultivable land) and *yeren* (those who lived in the open countryside). The effect of the integration was a more uniform taxation system that was no longer based on the performance of services on the land of the feudal lords (or for someone they designated), but on payment in agricultural products that varied from between 10% and 20% of the harvest. From the information we have at hand, it is clear that juridically farmers were moving farther and farther away from the concept of being slaves toward that of being serfs, but with a greater degree of personal freedom. Another development was that the use of land was slowly being distanced from the concept of being the property of the king to that of being a personal asset, and with it the first steps toward the notion of private land ownership were taken.

Greater integration of different peoples also produced a wider circulation of cultivable species; the most important were wheat, two species of millet, rice, pulses, cauliflower and various arboreal fruits. Mulberry and

sumac bushes (which produced lacquer) were cultivated and the yields used an industrial basis. This diversity, associated with the attention paid to the growth of the economy by members of the various philosophical schools of the period, most likely lay at the basis of the rotation of crops which, in the more favorable regions, resulted in more harvests per year. In addition, there was the gradual spread of iron farm tools and use of the ox-drawn plow which together represented a large increase in the production of crops and handcrafts in the 6th and 5th centuries BC.

The increasing travel between states, whether for the movement of armies or participation in summits, led to the transformation of local paths into interregional roads, the maintenance of which was often one of the obligations of the lords of the Warring States. Merchants increasingly used these ways of communication, by land and water, and many literary references are made regarding the presence of traders in 'feudal courts' and their social elevation. Many merchants were members of the intelligentsia, for instance, Duanmu Si, a disciple of Confucius, who, in addition to great wealth, acquired an eminent role

as a political counselor due to the experience he had gained by his mobility as a merchant.

These changes led, during the Spring and Autumn period (770–475 BC), to the development of a new system of exchange based on 'standards,' i.e., bronze coins. Some scholars think that these standards initially had a symbolic and ritual value. The first coins were made from copper/bronze and were cast in the area of the Zhou capital, Chengzhou. They were in the form of a two-pronged spade with a hollow, vertical handle. Some spade-shaped coins (called kongshoubu, a hollow-topped coin, or chanbu, a spade-coin) were cast in molds and bore either the single Chinese character wang (representing cheng, city or royal city), or two characters Dong Zhou (Eastern Zhou) to signify that the coins were from the Zhou kingdom. The appearance of standards was not unprecedented, however: an earlier form of coinage in the Shang dynasty made use of cowries (Cypraea moneta sp.). The value of cowries is shown by the composition of the character bao (precious) in oracular inscriptions in which the sign for a shell (bei) is part of the ideogram. Also illuminating are the mentions in Zhou inscriptions on bronze

of the use of a string of cowries (from five to ten) as a currency.

In any case, the circulation of cowries in the Shang and Zhou period was restricted to the aristocracy as was, it seems, circulation of kongshoubu. From the middle of the 6th century BC, three variants of kongshoubu bore the ideograms of at least ten different place names in Zhou territory, indicating where they were minted and the area of circulation. At the end of the Spring and Autumn period, the most powerful feudal state – Jin – dared to issue its own chanbu, with a solid rather than hollow handle. It was not for another century that Qin issued its own coinage.

The general growth created a market economy around the end of the Spring and Autumn period and the start of the period of Warring States. The rise of the private merchant, commerce, and coinage were all part of a circle of cause and effect that brought mutual benefits. In the period of Warring States, these revolutionary changes led to the validation of the concept of private property, general demographic growth, the development of a mature urban society and the birth of the Qin empire.

From Dukedom to Kingdom: Qin and the Warring States

The old feudal relationships were just a memory and the subject of political and ethical speculation when in 481 BC the head of the Tian family – which had held the position of prime minister in Qi for generations – placed a puppet on the throne after assassinating the duke and exterminating his supporters. He took direct control of the entire territory of Qi except for the area of the capital, which he left to the ducal lineage. The mechanism used by the Tian family to consolidate its power in Qi was not much different to that used several centuries later by Caesar in Republican Rome: gifts and philanthropic works in the capital (Linzi) and the recruitment of able counselors and administrators from various social levels who were not necessarily native to Qi.

In the half century preceding the assassination of the duke, even the 'ministerial' families in the dukedom of Jin had begun internal struggles, introducing a new mechanism of concentration of economic power and control to the territory. Once the rival families had been erased, their fiefs were transformed into districts (*xian*) and placed under the direct control of the dominant family, thus taking another step towards centralized control of power and the state. This control was underlined by the issue of regulations inscribed on bronze vases and by the blood oaths to sanction the alliance between families.

In 497 BC the struggle between the groups of ministerial lineage turned into a civil war that only ended in 424 with the victory of three clans that divided the land of Jin into the new territorial and political entities of Hann, Wei and Zhao. The Zhou only recognized these newcomers in 403 BC.

In the Yangzi valley, the tendency towards the centralization of power was manifested in the continual hostility between the states of Chu, Wu and Yue, and in the internecine struggles between the lineages of the royal family and the collateral families in Chu. Though the fortunes alternated between the two sides in Chu, the kingdom continued to grow in wealth and territory throughout the 5th century BC.

In this climate of territorial and institutional change, the aim of which was to optimize the management of resources for military and

❖

The powerful outline of an archer ready to shoot an arrow from his bow, sketched on a bronze hu *with copper decorations (7th-5th century B.C.), evokes the climate of social and political instability typical of an age in which tensions often resulted in open hostilities between clans within individual kingdoms or between states. (Paris, Musée National des Arts Asiatiques-Guimet)*

agricultural reasons, the dukedom of Qin also followed the transformations, though it was not in the forefront of change. After a period of conquest in the west and northwest, Qin suffered a phase of defeats and territorial losses along the stretch of the Huanghe River that separated Qin from the powerful league of Wei, Zhao and Hann to the east. The first one hundred years in Qin of the period of Warring States were marked by clan conflict, with the passage of the dukedom to various collateral branches of the Ying lineage, and a succession of young dukes whose reigns were significantly short. Less unstable seems to have been the tenure of ministers and counselors, to whom, no doubt, were due the consolidation of the western lands and the start of southwest expansion into the Sichuan basin. Sichuan soon became the main supplier of grain to Qin.

Duke Xian (ruled 384–362 BC) brought an end to court intrigues when, after spending a long period in Wei as a peace hostage (an expedient established in the Spring and Autumn period) supported by 'commander' Gai and the Rong and Di 'barbarians,' he returned to Yong in 385 BC and took power the following year. One of his first acts was to abolish the practice of sacrificial victims; then, for reasons of political and military strategy, in 383 BC he moved the capital east to Yueyang. To mark the occasion the city was walled. The advantages of the new capital (in the modern county of Lintong) were of being far from the old and untrustworthy noble families of Yong, and of bringing the center of power closer to the zone contested with Wei along the right bank of the Huanghe. In Yueyang, Duke Xian began his reforms, perhaps taking as his model the institutions of Wei, such as the registration of families in groups of five and the creation of districts (*xian*) administered directly by the duke. These reforms formed the base from which Duke Xiao (ruled 361–338 BC) and his counselor Shang Yang began to transform the dukedom into the most powerful political and military organization in the Warring States.

❖

These bronze objects date back to the same period as the hu *vase in the previous picture and exemplify the dual nature of the society of the period: an arrowhead, a sword encrusted with turquoise and jade, and a mirror, whose non-reflective side became the scene for symbolic decorations associated with the orderly vision of the universe at precisely this time. (Musée National des Arts Asiatiques-Guimet, Paris)*

Shang Yang (died 338 BC) is one of the most fascinating reformers and thinkers in archaic China because of his abilities to reconcile, appraise and draw up economic and political principles created separately in the various Warring States, and then turn them into a single body that served Duke Xiao's political designs. The son of a concubine of the lord of Wey, a small and weak dukedom in the lower Huanghe valley, Shang Yang (also referred to as Gongsun Yang, Wei Yang and the lord of Shang) learnt the techniques of bureaucratic control of the population from a master in the Legalist School. He then moved on to become the administrator and 'bursar' of the prime minister of the powerful dukedom of Wei. Following a standard practice during the period of Warring States, Xiao Gong of Qin called him as soon as he had ascended the throne. In this case, Shang Yang was invited specifically to advise on the reconquest of the lands to the west of the Huanghe. After arriving in Qin, Shang Yang obtained an interview with Duke Xiao and in the same year succeeded in being made a 'guest' officer of the duke. Just two years later, in 358 BC, according to Sima Qian, Shang Yang showed Xiao Gong a series of reforms necessary to bring vitality to the institutions and economy of Qin. This series included changes in the law, the imposition of fair but strict punishments, the development of agriculture, and the bestowal of suitable rewards for those who chose to fight and die in battle. The reforms were launched to the displeasure of the people, but three years later they understood the advantages. Shang Yang was promoted to the 11th grade to be a *zuoshuzhang*. After this initial success (as stated in Sima Qian's account), the reign of Duke Xian was simply a series of military successes, often obtained by Shang Yang, and periodic reforms like the transfer of the capital from Yueyang to Xianyang. This new site was opposite the ancient cities of Feng and Hao, the capitals of the Western Zhou, that are subsumed in modern Xi'an. Qin power was to remain centered in Xianyang until the fall of the dynasty in 206 BC. Politically significant is the fact that one of the first monumental works undertaken in the new capital (on the initiative of Shang Yang) was the Tower Gate (called the *Jique*) that gave access to the royal palace. Traditionally it was from this type of construction, called a *que*, that Zhou rulers used to issue their decrees and officially announce the laws.

It is difficult to classify Shang Yang's reforms into different categories as each one had multiple effects on all sections of the economy and institutions of the state. Shang Yang's main goal in drawing up a severe and detailed set of laws was the control of the court cliques and peasants' social behavior by declaring everyone equal before the law. However, the code also had effects on the economy and society by introducing the principle of collective responsibility and mutual monitoring. This mechanism bound together in civil solidarity the members of the groups of five or ten families in which the entire state was divided up; it also laid the foundations for an unprecedented degree of military solidarity as the members of each mutual monitoring and assistance group had to fight side by side.

Traditionally, historians have held negative views of the measure that introduced collective responsibility and mutual monitoring, as though it necessarily had to create bad relations between neighbors with its pettiness and mutual suspicion. If this occurred, we believe it was the exception rather than the rule; in fact, on the contrary scholars think that solidarity rather than mistrust was the norm. Another measure that had a dual effect was the writing up of the laws on pillars and on standards of weights and measures, the aim of which was to prevent people being able to deny they knew the law. It was also a powerful means of encouraging basic learning of the written language in social strata that were previously generally illiterate.

Analogously, the new levels of titles and rewards for courage shown in battle (measured by the number of enemy heads or ears taken), and balanced by very severe penalties, both individual and collective, for acts of insubordination and cowardice, created solidarity, camaraderie and ties to commanders. But, equally, it undermined the blood rights of the Qin nobility to whom the heredity of titles was almost unknown. As a result of Shang Yang's reforms, the army came to be composed of peasants, and this fact offered opportunities for social mobility and advancement, even for immigrants. These reforms were just as important as those in which parcels of land were assigned as large as a family with a single adult male was capable of cultivating. Taxes were placed on the head of the family and increased disproportionately with the increasing number of adult males who lived with the father. These taxes were offset by tillage of uncultivated lands and the assignment of lots to immigrants.

Even the most important reforms that Shang Yang launched straight after the transfer to Xianyang had effects on various sectors of society and the economy. In 350 BC, much of Qin was divided into administrative districts (*xian*), either 41 or 36 depending on whose count is accepted, each directed by a magistrate (*ling*), a vice-magistrate (*cheng*) and a military commander (*wei*). These three figures were directly accountable to the ducal administration and had beneath them a pyramid of local functionaries. The lowest level of these functionaries was the supervisors (*sefu*) who were distributed among the villages.

This reform created an efficient and well-structured administration that reached right down to local level, and also controlled society by documents that passed from the center to the periphery and vice versa. These documents could not be accepted as valid unless they bore the sign of authenticity that is still used to validate public deeds: a seal or stamp and the name of the official responsible.

The *xian* also became an essential instrument for military growth as enrolments were regulated on the basis of districts; this made a draft possible across all territories and therefore the creation of an easily mobilized infantry.

Qin was not the only state to innovate its military in this fashion; many of the Warring States created large armies based on a mass of conscripted peasant infantry supported by elite professionals.

Shang Yang's good fortune ran out in 338 BC on the death of Duke Xiao, though in the meantime he had accumulated honors and wealth. With his protector gone, and following a vendetta perpetrated by the tutors to the heir to the throne, he fell victim to the laws he had contributed to creating. His punishment was to be tied to chariots and pulled apart in the public square.

Despite the fate of their creator, Shang Yang's reforms were not abrogated; on the contrary, it was thanks to them that Duke Huiwen (ruled 337–311 BC) was able to resist the conflict with Wei, Hann and Zhao and to conquer lands and fortified cities to the east of the Huanghe. He also acquired lands to the north of Chu and united the middle Yangzi valley with the Sichuan basin. In this way Qin became a large kingdom, protected by the arid lands, mountain ranges and large rivers of western China. Duke Huiwen could count on the traditional aggressiveness of the Qin army, on the wealth of Chu's natural resources and large crops in Sichuan. It was in Sichuan ten years after the death of Huiwen that general Li Bing of Qin carried out one of the most spectacular hydraulic works in ancient China: the diversion of the Minjiang near modern Dujiayan. The water system – expanded during the Han dynasty with a series of dams, locks and artificial channels – was designed to divide the river Min and feed a series of canals for the irrigation of almost 1.5 million acres of cultivatable land in Chengdu Plain.

Huiwen succeeded in consolidating his power and enforcing the fearful respect of the lords of the Warring States, and in 325 BC he assumed the title of *wang*, as the duke of Wei had done in 344 and the duke of Qi had done in 341. In 324 even the duke of Hann called himself king, and then so did the lords of Zhao, Yan and Zhongshan in 322. The period of the growth of the states to become centralized administrations was about to end, as was the sacredness of the title that only the kings of the Zhou had until then borne.

Despite the importance of Yueyang, the capital from which the Qin began the reconquest of the entire Wei valley before they settled permanently in Xianyang, few archaeological investigations have been carried out on the site of the ancient city, which is estimated to cover an area of roughly 1.5 square miles. The only sections to have been investigated are the outlines of the walls, six gates, some stretches of the city streets, the remains of a few workshops, and piles of clay roof tiles that covered a series of largish buildings served by a drainage system of clay pipes. Research in the area of Xianyang has been much more extensive (to be discussed later) but it is not easy to tell what remains from the period preceding unification of the Warring States and what remains from the Qin dynasty. Once again it is the necropolises that provide the most information on the social and political growth of Qin.

The reason for the development of a new Qin model of funerary architecture during the period of Warring States is not understood. The rectangular shaft graves used in the Spring and Autumn period seem almost to have been replaced by tombs formed by a large burial chamber excavated on one of the sides of a deep access shaft. This form of burial is also an excellent marker of Qin expansion eastward, from the late Warring States period to the time of unification. After its first appearance in the Wei valley, the burial chamber grave can be traced throughout the middle Huanghe valley, though there the traditional shaft grave never entirely disappeared.

In general the new development featured small structures and few grave goods. In the many Qin necropolises of the 4th and 3rd centuries BC excavated in Shaanxi province (Keshengzhuang, Banpo, Baizhaizi, Lijiaya, Baoji and, above all, Taerpo) there are few tombs that contain either vases, or a weapon or other article made from bronze or iron. The norm is a few clay pots that often contain the remains of animals slaughtered as offerings. Anthropomorphic statuettes and personal ornaments are rare, whereas tombs without any goods at all are common and demonstrate that the graves belonged to low social classes; the poverty of the grave goods means it is even hard to recognize the deceased's profession or social role. It may be that the graves belonged to the peasant soldiers and low- and medium-level functionaries that turned Qin into a great state, and to their wives and children, these latter continued to be buried in clay pots as had occurred since the Neolithic era.

In a site just north of Xi'an, known as Minzhu Garden, many of the sixty graves excavated were not only without grave goods but in some cases several bodies were buried in the

❖

70 These "winged" or "grooved" bronze arrowheads were lethal weapons that were skillfully shot by the Qin archers — much feared during the Warring States period — using huge wooden bows. Although the material decomposed long ago, the imprint of the bows is often present in the graves. The wings aided the force of penetration of thee weapons, and once they had entered the target they also prevented them from being extracted. (Historical Museum, Xi'an)

❖

71 These painted gray ceramic equestrian figurines were found in Tomb 28057 of the Taerpo necropolis, which was established after 350 BC. It is hard to believe that they are just 100 years older than the statues of the Terracotta Army, for the subsequent progress made by the Qin in the art of molding is quite astounding. (Municipal Museum, Xianyang)

same trench in disordered and casual positions. Study of the bones has not yet been concluded so it is difficult to say whether these graves are the result of an unusual event – such as an epidemic, a famine or war – or an atypical form of burial that has not yet been well documented.

In the many necropolises in the upper Wei valley down as far as where it meets the Huanghe River, the graves that contain ceramic (rarely bronze) vases, weapons, mirrors, bronze seals, bronze belt buckles and ritual stone insignia are typical of the middle to high classes in Qin society. The decorations of the clay vases (which imitate bronze ones) are more cursive. Once their symbolic function was lost, they began to disappear around the middle of the Warring States period, and contemporaneously the vases took on elaborate shapes in which the internal volumes were increasingly reduced by raising of the bottoms until they almost reached the rim.

'Qin has the heart of a tiger or a wolf' said the neighboring states to the east, referring to the aggressiveness of the Qin army, and as the period of Warring States progressed, the grave goods show how true this description was. In Taerpo, the largest Qin necropolis uncovered in the capital Xianyang, objects of the everyday life of peasants, such as model granaries or ox-drawn carts, were accompanied by bronze and iron weapons: swords, different types of halberd, arrow tips, sharpened spearshaft tips, crossbow bolts and short curved knife blades. Little refinement was conceded, unlike in the grave goods of the nobility in the more eastern kingdoms, except for the varieties of Qin bronze mirrors with low reliefs and the zoomorphic hook buckles, for example, entwined dragons, which were the highest achievement of Qin metalworking.

One aspect is particularly interesting in this last category of items: the mixture of different elements, animals or monsters in movement demonstrates the familiarity of the Qin with the animalistic, intercultural art of the

❖

The grave goods, typical of Qin tombs, are models of subjects of contemporary everyday life, of the peasantry and aristocracy alike. Animal figures are commonly found, such as this horse with carriage, which reveals a certain familiarity with the world of the steppe and its animalistic art.

steppes. A brooch in pure 'animalistic' style was found in a late Qin grave at Zaomiao, close to the steppes of Ordos: it is of a tiger biting an ibex in the back. And at Badiqan a tiny bronze stud combines a human face with the head of a long-horned goat by means of two square spirals.

The Qin graves have revealed yet another aspect of major importance: the centralized control of handcrafts. This was the mechanism that made the construction possible of one of the largest funerary monuments in human history: the tomb of the First August Sovereign of the Qin dynasty, Qin Shi Huangdi.

74 This small terracotta head belonging to the Qin period probably depicts the face of a soldier. The presence in grave goods of miniature replicas of objects, such as human figurines, barns, and model carriages, testifies to the maturity of a process of change in funeral rituals that commenced at the beginning of the Spring and Autumn period and became widespread during the Warring States period.

75 In addition to bronze and terracotta artifacts, wooden and lacquer objects — such as this standing wooden figurine dating to the period between the end of the Eastern Zhou and Qin dynasties — were often found in the tombs of the era, particularly in the areas of the southern kingdom of Chu, conquered by the Qin armies. The popularity of substitute models, known by the obscure Chinese term of minqi ("spirit goods") gradually grew, but several centuries were necessary before they replaced real people and objects in the tombs.

Many of the vases found in graves were stamped with four-sided seals, the imprint of which usually bore four or six characters that stated the office supervisor and place of production. We do not know why these seals were included on the vases but it is possible that it had something to do with the control either of the pot quality or of its regular volume. A less plausible reason would be that they indicated the place of use of the object.

The style of the script in the ideograms is also of interest. It is very simple and linear, and in most cases easily read. This is very different from the inscriptions on the ritual bronzes or the styles in vogue in other Warring States, which were much more complex and archaic. The style of the ideograms on Qin pottery is one of the earliest examples of 'regular script' and was one that the Qin imposed on all its conquered territories at the time of the foundation of the empire. The style was to remain almost unchanged until the introduction of simplified ideograms a few years after the foundation of the People's Republic of China in 1949.

The stamps provide solid proof of the wide use that the Qin administration made of seals in control and certification. This was well attested in summer 2000 by the discovery of 325 stamped-clay seals near the village of Xiangjiaxiang. The site lies in the area of the imperial palaces from the period of the Western Han (206 BC–23 AD). These Han palaces were built over buildings from the Qin era that date from the late period of the Warring States to the early years of the Western Han dynasty, and were very probably offices used by the public administration. The seal imprints were made on lumps of raw clay and they provide important information on the geography of the capital (thanks to the many place names they bear). They also indicate the evolution of the administrative system through the change of titles or the appearance

❖

Over 1,000 clay seals stamped with slightly raised characters bearing the names and titles of people or administrative terms have been found in recent years in the area surrounding Xi'an. The custom of sealing official documents and missives in this way became very widespread during the Qin period and subsequent centuries, testifying to the complexity of the administrative system.

of new titles within the hierarchy of central and local administrations.

The use of seals was not exclusive to Qin as we know from finds made in 1987–88 in Grave 2 at Baoshan (Hubei province) roughly 9 miles from the Chu capital, Jinan, during the period of the Warring States. This grave contained the remains of the high functionary Zhao Tuo, the *zuoyin dafu* of the kingdom of Chu, who died in 316 BC. Of the 1,933 objects found in his grave, there were several small jars containing foodstuffs that were carefully closed with a leather strip beneath the wicker-lined neck, others by a rough cord wrapped around the vase from the upper part to the rim. In all cases, the loose ends of the tie that closed the lid were 'sealed' with a lump of clay on which the contents of the jar were written or rings were stamped. The intention clearly was to prevent the vases being opened without the owner being aware. What differentiates the seals of the Qin from those of the Chu is that they were used for administrative purposes.

These finds pose an interesting question: we know that the use of seals for storage control (whether public or private) has a long history, having been invented by temple administrations in Mesopotamia around the turn of the 3rd millennium BC. Seals made from bronze and precious stones were used in the western regions of Central Asia in the 3rd and 2nd millennia BC, but the use of seals in China in the Shang and Zhou dynasties is rarely documented. However, their use became common in the Warring States following the rise of centralized administrations. Therefore, as with metallurgy and the use of the chariot, a query arises: were these seals independent inventions or learned from other cultures? Currently, archaeology is unable to provide an answer.

Concrete evidence of the Qin centralized administration is not just provided by the impressions of seals on clay but by inscriptions on bronze weapons. And this fact is evidence

of the checks imposed on this essential field of production. Excavation work carried out in 1995 in Taerpo necropolis turned up a small bronze cap (27063:15) made to be placed on the end of a halberd; an inscription on the cap records that the piece was made in the nineteenth year under the supervision of minister Yang. In other words, it was made in 343 BC (the nineteenth year of the rule of Duke Xiao) under the supervision of Shang Yang. Other inscriptions on bronze weapons, three of which were also under the supervision of Shang Yang, reveal that direct control of the manufacture of arms was by the highest levels of the administration uninterruptedly and long after unification of the empire in 221 BC. However, the army could not count on arms made only in the workshops of the capital (as represented by the name of Shang Yang), so various weapons found outside the metropolitan area bear inscriptions that record the supervision of the *shangjun*, a high functionary in the local prefecture (*jun*). These latter inscriptions are proof that Qin had probably adopted for newly conquered territories an administration arranged on a different basis to the *xian* district; this new administration unit, the *jun*, is usually translated as prefecture.

These seals reflect the development of the Chinese script. It is no coincidence that the Qin style, which was to form the basis for the classic Chinese script following further refinement during the Han period, is known as xiaozhuang, *i.e., "small seal" or "lesser sealing."*

There is another category in Qin inscriptions on bronze weapons that is of key importance: these were short phrases inscribed in Qin script on weapons whose typology defines them as products of other 'kingdoms.' It seems that these weapons were war booty and are evidence of the advance made by Qin armies, especially during the 3rd century BC. The weapons with Qin inscriptions were found in Liaoning in the extreme north, and in Guanxi-Guangdong in the extreme south.

The best indicators of Qin expansion, though, are offered by Qin graves that lie outside the Wei valley, and are datable to the middle and late phase of the period of Warring States. In most cases they show the flexibility of the Qin culture, and its ability to adapt and incorporate elements of local cultures, for example, in the shape of the burial pits, the architecture of the internal spaces and the composition of the grave goods.

Many important finds have been made in the habitation areas and graveyards excavated in the territories of the Qin kings who ruled from the late 4th century BC. Near Houma (Shanxi province) about seventy graves have been excavated from the middle Warring States period, all characterized by the hunched position of the bodies. This detail and the typically Qin grave goods found with the bodies indicate that the graves were those of functionaries and officials from the kingdom of Qin, although the graves themselves are somewhat atypical in other ways. Specifically, they featured a small channel that marked the outer limit of either a single or a pair of graves, which often contained sacrificial victims. Some of these victims wore bronze collars, and others were dismembered, almost as if the channel and victims could offer a magical defense for the deceased in alien territories.

The Qin graves in Chengdu Plain (Sichuan province) contain bronze vessels and arms belonging to the local Ba culture. Meanwhile the Qin tombs uncovered in territories conquered in Chu contained not only abundant and refined items made from wood, lacquer, plant fibers, bronze, clay and jade, but also the form of burial was Chu, with the body wrapped in silk shrouds and garments inside wooden caskets. These were often lacquered and painted and placed inside each other, with spaces that contained the grave goods and symbolized the different functions of a luxury house.

Few of the Qin graves can equal the importance of those in the county of Yunmeng (north Hubei) which King Zhao (ruled 306–251 BC) won from the powerful kingdom of Chu in 278 BC. At the Shuihudi site, eleven graves from the end of the Warring States period or early Qin era were excavated in December 1975.

The finds at Shuihudi are of unrivalled importance: graves M7 (from the 51st year of King Zhao's rule, 256 BC) and M11 (30th year of the reign of Emperor Shi Huangdi, 217 BC) are of no less significance than the Terracotta Army. The grave goods included legal, jurisprudential, administrative, military, divinatory, pharmacological and philosophical codices written in ink on thin bamboo strips that provide an unprecedented body of information for the study of the entire early Chinese civilization. In M11 alone, the bamboo strips in the grave of a certain Xi, an expert functionary in the penal code, formed more than 1,100 codices after they were put back together.

These were accompanied by refined plates and lacquerware produced by the imperial workshops in Xianyang, plus writing brushes with bronze holders, silk garments (mostly decomposed), clay and bronze vases, and objects made of wood and bamboo.

79 top *Bronze mirrors were among the most important everyday objects from the time of the Warring States period onward, but they also had powerful apotropaic values. The non-reflective side was decorated with highly geometrized cosmological motifs, or more explicit patterns based on pairs of elements that appear to revolve in the field of the mirror, as in this typical Qin example found in distant Hubei province in southern China.*

❖

79 bottom *This lacquer basin was found in Shuihudi, near Yunmeng, in Hubei province, in a grave belonging to a Qin functionary called Xi, who died in 217 BC. The tomb also housed manuscripts containing juridical texts, which have proved important for the study of the Qin legal code prior to the foundation of the empire.*

The richness of the Qin functionaries' graves in the conquered regions of Chu is indubitably refined and perfectly exemplifies the cultural sophistication and 'quality of life' of the kingdom that the Hua Xia considered 'barbarous.' Yet the opulence of even these tombs is nothing compared to the magnificence and size of the tombs of the royal clan. To the northeast of Xianyang, near the town of Zhouling, two large tombs have been discovered, each covered by a pressed earth structure, that some experts believe to have been the burial places of the kings Huiwen (ruled 337/324–311 BC) and Wu (ruled 310–307 BC). If this is the case, then the area would have been the 'Bimo funerary garden' (*Bimo Lingyuan*) referred to by historical sources. More certain is the 'Eastern Funerary Area' or necropolis of Zhiyang that lies near the modern city of Lintong, a few miles from the tomb of the First August Sovereign of the Qin dynasty.

This lies in a flattish area at the foot of the western sides of Mount Li. Four funerary enclosures have been found in which a huge archaeological investigation was carried out in 1986 to establish the size of the necropolis (180 acres) and the distribution, size and shape of the tombs.

Enclosure I is surrounded by ditches and contains two main cross-shaped tombs measuring roughly 240 x 142 yards. Each has a burial chamber at a depth of about 75 to 82 feet with a ramp on each of the four sides; the east ramp was the one used for access to the grave itself. It is interesting to note that the cross shape was used in the largest of the royal Shang tombs in Yin. Connected to these two large tombs were two smaller ones and two sacrificial pits. The same area was found to contain the remains of four cult buildings associated with the tombs.

What distinguishes the royal tombs in the Eastern Funerary Area from the tombs of the Qin dukes in Yong is their visibility rather than their shape or size. Unlike the graves of the ancient aristocracy, these tombs are covered by large mounds made from layers of pressed earth that today still stand sixteen feet high, though that is nothing in comparison to the mound over the tomb of the First Emperor, which was ten times higher.

This change in funerary architecture and the conception of the tomb, in which the cult building was accompanied by a wooded hill, occurred sporadically during the 5th and 4th centuries BC in various kingdoms of the Middle Kingdom. Like metallurgy, the chariot and the use of seals, the mound may have been an imported feature, as the use of tombs covered by mounds (known as *kurgan*) began to be used in the northern steppes around the 6th century BC.

The steppe model is thought to have passed through the kingdom of Yan and been adopted first by several of the dukes and kings of the Warring States, then by the Qin emperors. And from that time the use of earth hills was a distinctive feature of imperial tombs in the centuries to come.

Another element in royal funerary architecture in the late Warring States period that remained in use until the Qing dynasty (1644–1911) was the practice of using the term *ling* to describe the complex formed by the main tomb, satellite tombs, sacrificial pits and cult buildings that lay within a ditch or earthwork planted with trees and plants. *Ling* is the term usually used to denote 'tomb' or 'mausoleum' (and often associated with the word *yuan*, which means garden); *ling* gives an idea of the magnificence of these complexes but it does not seem to fully match the reality of the fact nature, not architecture, was the predominant element,. For this reason, we prefer the term 'funerary garden' rather than mausoleum.

In addition to the graves of the Qin kings in Zhiyang, others are thought to belong to princes of the Qin household and high functionaries in Enclosure 3. They include pits with chariots, horses, sacrificial pits, a 'royal alley' paved with river pebbles, and earth platforms on which cult buildings stood. Although future excavations will certainly establish to which Qin kings the graves in Zhiyang necropolis belonged, we are sure that in Enclosure I (where the *Zhi Lingyuan* lies) the large cross-shaped tombs belonged to Queen Tang and King Zhaoxiang (ruled 306–251 BC). In 256, this king dared to attack King Zhou and succeeded in bringing down the dynasty of the Eastern Zhou.

Enclosure 2 contains a large pit with two ramps on opposite sides, three pits with a single ramp, two secondary graves, a sacrificial pit and the remains of a cult building that together form the *Shou Lingyuan* of King Xiaowen (ruled 250 BC) and Queen Huayang. Enclosure 4 has been found to contain a large cross-shaped tomb, two graves with a single ramp and the foundations of a cult building; this is the *Yang Lingyuan* in which King Zhuangxiang (ruled 249–247 BC) and his consort were buried. They were the parents of the First August Sovereign of the Qin dynasty.

❖

This pyriform jar, about 4.7 inches tall, is a typical Qin artifact dating back to the end of the Warring States period. The panel in the upper part with traces of red pigment bears a six-character inscription detailing the place of production and the standard size of the container. Similar small jars have been found in the necropolis of the Qin kings in Zhiyang, on the western slope of Mount Li, where the burial mounds of the First August Sovereign's parents are situated. (Terracotta Army Museum, Lintong)

QIN SHI HUANGDI AND THE TRIUMPH OF THE LAW

The drawing up of a body of laws and their strict application to the entire population was one of the strong points of King Ying Zheng of Qin's administrative and military organization: it allowed him to overcome his powerful adversaries, one after the other, in the space of just a few years. By 221 BC, he had created an immense empire, the like of which had never been seen. It ranged from the western highlands of Gansu and Qinghai to the modern southern provinces of Guangdong and Guangxi, and from the coastal regions in the east to the vast expanses north of the Yellow River, including even the remote peninsula of Liaodong. According to tradition, the excessive severity of the laws and the brutality with which they were applied concealed the strategic effectiveness of the policy of Qin Shi Huangdi, the First August Emperor of the Qin dynasty, as the king referred to himself once he had ascended the imperial throne. For more than two thousand years, the official (and mainly Confucian) historiography has branded the First Emperor and his first minister Li Si with

infamy. They stand accused of despotic government and atrocious deeds, such as the burning of the books in 213 BC, and the burying alive of more than 460 scholars a year later for not having handed over their writings as they were enjoined to do by imperial decree. Today, however, there are serious doubts over the veracity of these events and the tendency is to highlight the positive goals achieved by the First Emperor and his faithful minister, recognizing their broad and absolutely modern (for those times) political vision, admiring the large civil engineering works they completed in a short period, and appreciating the stability of the administration and judiciary. These last two elements were to remain, though with inevitable adjustments, the backbone of the imperial institutional system for centuries to come.

Traditionally, laws, punishments and fines — though necessary to control the people — were a secondary instrument of government, whereas

social rites and the conventions that derived from them were at the center of social harmony, as prescribed by Confucius.

'If government is carried out through laws, and order is maintained with punishments, the people will attempt to avoid being punished and will feel no shame for their shortcomings; if, on the other hand, government is performed through virtue and order is maintained through traditional ritual standards and conduct, the people will feel shame for their shortcomings and correct themselves' (*Lunyu*, 2.3).

Rather than being complementary, laws (*fa*) were long thought to conflict with ritual norms and norms of good conduct (*li*). This belief, given greater value by the rich philosophic tradition during the period of the Warring States (482–221 BC) handed down to us in literature written several centuries later (and therefore emended by imperial censors), is today seriously questioned. These doubts follow from closer reading of the works, and with more attention paid to the many manuscripts found recently by Chinese archaeologists from the period between the middle of the 4th and the 1st centuries BC. As they were not mentioned by traditional sources, these new documents were for the most part unknown, and their discovery has forced scholars of ancient China to revise much of the knowledge that had been considered definitive. Some of the recently found manuscripts contain laws and regulations, or instructions on the procedure to be followed in investigations, interrogations and the carrying out of trials; while others are more theoretical and discuss themes pertinent to the philosophy of politics and the law. The discovery of part of the legal code in force in Qin at the start of the foundation of the empire — which later became an integral part of the imperial codes — is of great interest.

As nothing can be fully understood without knowledge of the origins and successive development of imperial law, let us start by examining legislation in pre-imperial China.

❖

This bronze plaque is inscribed with an edict issued by Qin Er Shi Huangdi, the Second August Sovereign, of whom historiography has left us a negative image. (Archeological Institute of Shaanxi Province, Xi'an)

The Confucians considered social rites and rules of conduct (li) the ideal means of ensuring stability and social order, as important as the laws (fa) and their strict application were for the Legalists. However, the two opposing philosophies both agreed on one aspect that is well illustrated in this watercolor depicting a courtly scene: the need to respect social hierarchies.

Different legends recount the origin of the laws and punishments. One of these states that in the 23rd century BC the mythical emperor Shun and his faithful prime minister Gao Yao formulated the five corporal punishments (*wu xing*) and applied them with virtuous resolve. According to another legend, the five punishments – which were called for the occasion *fa* (laws) – were created by the Miao barbarians and inflicted by their governors with such ruthless severity that the abuses and excesses irritated the most important gods to the point that they decreed the end of the Miao line. The contrast between the virtuous severity of the Shun and the pitiless harshness of the Miao demonstrated the existence since remotest times of two distinct political approaches. The first was first based on an idealized vision of prudent government conducted by wise and enlightened kings capable of firmness, and the second founded on spreading terror of punishments in the population following the rigid application of laws that were little known, if not unknown or incomprehensible to most. This difference of approach is seen in classic texts, in particular those inspired by Confucianism. Not surprisingly, the history of the Miao – like that of Duke Mu of Zhou who lived in the 10th century BC (he also promulgated a body of laws to maintain order and restrain the cruelty of barbarian peoples) – is narrated in one of the oldest Chinese literary texts, The penal laws of the Prince of Lü (*Lü xing*), probably written around the 9th or 8th centuries BC (though some scholars think a few centuries later) and inserted in a later period in the Classic of History (*Shu jing*), one of the canonical Confucian texts. The passage runs:

'The Miao people was not the only one to cultivate the spirit and so was governed using the five punishments. It was this people that created the five repressive punishments and called them laws. Even innocent people were killed and they began to practice excessively cutting off the nose and the legs, castration and branding. Anyone who had anything to do with the law was treated in the same way, there were no distinctions even between the accused and the accusers. People began to trick one another and everywhere there was confusion and disorder; their faith did not come from their conscience, and so they broke oaths and alliances. All those who were punished with ruthless severity declared their innocence before Heaven. The highest god watched over the people but there was not even the smell of virtue, rather the fetid odor that emanated from the punishments. The August Sovereign felt sorrow and compassion for the innocence of those who were

punished and paid back the tyranny of the Miao judges with his virtuous severity, putting an end to all that and exterminating the Miao people, so that their descendants were no more.'

The unknown author of this passage briefly mentions the procedure to be followed in judiciary investigations, the correct administration of justice and how punishments are imposed, but he does not mention any specific texts or codes of law. The tasks of the legislator were to render the laws comprehensible to all, and to consolidate a principle to which the governors of later periods also wished to adhere: the purpose of the law was to protect the people from every excess and abuse. The responsibility of the ruler was to control the correct and impartial application of the laws. The question to be asked was whether the law was effectively the most suitable instrument for providing stability and social harmony or if the personal abilities and moral qualities of the ruler and his ministers were of greater importance and effectiveness. Philosophers differed in their answers on the topic of governing policy.

The introduction of the five corporal punishments, or wu xing, *is ascribed to the mythical Emperor Shun (left), the second of the three predynastic wise sovereigns. The section dedicated to him in the* Shu jing *– the* Shun dian *– attributes him with the creation of the first laws. Gao Yao, Shun's prime minister (right), is also said to have participated in the formulation of the first canons. A curious legend associates this statesman with a fantastic animal, the unicorn* qilin, *which Gao Yao would consult whenever he had trouble in passing a sentence, for the beast was capable of discovering the culprit by touching him with its horn.*

A couple of moralizing texts (*Kang gao* and *Jiu gao*) found in the Classic of History were actually written somewhat later but are considered to reflect documents from the period of the Western Zhou (circa 1045–771 BC); they discuss the control of the people of Shang, a region that had just been subjected, including through the use of laws. Apart from these two, references in classical literature to codes written in antiquity are few and far between. We do not know if at that time knowledge of laws was diffused orally or if they were written on materials that have not survived the test of time. It is assumed that they were also recorded in written form on wooden tablets or bamboo surfaces (these and silk were the most common media for writing before the introduction of paper). On the other hand, there are various texts relating to legal practices, penalties and punishments inscribed on bronze ritual vases during the era of the Western Zhou and the Spring and Autumn period (770–476 BC). These are records of disputes arising over land transactions, questions relating to the payment of duties or other episodes linked to the administration of justice; for example, a case of perjury and insubordination described in an inscription on a *yi* water vessel from the middle of the 9th century BC (the vessel is known as Ying *yi*), or the theft of a large quantity of grain during a famine described in an inscription on a *ding* tripod (known as the Hu *ding*, 3) from the end of the 10th century BC.

The existence of a written code regarding the

transactions between members of the royal family is documented in an inscription of the 9th century BC (Hu *ding*, 2). It describes the struggle that ensued after the consignment of a horse and a piece of silk that together represented the payment agreed for the work performed by five servants of a man named Xian – probably a rich nobleman – for an aristocrat named Hu (or, according to another interpretation, for their purchase). The negotiations were carried out by two intermediaries, one for each side, who, having taking possession of the horse and silk, attempted to extort a sum of money from the unfortunate Hu. Their argument was that the horse and silk represented the payment for their intermediation and that the sum of money they demanded was for the work performed by the five servants. Hu re-

ported the facts to the authorities, asking for the pledges made to be respected. The 'judge' called to resolve the matter had to decide if the norms that regulated the transactions between members of the royal household were applicable, because similar previous cases had required payment in cash. In the absence of legislation appropriate for solving the dispute, the final decision was that it was not possible to conform to that resolution. The reference to a set of codified rules for nobles of royal blood is an interesting one. The inscription concludes with the injunction to place at Hu's disposal five men as agreed, without depriving them of the possibility of maintaining their residence or looking after their fields. The traditional exchange of arrows, required by the ritual at the start and end of every lawsuit, confirmed the definitive acceptance of the verdict by the sides involved.

The case was a ceremonial act that fell within the administrative and religious activities of the ruler and his ministers. Since remotest times, legal practice had been intimately connected with religious and ritual activities, to the point of being transcribed on bronze sacrificial vases on which it was customary to register important events, donations and privileges conceded by the sovereign to his underlings and vassals. These vases represented the most important part of the aristocrats' rich sets of grave goods; they had an immense value and played an important role in he religious ceremonies held to communicate with the ancestors and gods in the Afterlife.

One of the most interesting testimonies associated with the administration of justice during the first part of the Zhou dynasty is a 157-character inscription known as Ying yi *(above), engraved on a bronze* yi *ewer (below) found in the village of Dong, in the county of Qishan (Shaanxi province). It recounts the conviction of a certain Muniu for having falsely accused Ying, his superior. (Qishan County Museum)*

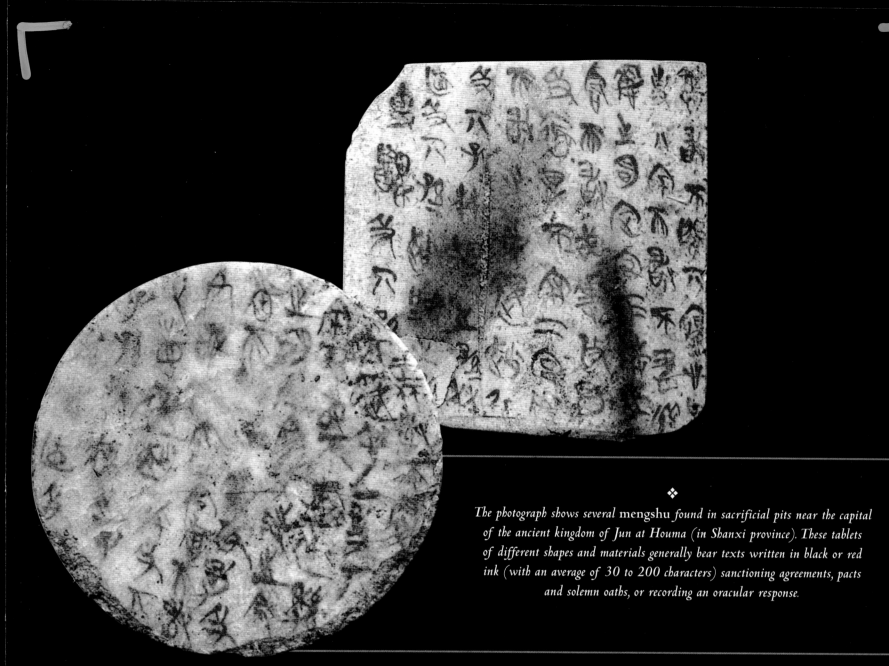

The photograph shows several mengshu *found in sacrificial pits near the capital of the ancient kingdom of Jun at Houma (in Shanxi province). These tablets of different shapes and materials generally bear texts written in black or red ink (with an average of 30 to 200 characters) sanctioning agreements, pacts and solemn oaths, or recording an oracular response.*

If the documents written by scribes on perishable materials like wood and bamboo were addressed to the living, it is certain that what was written on sacrificial vessels was for the spirits that lived in a parallel world to the terrestrial one. That this was the purpose of the legal inscriptions on the bronze vessels is demonstrated by an inscription dating to the start of the 10th century BC (Shi Qi *ding*) that discusses a case of mutiny when several soldiers refused to follow their commander on a military campaign. The case ended with the explicit injunction to transcribe the verdict both on the standard registers used (i.e., wooden or bamboo tablets) that were in all probability stored in archives, but also on a bronze vase, with the intention of rendering the proceedings as sacred as possible and of providing testimony of the decision to the spiritual world. The process of rendering the law sacred (begun during Western Zhou era) continued during the Spring and Autumn period. According to the Commentary of Zuo [on the Annals of the Spring and Autumn period] (Zuo zhuan), a work mostly compiled in the 4th century BC but which we only know from an edition of several centuries later, the first codification we are aware of dates to 536 BC when prime minister Zichan in the princedom of Zheng had the penal laws in force inscribed on bronze tripods. Some years later (513 BC) the princedom of Jin undertook a similar operation. The sophist Deng Xi (died

501 BC), an expert jurist and orator, was also from Zheng and the author of a code written on bamboo tablets that has not survived to the present day. An important step towards the compilation of imperial era codes occurred with the use, particularly from the 7th to 5th centuries BC, of sworn conventions (*meng*) inscribed on jade or stone tablets that formally sanctioned agreements and alliances between clans and princedoms. The solemn oaths were signed in blood in the presence of the powerful spirits of dead sovereigns that were invoked with sacrificial ceremonies. At the end of these ceremonies, those involved declared loyalty to their chief and wiped blood spilt during the rite on their lips. They pledged themselves to defend their chief's ancestral temple with their arms and accepted strict rules of behavior. The inscriptions that give the oaths sometimes list the punishments to be meted out should the obligations undertaken be violated. In general, the proceedings ended with the following invocation should defection occur: 'May the sovereigns of the past who are observing us from afar discover me on the instant and ruination afflict my entire family line.' The participants in these ceremonies were generally clan chiefs who bound themselves to the ruler of a more powerful princedom with a pact professing military and political loyalty. This created strong links between members of different clans, and aggregations of villages, towns, and small and

large cities grew in size. The rules imposed were eminently political but drew a religious significance from the evocation of spirits by means of blood sacrifices. Those that broke the rules were denounced during the ceremonies, punished severely and sometimes expelled from the coalition. This last possibility was often the equivalent of a death sentence. Some inscriptions list the names of those who, having been expelled from the community, were forced into exile. The requirement to have written rules as the basis of this form of mutual society led to the compilation of proper codes in which the principle of collective responsibility — the linchpin of legislation during the period of the Warring States and the First Emperor — was ratified to strengthen the power of the repressive measures taken. The ritual required that at the end of each ceremony the tablets were buried in sacrificial pits so as to remain available to the spirits, whose duty it was to watch over and check that the obligations undertaken by the members were respected. Several chance archaeological discoveries have unearthed thousands of these tablets. Particularly interesting are the Houma *mengshu* (a series of 656 inscriptions found in Houma in Shanxi province in 1965-66), the Wanxian *mengshu* (the inscriptions on more than 10,000 fragments, though not yet fully studied, found in 1980-82 in Wanxian, roughly 95 miles east of Houma), and the Qiyang *mengshu* (another set of inscriptions of the same type).

The first complete legal code to have survived is from the Tang period (618–907 AD). The first formulation of this was in 653 with new editions produced in 725 and 737. Until a few decades ago, the earliest code we had – though incomplete – was that of the second imperial Han dynasty (202–220 AD), written out in a section of the Dynastic History of the Han (*Hanshu*). This work was drawn up in the 1st century AD and integrated with various manuscripts of wooden or bamboo tablets found in tombs of the period. But what remains of the legislation of the preceding period?

Little or nothing. Not even the most authoritative representatives of the Legalists School (*fajia*) that developed in the princedom of Qin around the 5th and 4th centuries BC have left detailed information. Their works are mostly philosophical treatises on the law and the art of government. The Book of the Lord of Shang (*Shang jun shu*) and The Master Han Fei (*Han Feizi*) are cornerstones of Legalist literature of the 4th to 2nd centuries BC, but they do not cite any extracts from a code and refer only in passing to specific laws. Perhaps knowledge of the laws in question was assumed to be implicit. The little information at our disposal leaves many important questions unanswered. For example, in what measure were the Legalist doctrines implemented in the legal codes? And how many laws promulgated by the Qin influenced the code of the succeeding Han dynasty? We are still unsure if the rapid fall of the Qin dynasty not long after the constitution of the empire was prompted by the harshness of the laws and the unnecessarily strict application of the punishments, as the Confucians always claimed, or if other, more complex, reasons prevailed.

Experts have attempted to answer these and other questions in the absence of direct sources but in doing so have often reached different conclusions. Thanks to the analysis of several important archaeological finds made in the last few decades, we now have a more objective assessment of the political, religious and social situation in the 3rd century BC. Above all, there are now available many collections of laws, judicial cases and instructions on the procedures to be followed in investigations, interrogations and trials. In addition there are other documents that help to fill the gaps and

which have corrected our comprehension of a world that we thought – mistakenly – we understood, but our judgment was based on the selective recordings of a censorial and standardizing society that handed down only what conformed to its vision of the world.

I shall not linger on the analyses of the many aristocrats' tombs discovered pretty much all over the country, with their rich sets of grave goods that have included dozens of manuscripts and thousands of inscriptions on wood tablets, bamboo strips and pieces of silk. Nor will I linger on the fabulous Terracotta Army buried to defend the tomb of the First Emperor, nor on the finds uncovered in the sites of pre-imperial and imperial cities of Yong, Yueyang and Xianyang. More important is the 1975 discovery of a tomb in Shuihudi, near Yunmeng in Hubei province. The tomb was built in 217 BC and found to contain 1,125 bamboo strips, more than 600 of which bore exclusively juridical texts, including a large portion of the legal code in force in the princedom of Qin just before imperial unification. Also of importance are the manuscripts found in 1986 in Baoshan, also in Hubei, in a tomb from the early 4th or late 3rd centuries BC, and a bamboo strip found in 1979 in Qingchuan in Sichuan province that bears, in three columns, the text of a law on agriculture issued in 309 BC in Qin. In Mawangdui (Hunan province) in 1973 a tomb dating to 168 BC was excavated and found to contain various manuscripts on silk; several of these are referred to by the collective name of *Jing fa* and debate interesting questions of legal philosophy.

In Baoshan, Shuidui and Mawangdui the juridical texts were accompanied by manuscripts that apparently had little to do with codes and laws. They were works that until that time were unknown, and deal with astronomical and astrological calendars, divination, exorcisms and the practicalities of prophesying: all in all an expression of the traditions that lay between magic and the occult of which we knew little and had no documentation. These texts reveal the existence of complex magical and religious beliefs that were deeply rooted in all levels of society. They underline a conception of the world based on two parallel dimensions – the natural and supernatural – that communicate and interact constantly. The surprising novelty, which scholars have only re-

cently realized, is the presence of strong divinatory activities related to many facets of daily life, including aspects, such as law, thought till now to have been held strictly separate from the sphere of divination. The divination texts share a common vision of the social order with the codes and manuals of judiciary procedure in which the world of the spirits was as relevant as the actions of man. Any subversion of the order required specific rites officiated in ceremonial or judicial halls to restore it. The search for the agent responsible for an illness – a spirit that the exorcist had to placate or chase out using the appropriate rites – and an investigation into a crime – for which the criminal had to answer as much to the justice of man as to that of the spirits – followed very similar procedures.

The interdependence between religious ceremonies and legal practices from earliest periods remained unaltered during the period of the Warring States. It is not now surprising that at Shuihudi a collection of laws was found together with texts like the *Ri shu* (Book of Days), which was a sort of almanac of propitious and unpropitious days for particular activities. It was consulted by the magistrate before deciding the most suitable moment to hold an audience or, based on the crime committed, to interrogate a suspect.

Even the terminology used is sometimes the same, for instance, the terms *jie* and *zi*. The first indicates the faculty of entering into contact with a spirit by attracting it with the use of written magical formulas and, therefore, by subjecting it to a sort of formal control in order to induce it to act for the exclusive benefit of the postulant. In the legal field, the term refers to the stage of the proceedings in which the witnesses are listened to, questioned and their answers recorded by the functionary; in other words, this too is characterized by a sort of formal control. In both cases it was necessary to establish the cause of a problem so as to find the most suitable solution; this would either be the performance of a certain rite or the sentencing to a particular punishment. The second term had been used in the legal field in the Western Zhou era (in the Ying *yi* inscription mentioned previously) and signified the carefully recorded declarations released at the start of a trial by the parties in question, and also the sovereign's confession of his sins to placate the anger of the highest gods, manifested in the form of a calamity. For example:

'In every state sacrifices must be made to the mountains and rivers. For this reason, if a mountain stream or river should dry up, the sovereign must forsake lavish banquets, appearing in public in a sumptuous manner, traveling in magnificent carriages, listening to music, and staying in the opulent palaces of the capital. He must order the functionary in charge of ceremonies to prepare due offerings, and the functionary in charge of the archives to draw up a written confession of the ruler's wrongdoings. Finally, he must carry out the necessary sacrifices to the mountains and rivers.' (*Zuo zhuan*, Cheng 5).

In about the 5th century BC, the formation of proper independent states that arose from the increasingly large aggregations of urban centers led to the requirement for a new political, social and military organization. For close, well-structured control of such a vast territory, it was realized that the following were needed: an effective means of communication between central government and local administration, an efficient organization of agricultural and crafts' workers that took account of growing military activity, and an efficient system for registering the people and collecting taxes. With the aim of ensuring social order, it was essential that a series of written regulations and procedures was drawn up that would consolidate and control social change. And so a long phase of maturation came to an end that had covered the bronze inscriptions of the Western Zhou period, and the agreements ratified by ceremonial oaths and recorded on jade during the Spring and Autumn period. A more structured legislation was created that could adapt to the new bureaucratic, administrative and military organization of states that continued to struggle for supremacy and control of ever larger territories. The attention of the legislator turned more toward the individual than the clan. The practice of ceremonial oaths continued to play an important role, particularly with regard to the consecration of written laws or rituals required before the giving of evidence, as appears in the account of a trial included in the Baoshan documents that involved hundreds of witnesses. All were obliged to give a written oath ratified by blood sacrifices.

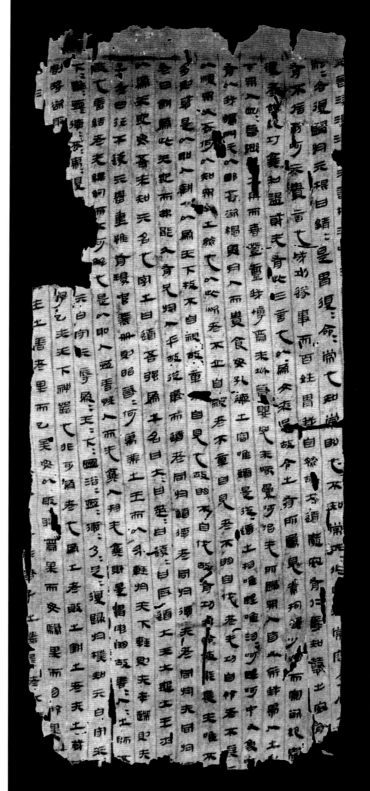

❖

One of the most important discoveries in Chinese archaeological history were the manuscripts on silk found in several princely graves near Mawangdui (in Hunan province), which can be dated to several decades after the fall of the Qin. Indeed, they include treatises on the legal philosophy of the Warring States and Qin periods, which revealed a link with magical and divinatory practices that were previously considered completely unconnected with the legal sector and its associated procedures.

At Shuihudi documents have been found in a set of grave goods belonging to Xi, a middle-ranking functionary. The documents are of great interest for the richness of the juridical information that they contain, including a body of 30 or so laws (*lü*), subdivided into almost 200 articles and many writings. Some experts consider the writings to be manuals of jurisprudence, others believe that they were a sort of procedural code for the carrying out of investigations and for the correct compilation of written reports (*Feng zhen shi*). The collection also contains texts that offer valuable information on the bureaucratic apparatus of the period: a manual that could be titled The Art of the Perfect Functionary (*Wei li zhi dao*), a chronological account of the events that occurred in the princedom of Qin during the period between 306 and 217 BC (*Pian nian ji*), two almanacs (*Ri shu*) and the copy of correspondence (*Yu shu*) between 'judge' Xi and a high functionary named Teng, an administrator in Nanjun. Born in 262 BC, Xi entered the public administration in 244 BC as a simple clerk and was promoted to the higher grade of Prefecture Clerk in 241 BC. From 235 BC he was made responsible with administering justice at local level. This prestigious appointment explains the presence in his grave of codes of administrative and penal law and divinatory texts.

Written on 625 bamboo strips (612 whole and 13 broken), they were placed beneath the body inside the coffin. It is not fully clear what significance this position had in the symbolism of the funerary ritual. In all probability it was a belief that the texts had to remain available to the deceased for when he restarted his profession in the world beyond the grave so that he would be guaranteed the same status as the one he enjoyed in life. Also these grave goods were the tangible sign of the great

privilege conferred on him by the sovereign and of his intimate link with his seniors in the hierarchy down though which power descended, and which he in his turn exercised over his subordinates. The deceased therefore had prepared his precious texts to be placed with him, not just as a symbol of his rank, but also so that he might preserve and exercise his profession in the afterlife.

The belief in a parallel kingdom beyond the grave that matched the earthly world and which was governed by its own bureaucracy and administration was already rooted in the period of the Warring States and remained so during the reign of the First Emperor. This is seen in the composition and symbolism of valuable sets of grave goods recovered in recent years, as well as by various instances in literature. An extraordinary find made in 1986 in Fangmatan in the province of Gansu was written on bamboo strips and in all probability came from the Qin archives. It was drawn up in 269 BC and tells the story thirty years previous of a man named Dan who, having wounded someone, killed himself to avoid the shame of being punished for his misdeed. As was customary for those guilty of serious crimes, his dead body was displayed in the public square and buried outside the South Gate of his village, Yuanyong. Three years later, Xi Wu, a general from Wei who had been Dan's employer, was convinced that Dan had died earlier than the gods had wished, so he sent a missive to the scribe (*shi*) of the director of Heavenly Mandates (*Siming*) requesting the prompt resurrection of his employee. Gongsu Qiang, the director, considered this a valid request and charged a white dog to search for the soul of the deceased. The dog hurried to dig up the trench where Dan had been buried. Returned to life, Dan had found himself wandering through the Northern Ter-

ritories, which still belonged to the world beyond the grave, before retaking his proper place among the world of the living, though not in full possession of his faculties. This unusual case is not just interesting because it increases our understanding of the religiousness of the period, but also because it clearly demonstrates how deep was the conviction of the existence of two parallel bureaucracies able to communicate effectively to correct any errors made by man.

An examination of the Shuihudi documents provides interesting reading; in part it confirms what we already knew from other sources, and in part it firms up our knowledge of the time between the end of the Warring States period and the first phase of the imperial epoch. The information refers to the administrative and judicial organization of the empire as well as to several aspects of daily life that our traditional sources hardly touch upon. We find a surprising number of laws which, far from constituting the complete code of Qin, signify the existence of a more complex legal system that could have been expected, since, according to tradition, there were only six basic laws in force in the kingdom during the life of Shang Yang (390–338 BC). From this we can deduce that the Qin code had already achieved the completeness and systematic nature that were characteristic of the successive Han code.

The Qin governors believed in the right to intervene in matters relating to central and local administration in order to safeguard the human and material resources on which the empire's successful administration depended, They also intervened in an entire series of aspects (of little apparent importance) that concerned the private life of the people. The degree to which centralized control had stretched had arrived at extreme levels; for example, the law even regulated the quantity of grease used to lubricate cart axles and the measurements of prisoners' clothing. Making this unbending regime even more oppressive was the fact that the Legalist principle of collective responsibility theorized by Shang Yang – which, as we have seen, went back to the mutual solidarity of the clans and was sanctioned by blood vows inscribed on jade or stone tablets – was broadly acknowledged.

As the documents found reveal, the Qin code mainly dealt with questions of administrative and penal law, and this characteristic was to remain pretty much unaltered in Chinese legislation for many dynasties. The punishments meted out for various offences were substantially those for which the Han code was to specify: the death penalty, forced labor, exile, mutilation and fines. In many cases it was possible to commute the penalty (though not the death penalty) to the payment of a fine or work for the local administration for a suitable period. In the event of pecuniary hardship, which was usually the case with functionaries, the amount was often expressed in supplies to the army, generally suits of armor, shields or the number of leather ties used to attach the plaques that provided body armor.

Flogging was the punishment given to prisoners who had attempted to escape or damaged property after being condemned to forced labor; it was also a possible punishment for those who told lies or were reticent during interrogation. In such an event, the enquiring magistrate was obliged to write a report following a particular procedure: the *Feng zheng shi* prescribed that:

'The best examination method lies in avoiding flogging and basing itself on the evidence provided by documents and facts; flogging is a poorer method; an interrogation based on intimidation is the worst of all. When hearing opposing parties, the first thing to do is to listen and record faithfully what is said, letting each person make a full statement. Even if it is clear that the person involved is lying, there is no need to press him or accuse him for the moment. When his statement is completed and fully recorded, if there are any doubts about his declaration, interrogate him again but more specifically. Also during this stage, no interruption should be made to the answers given, and everything should be carefully written down. Once the weak points of his statement have been identified, he must be questioned again. If he continues to lie or change his version of the facts without plausible justification, and if he is liable to flogging [*i.e. if the person in question is not in one of the protected categories, such as the very elderly or very small children*], then flogging may be used. In this case the magistrate must compile a document as follows: "As Mr. X has repeatedly changed his version of the facts without supporting these changes with plausible explanations, the interrogation has moved on to flogging."'

The most common method of execution was decapitation, and this may have been carried out in the public square if for particularly serious crimes; display of the body for a certain period after death was considered an even more severe and exemplary punishment. Other methods of execution could be quartering, dismemberment or drowning, depending on the brutality of the crime. There were several methods of mutilation: castration, the cutting off of one or both feet, the cutting off the nose, and branding. Shaving of the head and beard (considered a shameful procedure) was reserved for those condemned to forced labor.

Forced labor was the punishment for most crimes. Prisoners were made to work in the fields or build pressed earth defensive walls, though both of these were activities that much of the population was periodically obliged to perform. All those who participated in the construction of defensive walls were made responsible for the solidity of the construction for at least a year. Should the walls crumble before that time, the people responsible were obliged to rebuild them without payment.

There was a clear distinction in the code between premeditated murder and injuring or killing a person unintentionally or involuntarily, for example, during a game or a scuffle. An interesting exception is described in this article: 'Consider the case of a policeman who, in attempting to arrest a delinquent, is punched and killed by the latter. Question: did the delinquent act with the intention of killing the policeman or was the death accidental? The answer is accidental, during a scuffle. According to Court Precedents, however, this case should be treated as premeditated murder.'

This is clearly an existing law that has been modified, in compliance with Court Precedents, at high level but the original text has unfortunately not survived.

The position of someone who assaults another by punching, or pulling the hair or ears of another person wielding a blunt instrument or weapon was quite separate. Particular attention was paid to infanticide or the killing of servants or slaves. Killing a newborn but deformed baby was not considered a crime, however, killing a healthy baby because the parents already had too many children was murder. The law introduced further distinctions to protect adopted children: 'A father who steals from his own son is not to be considered a thief. But how should a father who steals from an adoptive son be considered? The equivalent of a thief.

A parent wishing to punish a child that showed a lack of respect had the right to mutilate the child or even kill him or her, following special permission from the authorities. However, in the absence of this permission, the parent who inflicted such a punishment would be considered guilty of injury or murder.

The report given below is interesting in that it reveals that the maximum respect for Confucian principles existed, even where the facts were inconsistent. 'My son does not behave like a son to me; I therefore ask that he be put to death. I dare make this report.' The father succeeded in having his son arrested immediately and interrogated; this is the son's declaration: 'I am his son and I admit that I am not very respectful towards him, I admit my guilt.'

The death penalty was the punishment for such disrespectful behavior. In a similar case, a father asked for his unloving son to be exiled for life to the borders of the Shu kingdom (in the modern province of Sichuan) and perhaps condemned to have his feet cut off (the text is not clear, and it might simply be the attachment of shackles to his ankles). Lack of filial love was included in successive imperial codes as one of the most serious crimes. Scholars think that the severity shown against those who were derelict in their family duties was the result of 'Confucianization' of the law, which occurred after the fall of the Qin dynasty. It is therefore surprising to learn that this crime was also thought serious in the Qin codes, which were inspired, as has been said, by philosophical principles very distant from those that underlay Confucianism.

Other articles in the legal code indicate a care and delicacy seemingly unthinkable for the Legalists, and certainly different to those attributed to them by later tradition and by Legalist philosophical literature itself. An example is the article that follows, which would seem to be taken from a Confucian or even Taoist work:

'In the second month of spring, the trees in the forests must not be cut down and the streams must not be blocked. With the single exception of the summer months, weeds must not be burned in the fields, nor must indigofera, eggs, young birds or the young of wild animals be collected. Fish and turtles must not [*six characters are missing here*] poisoned or traps or nets for fishing be put out. From the 7th month onwards, these prohibitions are suspended. Only in the ill-omened case of a sudden death may wood be cut to build the coffin and sarcophagus regardless of the wood-cutting period. In settlements near enclosed areas and parks to which access is prohibited, do not dare to enter with hunting dogs in the period that the young of wild animals are being weaned. If dogs belonging to commoners enter parks prohibited to the public without the intention of hunting game, do not dare to kill them; those that enter to hunt, however, must be killed. Dogs killed in areas monitored by gamekeepers must be handed over entire to the authorities; those killed in other prohibited parks can be eaten but their coats must be handed in.'

Stealing and the receiving of stolen property were punished heavily. The penalties depended on the value of the goods stolen. Even slander in a legal proceeding was punished. The code distinguished between various possibilities: if the accusation was deemed unfounded, then the accuser was treated as though he had committed the offence in question when it could be demonstrated that he had lied in order to harm the accused. However, if it was shown that he had no intention of harming the accused, the charge was reduced to 'an imprecise report' and a light punishment imposed. Several examples throw light on the intention of the legislator: 'A reports B for the theft of an ox and for having intentionally slandered a person. It is shown that B has committed no crime. Question: how must A be judged? If he has acted with the intention to harm B, he is a false accuser; if he has acted without harmful intention, then it is a case for a report presented imprecisely.'

The logic that underlies the judgment in the following case is very subtle: 'A is reported for having stolen 1,000 coins. It is shown that he has stolen "only" 670. How should the person who reported the crime be judged? He should be absolved.'

The law established different punishments for thefts of money depending on the sum stolen and the punishment was severe if it ex-

❖

The characters on the bamboo strips discovered in Zhangjiashan, in Hubei province, include important testimony of the law during the Han period and feature a total of sixteen laws (lü) and ordinances (ling), along with a series of unresolved judicial cases. These texts contributed to clarifying the extent to which the Qin legal code was inherited by the Han dynasty.

ceeded 660 coins. In the case above, the plaintiff was absolved because, as the sum stolen was greater than 660 coins, the thief would receive the same punishment as for 1,000 coins, therefore the report, though imprecise technically, did not formally fall within the crime of false accusation. If the sum actually stolen had been fewer than 660 coins, then the false accuser would have been guilty of presenting an imprecise report.

In the case of criminal association related to robbery, the penalties were shared equally among the group and even to the receiver of the stolen goods, provided that it could be shown that he was aware of the goods' provenance.

A large part of the Shuihudi documents contains administrative law. Precise regulations defined every aspect of prisoners' life, in particular for those condemned to forced labor. Equally detailed were the norms drawn up regarding the conduct of local functionaries. The painstaking checks to be carried out during the collection and storage of crops were specified, the quality and quantity of seeds to be used in the fields were set down, and so were the procedures for the use and maintenance of tools. Also regulated were the various stages involved in the breeding of livestock. Functionaries were instructed on the complicated formalities to be performed in the drawing up of records and inventories, on the procedures to be followed in sending regular progress reports to central administration on projects and on the crops themselves, on what to do in unexpected events or disasters, and on how to make out reports to central government, etc.

Notable importance was given to the method used by the local magistrates, the disciplinary proceedings, the accuracy of the investigations that had to precede the verdict, the decision criteria and the writing up of the sentences. The most important laws were supported by many explanatory notes and reference examples. The Shuihudi texts show clearly the emphasis placed on the competence, efficiency and honesty of the bureaucrats. The ideal profile of a new Qin functionary (an essential link between the central and local administrations) is delineated in The Art of the Perfect Functionary, found

among the Qin legal codes: loyalty towards his superiors, maximum obedience and deference, iron discipline, utter self-control, exemplary behavior, sobriety, and an absolute lack of both autonomy and argumentativeness. These were the characteristics of the perfect functionary, the fulcrum of the elaborate Qin bureaucratic machine that enabled the huge empire to be governed. The Qin code required that lazy, inept, annoying or dishonest functionaries were punished and possibly removed from their posts.

Another commonplace revealed by the recently discovered documents regards impartiality in the application of the laws which, to avoid abuse, should be clear and comprehensible, and, in accordance with the intentions of the Legalist theorists, should be applied with the greatest impartiality across the entire population. The rank and functions performed by the accused, however, had a significant effect on the assignment of punishments. Privileged treatment was meted out, in particular to those who had acquired a position of prestige through military merit, even if honors awarded directly by the sovereign as a reward for services rendered could be limited or annulled in the event of serious violations. Generally the punishments were fines, mostly in the form of weapons, armor or leather laces to be furnished to the army.

Overall the Qin code varied little from the one drawn up subsequently by the Han dynasty. This is revealed by a comparison of the Shuihudi materials with the traditional sources, and is further supported by the study of sixteen laws (*lü*) and ordinances (*ling*) from the Han era written on more than 500 bamboo strips found in 1983–84 in a tomb in Zhangjiashan (Hubei province). An equal number of bamboo strips reports a series of unresolved judiciary cases, almanacs and divinatory, medical, mathematical and historical texts. They have not yet been studied in detail but from what has emerged so far, it can be said that most of the changes made by the Han legislators concentrated on form rather than substance. The penalties laid down by the Qin codes were not particularly severe if compared to those in the legal codes of later periods. Nor is there a suggestion of an overstrict application of the laws for reasons of

deterrence, as recommended by the Legalists. On the contrary, the justice meted out was devoid of any moral rigidity and it assigned punishments for criminal acts as an obligation. The guilty party had to absolve his wrongdoing by providing compulsory service to society or by paying a fine, mostly in the form of supplies to the army. Only in the most serious cases was the death penalty, mutilation or exile considered.

The Qin and the representatives of the Legalist School have passed into history as ruthless administrators, however, even if today we have reasons to suspect that undue criticism has been made of the Qin in the traditional historiography, the real reasons that led to their sudden downfall are obscure. Perhaps the most serious error committed by the Qin governors was to have imposed laws, that for years had been in force in their own princedom, on the new lands they conquered. Maybe the laws were applied too quickly and intransigently, without taking into account local customs and regulations.

The advent of the Han dynasty did not alter the juridical and administrative institutions very much, certainly not in the early phase of its regime. The Han rulers were aware of the errors their predecessors had committed and thus they attempted to distinguish their style of government from the iron hand of the First Emperor. They did so by ruling with greater flexibility, applying the laws gradually, being tolerant of local traditions, and, most importantly, exploiting as much as possible what they had learned from the previous decades.

The Han conceded numerous, wide-scale amnesties for crimes that had already been to trial, and they delegated to functionaries the thankless task of adapting the laws to the changing times. In fact, this responsibility cost the life of more than one minister. Sima Qian (circa 145–89 BC), the Great Historian of the Han era, concluded his biography of Chao Cuo (died 154 BC), a powerful minister executed after having attempted, on the emperor's orders, to modernize the laws inherited from the previous dynasty, with these words: 'Changing what is longstanding and fiddling with what has always been only leads to disaster, if not death.'

THE DEVELOPMENT OF PHILOSOPHIC THOUGHT IN CHINA IN THE PERIOD OF THE WARRING STATES

The final period of the third Chinese royal dynasty — the Zhou (1045–221 BC) was characterized by a deep economic and political crisis that resulted in bloody wars between the various feudal states which, nominally, were accountable to the increasingly less effective central power. The epoch was later named the period of the Warring Kingdoms or of the Warring States and lasted from 476 (or 481) to 221 BC. Political fragmentation and the progressive decline of institutions brought about substantial alterations in ideologies and many currents of thought, as in the case of later Confucianism. New doctrines sprang up, often in continual conflict with those more ancient, and also amongst themselves. These new currents were called the 'Hundred Schools' (*Bai Jia*) by the Chinese, but it should be understood that the number 'hundred' is not literal and only indicates 'many.'

It should also be remembered that the main problem the new schools of thought attempted to solve was the existing political crisis. There are those, in the West and China, who claim that Chinese thought cannot properly be called a philosophy in that its attempts at tackling ontology and metaphysics — which were fundamental to Western thought — were either inadequate or occurred very late. In short, the most ancient Chinese philosophy (we will continue to use the term) was principally focused on politics and ethics.

The Chinese Iron Age had only recently begun, but it had substantially modified the country's economy that was, and was to remain until modern times, based prevalently on agriculture. New techniques were introduced in the fields of agriculture and the military.

Disturbed by continuous wars and their consequent economic crises, the peoples no longer believed in traditional forms of popular religion. As always occurs in any age and in any part of the world, political and economic crisis was added to by a profound spiritual crisis.

❖ 94 Confucian theories had a far greater influence on the political philosophy of the Han dynasty that they did during on that of the Qin period. Indeed, the Han were the first to establish the purely secular cult of the Master. Confucius was an exclusively cultural hero and never canonized, and his birthplace, Qufu (in modern Shandong province) — shown here in a painting on silk dating to the Qing period (1644-1911) — became the main center of veneration, where his descendents have perpetuated his memory up until the present day. (Bibliothèque Nationale de France, Paris)

❖ 95 This ink and color painting on silk from the Song period (or a Ming copy of a Song original), signed by the famous painter Li Tang (1050-1130) depicts Kong Fuzi, "Master Kong," Latinized to Confutius (or Confucius) by the first Jesuit missionaries to reach China during the 16th century. The Master is depicted debating with his disciples, but the structure of the composition, featuring figures climbing toward the venerable personage almost in a procession, suggests that they are followed by others — in both space and time — in an unending sequence.

The earliest form of Confucianism, that of its first master, Confucius (551–479 BC), never considered the themes of the creation of the world and what awaited man after death.

The answer given by the Master to his disciple Zi Lu, when the pupil wanted to know something on the subject, was as follows: 'How on earth can those who do not know life ever know death?' (Dialogues, XI/II). This was an implicit exhortation to concentrate on contingent problems rather than the ultramundane. In another passage from the Dialogues (VIII/20), it is recorded how 'The Master never spoke of extraordinary things or transcendent beings.'

Confucian doctrine and the Master's preaching were not addressed to the people, rather at the fief-holding class that governed the various states of China in the 6th and 5th centuries BC. Confucius never considered himself an innovator, nor the founder of a new doctrine destined to last centuries. His famous statement, 'I transmit and do not create; I love and believe in the past' (Dialogues, VII/I) characterizes him fully. The Master had hypothesized a mythical golden age at the start of human civilization from which Man had progressively declined, eventually reaching his condition of contemporary material and spiritual chaos. It was necessary to restore that original happy state. This Confucian theory was later defined as 'historical regression' and the Chinese only accepted the idea of progress in the modern era.

In order to return to the mythical golden age, Confucius believed it was essential to restore adequate ethical standards to regulate relationships between people. Therefore, in his doctrine he exalted the practice of certain "virtues" (*Dé*), such as goodness, altruism, sincerity, loyalty, justice, wisdom, and respect for the ancestors and tradition. For Confucius the first wise rulers that had governed the country in the ancient golden period were above all virtuous. The natural consequence of this was good government and the good conduct of their subjects. So how was it possible to return to that state and to lead the people to a new happy age?

The priority was to practice the 'virtues,' but so they could be better implemented, the people should study the ancient texts. According to tradition, Confucius or his immediate disciples published philosophical and literary tracts in which the deeds of the men of the past were highlighted: the positive ones to be imitated

and the negative ones to be condemned and their errors avoided. This was the period of the first editions of three works that became the prototypes of future Chinese literature: *Shi jing* (the 'Classic of Poetry'), the first literary work; *Shu jing* (the 'Classic of History'), the first historic document; and *Yi jing* (the 'Classic of the Changes'), considered in some way a philosophical text. Study was therefore used as a means of learning how to behave ethically in society. Chinese literature was influenced for many centuries to be an educational tool rather than to satisfy the creativity of the author.

The fief-holding class that Confucius addressed did not pay him or his advice much attention. There was only a brief period in his life, when Duke Ding of the feudal state of Lu (Confucius' home state), first appointed him governor of the city of Zhongdu, and, later, as superintendent of public works and minister of justice. To Confucius it seemed the right moment to put his theories into practice. The consequence was that the duke of Qi, a rival state of Lu, was afraid that such a wisely administered territory — in which improvements were soon evident — might one day extend its power over all China. So, in order to alienate Confucius, he sent eighty dancing girls and musicians and several teams of fine horses to Duke Ding as a gift. Distracted, Ding no longer followed Confucius' advice, and the indignant Master resigned his post and left the dukedom.

This marked the beginning of his wanderings in other feudal lands. He would argue that it was essential to implement what he used to call 'the amendment of the names,' in which 'Princes should behave like princes, ministers like ministers, fathers like fathers, and sons like sons.' In other words, already in that period, the rulers and princes were being deprived of their power, ministers abused their privileges and, even in family life, the respect for age was not as strong as it had been. The state was conceived of paternalistically as a large family with the ruler as the father of his subjects.

But not having found a single feudatory who would listen to him, Confucius returned to Lu in 483 BC where he died four years later, convinced he had failed in life. His last words to his disciple Zi Gong were, 'For a long time there has been no more wisdom in the world and there has been no-one who wanted me as a teacher.'

This ideal picture of Confucius portrayed as an old man reveals the respectful deference that has been reserved for this venerable master. The work has been realized by a contemporary artist, Dai Dunbang, a painter specializing in the depiction of characters and figures from Chinese history and literature.

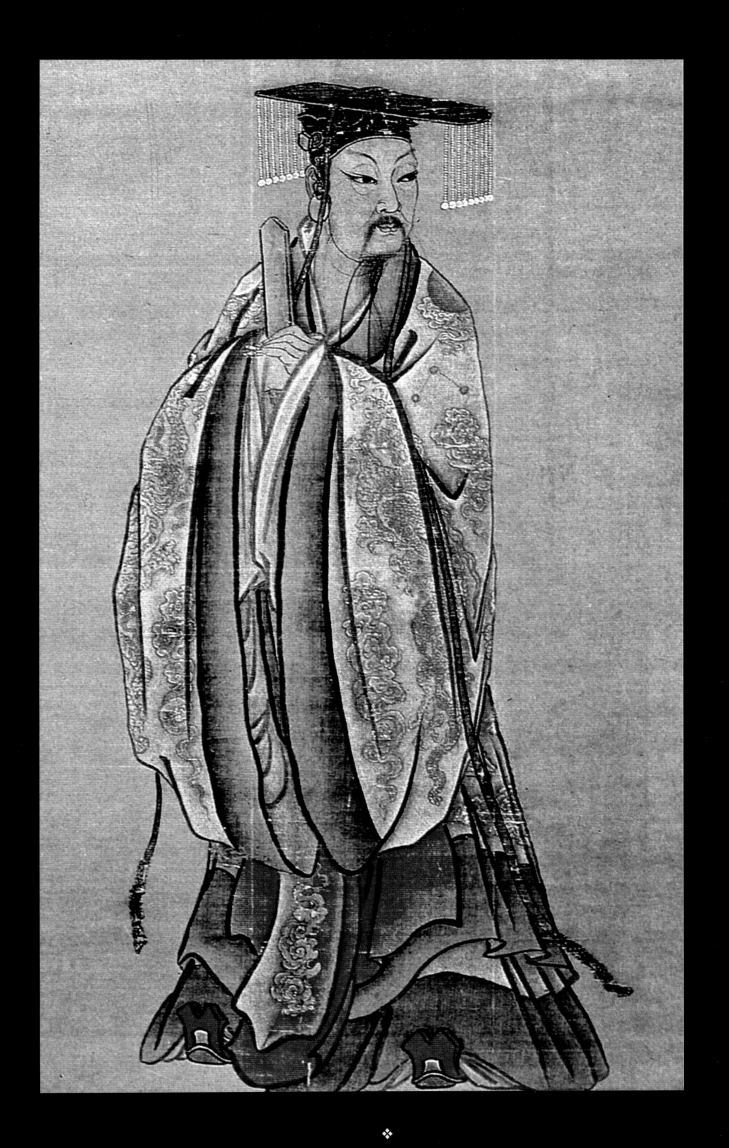

According to Confucius, a good "servant of the State," whether ruler or subject, should model himself on the wise virtuous sovereigns of antiquity, such as the Great Yu (Da Yu), the last of the three wise kings and mythical founder of the Xia dynasty, who is traditionally credited with having achieved control over the waters.

Confucianism survived its founder's death and Confucius himself was remembered, even by his adversaries, simply as 'the Master,' rather than by his name. The expression 'Zi yue' (The Master said), for millennia corresponded to Aristotle's 'Ipse dixit.'

The greatest exponent of the Confucian doctrine in antiquity was Mencius (Meng zi, Master Meng), who lived from 372 to 288 BC.

During the era in which Mencius lived and worked, one of the themes that greatly enthused the various schools of thought was human nature at the moment of birth. There were those who claimed that human nature was evil and that it had to be corrected; there were those who considered it neutral, and there were others, of course, who believed it to be fundamentally good. Disputes of this nature would take place even within the same school. Mencius tended toward the natural goodness of human nature, convinced that we are spoiled by external elements like the society in which we live or individual motives, like the desire for personal advantage.

As a good Confucian, he too was persuaded that the practice of the virtues and study of books were indispensable means of rediscovering 'the heart of the red child,' i.e., the stage of innocence enjoyed by a newly born baby. For Mencius the individual has the duty to perfect himself so as to contribute to the improvement of society as a whole, but Mencius believed that the individual has greater freedom than Confucius did. In the meantime, society and the political climate had worsened even more, and, for the first time, Mencius declared that ministers and thinkers had the right to criticize their rulers and to advise them when they behaved badly. He even considered regicide justified if a ruler behaves like a criminal.

To some degree, Mencius democratized Confucian thought; he adapted it to the changing times and made a sizable contribution to its diffusion around the country. For this reason, Giuseppe Tucci, a great 20th century Italian Orientalist, referred to Mencius as the St. Paul of Confucianism.

A century before Mencius, just about the time Confucius was dying, the thinker called Moti or Mozi (Master

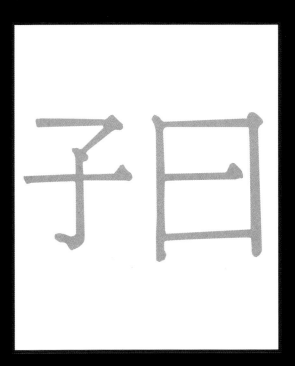

❖

The expression Zi yue, which literally means "the Master says," was often used by the Confucians to legitimate texts or theories that were often not actually directly ascribable to Confucius. The custom of attributing him with a certain claim constituted a sort of guarantee from the point of view of reasoning.

98

Mo) was born. His birthplace and dates of birth and death are uncertain, however, he may have been born around 479 BC and died ca. 381 BC. Little is known of his life, but his theories are clearly expressed in the work he wrote, in line with the custom of pre-imperial China. Tradition has it that as a young man he too was a Confucian, but that he soon moved away from this movement in disappointment at the mediocrity of his contemporaries in the school. Born in a different social class to the aristocratic Confucius (whose teachings were above all aimed at the governing class), Mozi came from a more modest background. He was the theorizer of universal love and a certain kind of pacifism, very different from the asocial and anarchist teachings of the Taoists. At the same time, Mozi wished for a strongly hierarchical, autocratic state tempered by mutual respect between men.

His anti-Confucianism was more directed at the Confucians of his own lifetime than against the Master of Lu. He criticized the excessive formalism of the Confucian rituals and etiquette; he preached an almost ascetic life and censured the luxury of houses and music. He considered Confucians atheists and inert, and disapproved of the three-year mourning practiced by Confucians on the death of a father. It was expected that for three whole years one should either cease working or take up a public post (note how this typically Confucian practice was rigorously observed by the son of Kim Il Sung on his father's death in the 'old Communist' state of North Korea).

Mozi was among the first to find a link between demography and economics, and wished for a large increase in the population so as to increase agricultural production. He was a great Utopian and his ideas enjoyed a certain popularity in China, but his school slowly declined and disappeared at the dawn of the Vulgar Era. Salvatore Cognetti de Martiis, a famous 19th-century Italian economist at the Reggia Accademia dei Lincei, is said to have dedicated a work to Mozi, entitled 'Mihteih, a Chinese Socialist in the 5th century BC.' De Martiis was among the first Western scholars to undertake a thorough study of Mozi.

❖

Mengzi (Mencius), the most important follower of Confucius's philosophical teachings, was the author of the book that bears his name, considered of such importance as to be included among the four texts that comprise the Confucian canon. He was responsible for the definitive elaboration of the concept of "Heavenly Mandate", or tianming, which played a fundamental role throughout Chinese history.

The Taoist school claimed its origins from the famous Laozi, who, it was claimed, wrote a brief treatise that at first bore his own name, but was later titled *Daode jing* ('Classic of the Way and of Power'). The most profound account of this important school of thought is found in the work by Zhuangzi (369?–286 BC) which, like the works of other Chinese thinkers, was not in fact a systematic treatment of the theories of the school.

It was a corpus of various anecdotes, maxims, dialogues and paradoxes presented in high aesthetic literary form. Unlike the Confucians, who thought of individuals as members of a family and state whose duty it was to correct society, followers of the Taoist school refused any form of social collaboration. The anecdote is well-known of when Zhuangzi met two legates from the state of Zhou while he was fishing: the legates invited him on behalf of their prince to go to the court to accept an important administrative appointment. Zhuangzi refused the offer, saying that he did not want to be like just another sacred tortoise dead for three thousand or more years, and venerated in Zhou, but would prefer to be alive, sloshing his tail about in the mud and without losing his freedom (*Zhuangzi*, chapter 17).

In brief, Taoism is a doctrine of individual 'salvation.' It rejects science, study and culture as useless erudition and does not believe in the virtues argued for by Confucius. The author of the most wonderful and profound work of philosophy, Zhuangzi paradoxically considered books the 'dregs of the world,' An individual must renounce every ambition, whether political or literary, and must detach himself from the world and society into which he was born. He should reject its values as a whole and practice *wuwei* (non-action); he should even doubt his own existence. There is the famous story of Zhuangzi who awoke after dreaming he was a butterfly, no longer knowing what was real and what not: was he a man who dreamt of being a butterfly, or a butterfly dreaming he was a man called Zhuangzi? Life is a dream, but where is truth, if it in fact exists? (Zhuangzi, chapter 2).

Taoists had to believe in the *Dao* (The

Way), which lies at the origin of all things, of the ten thousand beings of which man is just one. We are no different to the plants, animals, sky or earth. But, as Zhuangzi warned, the *Dao* could not be understood through study, through use of reason or by forcing it in any way: it was only through a mystical event that comprehension would occur.

Philosophical Taoism differs from popular religious Taoism. The latter has various currents and subschools and encourages personal physical and mental health through careful breathing, diet, and sexual and alchemical practices with the aim of reaching immortality or, if not, at least longevity. It is difficult to date the start of religious Taoism, though it was probably extant to some degree in the 4th or 3rd centuries BC as a mention of these practices is given by Zhuangzi's work and in the one written by the third Taoist master, Liezi.

It should be emphasized that the terms Confucianism and Taoism are broad labels that cover several currents within the same school, but which are themselves often rivals if not actually divergent. Each one tended to stress a particular aspect of the original doctrine. For example, with regard to Zhuangzi's refusal of a post at the court of the prince of Zhou, a later Taoist poet, Dongfang Shuo, claimed that the best way to be alone was to be in the middle of a crowd in court. This paradox is typical of the Taoist school.

In Liezi's work, fragments were included of a lost text attributed to a thinker, Yangzi, of another current. He was active around the middle of the 4th century BC. In the work, Yangzi was asked if, to save all of humanity, he would be willing to sacrifice a single hair from his head; the cynical reply was no, an expression of the most absolute individualism.

❖

100 left Laozi, the "Old Master," is often depicted astride an unusual mount — a buffalo — as he flees westward. Indeed, according to tradition, this semi-legendary figure abandoned his post at the Zhou court and took refuge in the desolate western lands, where he recorded his teachings in written form in the fascinating and ambiguous work entitled Dao De jing.

❖

100 right The Taoist philosophy gave rise to a form of religious Taosim that was gradually enriched with a series of deified and immortal figures and spirits often associated with cosmological and cosmogonic aspects. This detail of a wall painting in typical Ming style depicts the three deities, Fu, Lu and Shou, also known as the "Three Stars," or sanxing, *that represent happiness, prosperity and longevity respectively.*

This photograph depicts the eccentric Taoist poet Dongfang Shuo (ca. 154-93 BC) — who maintained that the best way of ending up alone is to throw oneself into the midst of bustling court life — holding a large peach, which is immediately recognizable as the fruit of the Tree of Immortality that grows in the garden of Xiwangmu, the Queen Mother of the West, one of the principal deities of the Taoist pantheon. Achieving immortality was the most important aim of all the Taoist schools, particularly the alchemical and esoteric ones.

The Logicians school of philosophy (Mingjia) was represented by two thinkers, Hui Shi and Gongsun Long, the authors of treatises that have only partly survived to the modern day.

Hui Shi (380–300? BC) was famed for his erudition and polygraphy. He had written so much that it was said that to hold all his works more than five carts would be needed. However, nearly all his writings were lost in Emperor Shi Huangdi's book-burning of 213 BC, and only a brief fragment attributed to him can be found, mentioned by Zhuangzi.

The school of Logicians often made recourse to paradoxes. In politics they were moderate and inspired by pacifism, which was an easily understood stance during a period of disastrous wars. Here are some of the significant paradoxes mentioned by Zhuangzi (chapter 33): The sky is lower than the earth, a mountain is flatter than a plain; a newborn baby is a being that is dying; today I am going to Yue and yesterday I came back from Yue; an egg contains the feathers; a hen has three feet; fire does not burn.'

Zhuangzi mentions how this philosopher had many leanings that pleased the school of Logicians. According to the Taoist master, they 'were capable of dominating men's mouths with their paradoxes, but not their hearts.'

Gongsun Long (320–259? BC) is thought to be the author of a five-part treatise of the same name that is filled with sophisticated arguments. A famous one demonstrates that 'a white horse' is not 'a horse' in a logic that is reminiscent of Plato.

This was the philosophical climate in which the intellectuals of the period of the Warring States lived and discussed. Their purpose was in essence to find political programs that would bring society through a crisis that had existed for centuries and which was destroying the country, both economically and demographically. There were conservatives who wished for a return to an ideal past, and there was the utopia of those who hoped to put into practice universal love and brotherhood. To the Confucians and Mohists, the Taoists replied that it was necessary to withdraw from social life in an anarchical conception of the social system. Yet when in the 2nd century AD the Taoists inspired revolts and the movement of the Yellow Turbans, they were constrained to formulate a type of social organization. Participation in political life can be contested as a whole, but, if one achieves power, it is necessary to create a social organization of some sort.

❖

102 Gongsun Long, who lived during 3rd century B.C., was a leading representative of the mingjia, *the "School of Names" or Logicians, whose members resembled the Greek sophists in some ways. The school is famous for its logical and linguistic paradoxes, the best known of which is the famous* baima fei ma, *"a white horse is not a horse."*

❖

103 Gongsun Yang (4th century B.C.), later known as Shang Yang, commenced his career as a functionary in the state of Wey, before arriving in Qin, where he won the trust of Duke Xiao along with the title of Lord of Shang This name was given to the text attributed to him, the Shangjun shu, *whose title is shown here*

In the feudal state of Qin, where the future First August Emperor would be born, like other philosophical currents, Confucianism had not arrived in any measure. The state of Qin, though strongly organized militarily, was backward and coarse on a cultural level. However, important reforms were implemented to a certain point, all of which are attributed to a man known either as Shang Yang or the Lord of Shang.

Shang Yang (390–338 BC) can be considered the founder, or at least the first known exponent, of the Legalist school (*fajia*). It was not he who coined the term, but one of the first to use it was the great Chinese historian Sima Qian (145–89 BC) when he listed the ancient schools of thought in his monumental work *Shi Ji* (Historical Records).

The Confucian Sima Qian defined the Legalist school in detail:

'The Legalists do not make a distinction between relations and non-relations, everyone is considered equally by the law, for whom both the love shown to one's relations and the respect to those who are deserving of honor disappear. This doctrine can only be practiced at a particular moment and for a determined purpose, but it cannot always be applied. No theory could ever modify the principle of clear separation that must exist between the eminent position of a ruler and the submission of his subjects.'

With his Confucian conception of a strongly hierarchical state, the great historian found it inconceivable that the law could place subjects and their ruler, relations and non-relations on the same plane. In previous centuries, it had been discussed what the behavior of a son should be if he had surprised his father committing a crime. In that case, should the love for one's parents, so exalted by the Confucians, rule the son's actions or should he report his father so justice could prevail? In the society desired by Confucians, the hierarchy was ever present: between ruler and subjects, father and children, the elderly and the young, husband and wife. In Chinese society until the modern era, male chauvinism reigned, just as the hierarchical principle did.

Nonetheless, the admission made by Sima Qian is interesting, in which the doctrine of the law could 'only be practiced at a particular moment and for a determined purpose.' This is reminiscent of the institution of a dictator for a set period, as occurred on several occasions in republican Rome.

Some experts have wondered whether the first exponent of the Legalists was the thinker Guanzi (died 645 BC), to whom the text of the same name is attributed. Little is known about this man, but the writing that bears his name (despite a philological study suggesting it is a much later work) is not so much a typical expression of the Legalist school as a late philosophical syncretism.

Lying at the base of the school of *fajia* was the law (*fa*), which was exclusively penal law. That of course did not mean that previously laws did not exist in China and that heavy punishments were not applied to offenders. Confucians, who dreamed of an ideal state run on ethical principles as opposed to the period of moral decay extant, had to find

some way to justify the range of punishments that included the removal of parts of the body and capital punishment. Unable to attribute such cruelty to the mythical rulers of the Golden Age who had created everything for mankind, they claimed that it was barbarian peoples who dreamed them up and applied them. Barbarians lived on the edges of the civilized Chinese world and the Chinese could apply their laws only in periods of crisis, like the present one. A perfect people and society, like the state they wished to restore, would not need laws and punishments.

Shang Yang, the leading Legalist in the service of the Duke Xiao of Qin (an ancestor of the future First Emperor), was the reformer of the Qin laws. He also reformed the administration, the tax system and had a new capital built. The state of Qin began a series of wars of conquest, and one of the first states to suffer was Wei, where Shang Yang had grown up. On the death of Xiao, Shang Yang fell into disgrace and was persecuted by the new duke, so he sought refuge in another state and died in battle.

The dates of birth and death of Shang Yang are not certain, but it is known that during that period the state of Qin implemented important reforms. One of the principal ones was to divide the population into groups of five or ten persons who were responsible for monitoring each other, and to be responsible as a unit if they did not report any offences committed within their group. Classes and social distinctions were clearly defined; housing, land and domestic staff were assigned to match a family's hierarchical level. When the state capital was moved to Xianyang, further reforms were carried out including territorial reorganization based on counties, the implementation of uniform taxation for everyone, and the unification of weights and measures which, with other reforms, would later lie at the base of the empire. The life of the second promoter of the Legalist school, Han Feizi (?–233 BC), is well known. As a youngster, he was a pupil of the heterodox Confucian Xunzi, together with Li Si, the future minister of the First August Emperor.

In contrast to the theory propounded by Mencius, Xunzi (298–238 BC) asserted that human nature at birth is evil and that it must be improved with study and using the coercive Confucian concept of *li* (rite or etiquette). Xunzi too had political and administrative responsibilities. On one of his trips to the state of Qin around 264 BC, he wrote a description of what he saw, which was included in the work that bears his name. 'When I crossed the borders [of Qin] and saw their customs, I saw that their people were simple and unpretentious. The music was not corrupt or licentious; the clothing was not frivolous. They respected their superiors and obediently followed those who led. When I reached the offices of their cities, I saw that their administrators were treated with respect and that there was not one among them who was not courteous, moderate, honest, serious, sincere and tolerant. When I entered their capital and observed their high dignitaries, these officers left their houses to enter the public offices and then left these to return to their homes; no-one attended to personal matters, nor used favoritism, nor participated in cliques. They were dignified and there was none among them who was not sympathetic and composed. Dignitaries from the Golden Age! When I watched their court, I saw that they listened in complete tranquility and calmly made their decisions, almost as though they were not attending [to their functions]. Court of the Golden Age! It was for this that they were victorious for four generations and not just due to good fortune, but because they reasoned. This is what I saw. It is said that the best government is calm government, taking into consideration what is general in order to arrive at the details and to achieve results without confusion. Qin is [a state] of this type.' (*Xunzi*, chapter 11). Xunzi was a Confucian, though heterodox, and, though he made no mention of the principles of the Legalist school on which the state was run, he was favorably impressed by everything he had seen in the state of Qin. The difference between the new political and social order of Qin and the chaos and corruption in other states was evident to Xunzi. Might it have been about to return to the great times of the past? His nostalgic and emphatic acclamation of the 'Golden Age', which he referred to twice, makes one think so.

❖

104 The themes dear to Confucianism are treated systematically and concretely in the writings of Xunzi, here in an ideal portrait. The influence of Legalism on his thought is very evident. His reflection on the problem of evil, summed up in the famous assertion ren xing e *("the nature of man is evil"), led him to distance himself from the vision of Mencius, who was convinced of the fundamental goodness of human nature.*

❖

105 Han Fei was a pupil of Xunzi. His work, an Feizi ("Master Han Fei") – here is a page of his Book Sixth – effectively sums up the Legalist conception. An innovative aspect of his teachings was the concept of historical evolution: as each historical age has its own specific conditions, Han Fei reached the conclusion that the present required a system of government based on a strong central authority – that of the sovereign. The Qin empire, using his teaching, found solid bases.

Han Feizi

Han Feizi came from an ancient aristocratic family in the state of Han. He soon realized that in a period of bloody wars one of the first things to be done was to strengthen the authority of the ruler, but that it was also equally necessary to make the army more efficient. Furthermore, the laws had to be clear to all subjects and selection of members of the administrative staff should not be based on heredity but ability. Therefore, a strict system of rewards and punishments had to be implemented relevant to all the administrative staff in the state. His work contains harsh criticism in the style of the Confucian school, a signal that heralded the end of a dying feudal state and the rise of a new conception of the state and society.

The Legalist school laid the foundations for an authoritarian state in which the ruler was not supposed to be a virtuous model for his subjects, but an individual able to lead the entire country in accordance with strict rules that reward well those whose behavior is beneficial and punish those, perhaps heavily, whose behavior is detrimental. It was an extremely modern notion even for whoever conceived and implemented it.

The basic instrument was the *fa* (the law). The Legalist riposte to the Confucians who wanted a virtuous leader, and to the Taoists who said the best ruler was one that abolished the laws and did not govern at all, was that the person who led the country should be neither a despot nor conditioned by ethics, but different

to others and capable of ensuring respect for the law. In modern terms, the ruler had to exercise notarial functions of control.

In his writings, Han Feizi makes interesting statements, for example:

'An intelligent ruler will ensure that it is the law that chooses men and that he does not make arbitrary promotions. He must ensure that it is the law that measures abilities and that he does not employ arbitrary standards. Capable men, therefore, will no longer be set to one side, nor will the wicked be able to hide themselves any longer. Those who have been wrongly praised shall no longer be promoted and those who have been wrongly defamed shall no longer be humiliated. In consequence, the difference shall be clear between the ruler and his ministers and order will thus be achieved. It will be enough that the ruler employs the laws.' (*Han Feizi*, chapter 6).

As mentioned, Han Feizi had studied at the school of Xunzi with a youngster who was to be decisive in the history of the first Chinese empire, Li Si. It was his schoolfellow who introduced Han Feizi to the court of Qin and, years later, to implement many of his ideas. Implicated in a palace intrigue motivated by Li Si's political jealousy, Han Feizi was imprisoned in Qin and, according to tradition, committed suicide in 233 BC. This would have been too early for him to see the birth of the first empire, which was based on his ideology.

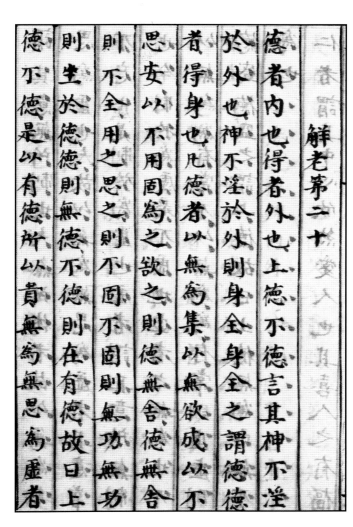

THE FIRST LEGALIST REFORMS

What really happened in China at the time of the birth of the empire in 221 BC? The imperial state was unified as even the Confucians had imagined it, but it was certainly not a simple restoration of the past or the passing of power from one dynasty to another. The country was no longer a kingdom in that the ruler, instead of taking the title of *wang* (king), had chosen that of *di* (emperor), as had been used by those rulers at the dawn of civilization. It was an empire. It was not a dynastic transfer of power forced by the greatest power, *Tian* (Heaven), which, according to an ancient Confucian theory, removed the *tian ming* (heavenly mandate) from a decadent and corrupt ruler to pass it to a new and highly capable man for him to initiate a new dynasty.

A revolution had taken place in Qin which, thanks to the strength of the armies and greater internal compactness, had succeeded in defeating the other states one by one. Feudalism was done away with and the aristocracy eliminated. As a result, the emperor became the guarantor of practical law rather than the moral law the Confucians theorized about. The idea of an ancient state to be restored was discarded and the emphasis was placed on the present. The emperor implemented a radical transformation of the administration by doing away with the feudal system and creating, in its place, new institutions. Prefectures governed by civil servants were set up, as were several special zones run by the military. Modernization of the economy and agriculture led to the formation of a newly rich class and, in particular, the work performed by the peasants (always the majority of the Chinese population) was liberalized. It was understood that the work of individuals in the fields could sometimes be more productive than that of collectives.

The political unification of 221 BC brought about a series of measures that led to the standardization of weights, measures, coinage and even cart axles, both military and civil, as their length had varied for a long time

from state to state for military purposes and reasons of customs duties. An attempt was also made to unify thinking. In 213 BC the burning of books took place. It was the minister Li Si who presented a memo to the throne to send to the flames the books of the Hundred Schools, the Classics of Poetry and History, and all the official historical texts of all the states except Qin. In the words of Li Si, 'The literati [i.e., the Confucians] do not take the present as their model, but study the past in order to denigrate the present.' Scientific books were excluded from the auto-da-fé as they were not ideologically dangerous, and the Classic of Changes, also because, as a divinatory text, it fell within the definition of scientific works. Those who suffered most were the Confucians, many of whom were put to death and many more sent to work on large public works like the Great Wall.

The exclusion of scientific works from the pyre and the implicit recognition of their importance can be interpreted as the first clash in the world between the humanities and science. But the episode of the burning of the books was considered in a later period – influenced by the restoration of Confucianism – as the greatest crime committed by the First August Emperor.

With the next dynasty – the Han (206 BC–220 AD) – Confucianism flourished once more, but the greater part of the reforms the Legalists has carried out remained in force. The façade of the empire was Confucian but many of the supporting columns were the Legalists' reforms. Many currents of thought extant during the period of the Warring States had passed away, but Confucianism and Taoism survived, even though divided into many schools.

---

106 The most important archaic Chinese deity, Tian (Heaven) never acquired an anthropomorphic form, despite the fact that the emperor continued to consider himself the Son of Heaven up until the beginning of the 20th century. Nonetheless, the great painters tried to express the reflection of this superior force and undefined entity.

107 left In 219 BC Qin Shi Huangdi celebrated the first sacrifices on the sacred mountain of Taishan and many emperors of subsequent dynasties repeated the act as a ritual of appropriation of the land. This photograph shows the cast of a stone inscription that celebrates the event and is said to have been written by the Prime Minister Li Si.

107 right The image of two intertwined divine figures with the body of a snake, Fuxi and Nüwa, exemplifies the idea of alternation between the two opposing principles of yin and yang on which the school of the same name was founded and whose chief representative was Zou Yan (305-240? BC).

After having achieved all that he could have wished for, the founder of the first empire undertook long journeys through his domains to check that all the reforms implemented had been carried out. In 219 BC Shi Huangdi celebrated important religious rites and sacrifices on the sacred mountain of Taishan. Later monarchs of different dynasties repeated these sacrifices as though to consecrate their imperial investiture. In that same year the emperor met a man named Xushi, who spoke to him of the islands in the Eastern Sea, the largest of

not be surprising that an emperor whose rule was based on the ideas of the Legalist school should be attracted by the Taoist myth of Immortality. Belonging to a particular philosophical current or religious faith had no correspondence with the three monotheistic religions of 'the Book,' and China never placed insuperable barriers between the various schools. It was in the Han period that classification began into various schools of thinkers from the past, and especially those from the time of the Warring States. These included the Confucians, the

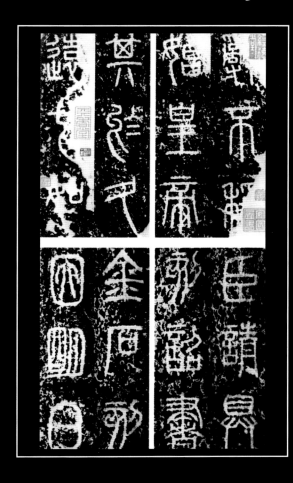

which was Penglai where the Immortals lived. This was a Taoist belief, but as Sima Qian records, the ruler allowed Xushi to go to sea to search for the islands with a retinue of three thousand men and women. The expedition departed but never returned. In 215 BC, the emperor sent a second mission of just three people in search of the islands where the Immortals produced the elixir of immortality, but again he was disappointed. Whether history or legend, the episode attests a certain type of syncretism: it should

Legalists, the Taoists, the followers of the school of the two opposing principles of *yin* and *yang*, the Mohists, the Logicians, the Eclectics and also minor groups. And so thinkers were conveniently pigeon-holed, though not necessarily accurately. What has always typified Chinese civilization and its philosophical thought has been the tendency to syncretism, thanks to which it has often been possible to assimilate elements from different currents, merging them with one or another original doctrine.

THE FIST
EMPEROR

秦始皇

姓嬴名政始自始皇乙卯即王位庚辰併天下稱皇帝
在位三十七年居王位二十五年即帝位十二年壽五十

廿

THE FIRST EMPEROR, HIS CITY, AND HIS TOMB

According to Sima Qian, before the mother of Qin Shi Huangdi married King Zhuangxiang, she was a very beautiful and expert dancer and the concubine of the rich and cultivated merchant Lü Buwei. Before ascending the throne of Qin, Zhuangxiang was the unfortunate peace hostage in Handan, the capital of the kingdom of Zhao. He was treated with little respect and less generosity because his grandfather, King Zhao of Qin, almost heedless of the fact that one of the youngest of his twenty or more grandchildren was a hostage, continually attacked the kingdom of Zhao. Fortunately for the future King Zhuangxiang (at the time called Zichu), the merchant — of whom Sima Qian said, 'he bought cheaply and resold dear' — noticed the youngster's talents during a visit to the court of Handan. Counting on the fact that the heir to the throne of Qin was without children, Lü Buwei struck up a friendship with Zichu and began to plan to bring him back to Qin and have him adopted as the heir to the throne. In his biography of Lü Buwei, Sima Qian says that the merchant and young Zichu were on a serious drinking bout when the hostage saw the beautiful dancer who lived with Lü Buwei and fell in love with her (Sima Qian, *Shi Ji*, chapter 85). Without mincing his words, Zichu asked the merchant for the girl

and reluctantly Lü Buwei agreed, however, the young girl kept quiet on one fact, and that was that she was already pregnant. In the forty-eighth year of King Zhaoxiang of Qin, in 259 BC, she gave birth to a boy named Zheng (True, Just, Candid) or Ying Zheng (Zheng of the Ying household), the future First August Sovereign of the Qin dynasty.

Was Zheng then not the son of King Zhuang? Was he the natural son of a merchant? Of course not; it seems certain that the defaming passages in *Shi Ji* are slanderous insertions by an unknown Confucian commentator added to denigrate the First Emperor and his line. In addition to recording this cowardly attempt to hide ideological hatred behind a disparaging historical untruth (not rare in Chinese or other national historiography), it is curious to note how much scorn Confucian intellectuals poured on the merchant and commerce in general. This is particularly noticeable from the Han dynasty onwards, to the extent that Confucians relegated trading to the lowest level in society, on a level with or just above that of the fishermen, who were traditionally considered coarse.

The curious fact is that Confucius himself never made negative judgments on merchants. Rather, as already mentioned, one of his first disciples was a trader.

Unlike earliest Confucian thinking, it was the great legalist reformer Shang Yang who imposed anti-trading regulations in his reforms of the mid-4th-century BC, and obliged merchants' families to be registered as 'inferior persons.' This was not for reasons of dislike but because they were itinerant by the nature of their profession and thus difficult to control; they could move their capital around at will and were free thinkers.

Returning to the 'spurious' origin of the August Sovereign, it is clear that there was a dual purpose in his denigration: not only was he the illegitimate 'son of a dancer' but also of a merchant.

In any case, Zhuangxiang became king of Qin in 250 BC and made Lü Buwei his 'prime minister' with the title of Marquis of Wenxin and an income provided by some hundreds of families. In Sima Qian's account of Lü Buwei we are aware of the effervescence of the cultural circles of the Warring States period when art patronage was more widespread than at any other time in the history of Chinese culture. Lü Buwei 'gathered around him a circle of guests and itinerant scholars with the hope of uniting the world, and one of these was Li Si.' In a single phrase the Great Historian summarized the essence of the Warring States period: guests were defined as foreigners that exercised their art (political, military, medical or magical) at the court of the lord of a state, for example, Shang Yang was a native of Wey and a guest in Qin. Itinerant scholars were called *shi* and, during the era of the Western Zhou, *shi* were the aristocrats invited to serve the ruler having been educated as 'officials and gentlemen' with the Six Arts (rites, music, archery, driving a war chariot, calligraphy and mathematics). Later, during the turbulent Spring and Autumn period, the youngest sons of the lower aristocracy and the offspring of impoverished families slowly abandoned the handling of arms to concentrate on philosophy and literature. It was on this class of intellectuals that the feudal lords drew for the theoreticians of the new social and political order: Confucius, for example, was a *shi*. It is probable that the 'circle of guests and itinerant scholars' mentioned by Sima Qian was the same one from which Lü Buwei commissioned the well-known historical work *Lü Shi Chun Qiu* (Annals of the Springs and Autumns of the Lü family). As for 'the hope of uniting the world,' this was the aim of all lords of the Warring States, and the learned calligrapher Li Si, a convinced supporter of Legalism, became the last artificer of the centralization of power and the state when he was made counselor to the First Emperor.

The early years of the new ruler began with difficulty following the death of his father, King Zhuangxiang, in 246 BC.

❖

Sima Qian recounts that Qin Shi Huang Di made various inspection tours of the newly founded empire, possibly to symbolize his domination of the territory. A silken page from an 18th-century album of watercolors (Bibliothèque Nationale, Paris), depicts the emperor traveling in a palanquin along a seashore or the bank of a great river: this may have been his last voyage. After having crossed the Yangzi twice, he headed north along the coast of the country of Wu accompanied by presentiments of misfortune. Indeed, he fell ill at the ford of Pingyuan and died soon after at a place known as Ping Terrace, near Shaqiu (Sand Dune) during the seventh month of 206 BC.

The young Zheng was only thirteen at the time and his first years as ruler were practically under the guidance of Lü Buwei. Various attacks were made by other Warring States (in 241 BC Hann, Wei, Zhao, Wey and Chu formed an alliance against Qin but Qin responded well) and court cliques intrigued for control of the young king. One of these was probably inspired by the mother of Zheng, whose name, significantly, was never recorded by Sima Qian or by other sources. The faction of the queen mother seems to have been supported by a certain Lao Ai, a powerful palace intendant. Confucian historiographers and Sima Qian, or someone after him, have treated this figure acidly, as always to the detriment of Qin Shi Huangdi and his family.

In Chapter 85 of *Shi Ji*, the 'Biography of Lü Buwei,' we read that Lao Ai was well endowed sexually and that the queen — having seen him support a heavy wooden wheel with his considerable penis — took him as her lover and had two children by him. The weak Lü Buwei favored this union, but the queen was so in Lao Ai's power that almost all the affairs of state passed through his hands. The affair was both sexual and political and together they hatched a plot to eliminate Zheng and replace him with one of their two own children.

Zheng, however, came of age in time and, in the 4th month of 238 BC, at the age of twenty-two, he went to Yong where in the Qin ancestral temple he received the cap that symbolized male adulthood and became eligible to wear the insignia of royalty: the sword and the belt that were probably made of jade. Consequently, Lao Ai thought that events would have to move along a little faster so he brought his private troops together (to whom were associated contingents of Rong and Di 'tribes') and decided to attack Zheng at Yong. But he was too late.

The king had learned of the plot and ordered his prime minister, Changping, and the lord of Changwen to attack the conspirators. The clash in Xianyang was practically a civil war and resulted in a bloodbath. All those who could bring in the head of a rebel were

promised a noble title, and even the eunuchs would be advanced a grade. Lao Ai was defeated but escaped with a reward of 10,000 coins on his head if he were captured alive. His closest conspirators, all high functionaries, were decapitated and their heads exposed to public mockery, but Lao Ai, when he was captured, was torn apart in the public square and his clan completely exterminated. There were 4,000 noble families involved in the resulting purge, with high-ranking individuals being deported to

Fangling on the border of the kingdom in Sichuan province. The next year it was discovered that Lü Buwei was also implicated and, having been removed from office, he was exiled to Sichuan where he committed suicide in 235 BC.

Following Lao Ai's plot, the removal of Lü Buwei and the ascent of Li Si to the position of prime minister and counselor, Zheng's rule was marked by his victories over and annihilation of the Warring States. In 230 Hann was routed and its territory turned into the *jun* prefecture of Yingchuan. In 238 it was Zhao's turn and then this was used as a base for attacks on Yan, which was conquered in 226 BC. A year later general Wang Pen of Qin attacked Wei but the kingdom surrendered without giving fight

when a flood channel of the Huanghe was opened and gushed water onto the earth walls of Daliang, the Wei capital, liquefying them. In 223 the kingdom of Chu in the Huai and Yangzi valley was taken and the following year it was the turn of the northern kingdom of Dai (what remained of Yan in the Liaodong peninsula on the border with modern Korea). In the lower Yangzi valley, the kingdom of Yue was transformed into the Qin prefecture of Kuaiji and the kingdom of Qi in the Shandong peninsula, the last bulwark of the Warring States, was swept away in 221 by General Wang Pen with an attack from the north. At this point, Qin dominated all the states of the Middle Kingdom.

It was then, in 221 BC, after stating the wrongdoings of the six large states that had just been subjected, that King Ying Zheng declared the historical change with words that Sima Qian quotes exactly:

'Insignificant as I am, I collected troops to punish violence and rebellion. With the help of the ancestral spirits these six sovereigns have recognized their wrongdoings, the world enjoys great order. If now there is no change of title, the successes will not be exalted and cannot be passed down to the generations to come. Decide therefore on a ruler's title.'

A committee of learned men, which included the Confucian Wang Wan and the Legalist Li Si, was appointed with the tricky task of deciding upon a new title. This would express the sacredness that had characterized the regality of the Western Zhou but not use the term *wang*, which had been first discredited by the Eastern Zhou and then usurped by the lords of the Warring States. Yet the new title had also to express a concept of superiority to the Zhou title as the majesty of the Zhou had resided in its ability to acquire and maintain the consensus of the feudal households though it was without coercive power. As the members of the committee remarked:

'... some of the feudal lords came to court to render homage, others no, but the Son of Heaven could not impose his will on them ...'

The members of the committee realized

that the centralization completed by King Zheng had produced a radical change in the institutions and they said:

'Now Your Majesty ... has pacified the world, has established districts and prefectures in all the lands surrounded by the seas and has ensured that laws and regulations all ensue from a single authority. From the earliest of ancient times, this had never happened...'

In order to find a figure that was conceptually comparable with King Zheng in terms of sacred aura and power, the learned men were obliged to go back to the *San Huang* (Three Noblemen) from the age of myths. The third of the three, Tai Huang (Greatly August) was chosen for the creation of a new imperial title. King Zheng accepted provided that, with unexpected modesty, the 'Greatly' was dropped. However, he wanted to add the title *Di* (Lord or Emperor) that had been granted to *Wu Di* (Five Emperors) who were successors to the *San Huang* who had created civilization. *Di* was also the name that the Shang had given to the most powerful 'supernatural power,' for example, *Shang Di* (Di on High), who for some was their Supreme Ancestor, residing in a religious realm of spirits and invisible powers. In addition, the term *huang* ('shining,' usually translated as 'august' as this is a more familiar concept to us) sounds like the term *huang* that means 'yellow' when referring to *Huang Di* (the Yellow Lord or the Yellow Emperor). *Huang Di* was also the first of the *Wu Di* from the mythical age and an object of cult worship just from the later Warring States period. The Yellow Emperor/*Huang Di* not only was symbolically associated with earth, the color yellow, dragons and the concept of centrality, but he had also close connections with the immortality cults widespread in the extreme western regions of China. It is therefore possible that the choice of *Huang Di* (Shining Lord or August Sovereign) as title was determined by the ritual power of the connection with the *San Huang* and *Wu Di*, and, as a result of the word play between the two homophones of *huang*, by the allusion to the power of the *Huang Di* in the guise of the Yellow Emperor, lord of the immortal spirits

and of the center, lord of the *axis mundi* and central regions that lie beneath Heaven. In other words, the Middle Kingdom or *Zhongguo*. The choice of title assumed by Ying Zheng would have included all this and maybe more.

Placing the emphasis on filial piety (typically Confucian in concept, and not Legalist), King Zheng, who was later to symbolize all that the Confucians loathed in future eras, abolished the practice of having a name posthumously conferred on by the new one to

the previous ruler. Posthumous names usually alluded to the virtues of the dead ruler or a characteristic of his reign:

'... posthumous names were assigned on the death [*of the ruler*] on the basis of his actions. So the son expressed a judgment on his father, the citizens on their ruler. This is improper and We do not accept it. From now on, it is abolished. Our Person will be called Shi Huang Di [*First August Sovereign*] and successive generations will be counted consecutively, Second, Third up to Ten Thousandth, in a sequence without end.'

As we know, Zheng's expectations were disappointed and the succession ended with the Second August Sovereign.

In the same year as political unification

took place, the emperor concentrated on bringing into force in all his newly conquered territories the reforms that had made the kingdom of Qin stable and powerful, as, now that the empire had been created, it was necessary to administer it. Supported by the *ting wei* (high justice official) Li Si, the emperor prohibited feudal control of land by members of his own household and the families of his ministers; on the contrary, he divided the empire into thirty-six prefectures each of which was administered by a 'governor' (*shou*), a military commander (*wei*) and an imperial inspector (*jian yushi*) as Shang Yang's reforms had established. He then confiscated all the bronze weapons from the newly-subjected states and had them melted down (these probably belonged to the private militias of the large noble families) and made into bells and twelve large statues that represented the 'barbarians.' According to descriptions made during the Han era, each statue bore a long inscription on the chest and weighed about 29 tons, though this may be an exaggeration. During the era of the Eastern Han dynasty (25–220 AD), these bronze giants still stood in front of the entrance of the Changle Palace in the capital Chang'an but today they no longer exist: ten were melted down at the end of the 2nd century AD to make coins and the other two in the 4th century.

A fundamental advance was the standardization of weights, measures, laws and, in particular, writing so that the empire would have a common means of communication. Other standardizations were the width of cart axles and bronze coinage to encourage the construction of a large road network; in turn, this provided for the easy movement of troops and promoted commerce. The defensive walls that the Warring States had erected around their borders were knocked down and the northern sections joined up to defend the country from raids by nomadic herders. This measure created the nucleus of the Great Wall.

All these reforms — those of Shang Yang, Qin Shi Huangdi and the edict that brought them into force — are supported by archaeological evidence.

116 left This bronze tablet was discovered in 1961 near Xianyang, the capital of the Qin empire. It was once affixed in a public place so that it could be read. The inscription, in xiaozhuang script, declares: "26th year, the August Sovereign has united all the feudal lords beneath the heavens, and the people enjoy great peace. Acknowledged as August Sovereign, the Emperor has issued an edict delivered to Chengxiang, Zhuang and Wan: let the measures be standardized. If they are not uniform or if they are doubtful, they must be clarified and regularized." (Xi'an, Historical Museum)

116 center This oval vase is a standard grain measure dating from the end of the period of the Warring States or the dynastic period. (Xianyang, Municipal Museum)

116 right This four-sided bowl, found at the site of Yaodian near the ancient Qin capital of Xianyang, is a sheng, i.e., a measure for grain, and represents concrete testimony of the reforms launched by Qin Shi Huang Di in 221 BC. Indeed, two edicts are engraved on the sides of the container: the first is that regarding the unification of weights and measures of the entire empire announced by the First August Sovereign, while the second is its reiteration ratified by the edict issued by the Second August Sovereign upon his accession to the throne in 210 BC. (Xi'an, Historical Museum)

The coinage system is evidenced by the finding of typical Qin bronze coins, called *banliang* ('half a liang') and the discovery in grave M11 at Shuihudi of a royal edict — the *Jin Bu Lu* (Regulation Standard of Gold and Fabrics) — which provides detailed information on the coinage. The edict clearly shows that there were two coins current in Qin at the end of the Warring States period: the *qian*, a round coin with a square hole at the center worth half a *liang*, and the *bu* or *bubo* (cloth or material), which was a piece of material, probably hemp, about 8 *chi* long (roughly 6 feet long) and 2 *chi* 5 *cun* wide (about 23 inches) that was worth 11 *qian*. As quantities of *banliang* coins were always given in multiples of 11 in other Qin standards, this suggests that the original reference value was the *bu* and that metal coins came after the cloth currency. This fact is confirmed by the chapter *Liu Guo Nianbian* (Yearbook of the Six Kingdoms) in the *Shi Ji* where it is recorded that Qin, last among the Warring States, had only issued a metal coin in 336 BC. The use of the *bu* very probably only occurred following unification and the creation of standardized systems, starting with the traditional form of the Chinese coin, i.e., that of the *qian*, round with a square hole, which remained unchanged until the 20th century.

Many objects have been found that were used as standards for the weights and measures system, on which the edict of the emperor was inscribed. These include, for example, weights for use in bronze or iron steelyards (which varied from 1 to 120 *jin*), and measures of capacity in the forms of square or oval clay or bronze cups used for grain and liquids. These varied from 1 *sheng* (about a fifth of a quart) to 1 *dou* (just over half a gallon). The codices found at Shuihudi have recently clarified one of the uses of these measures: standard rations for forced laborers are set down in the *Canglü* section of one such codex. Adult males building pressed earth walls or engaged in equally physically demanding work received a morning ration of food equal to half a *dou*, and an evening ration of one third of a *dou*. Women received one third of a *dou* for both morning and evening meals. Another document found in grave M11 at Shuihudi records the fines handed out to functionaries who were found using non-standard measures; payment was made either in the form of a weapon or a shield.

Whereas the written codices found at Shuihudi reveal the theory and praxis of Qin law and administration, the discoveries in grave MI in Fangmatan necropolis near Tianshui (Gansu province, northwest China) in the heart of traditional Qin territory, are indicative of the efficiency of their ad-

117 These pictures show several typical Qin bronze coins (known as qian in Chinese), called banliang, whose face value was equivalent to half (ban) the unit of weight referred to as a liang, as stated in the inscription either side of the central hole. Following the unification of weights and measures and the creation of standardized systems, Chinese coins retained the traditional form of the qian — round with a square hole in the center — right up until the early decades of the 20th century. These metal coins were cast in tree mother molds (above). The rectangular molds had a central casting channel, which branched out into smaller channels that conveyed the molten metal to the circular depressions engraved with the pattern of the coin. Coins of this type, which started being used from 336 BC, have been found at all Qin archaeological sites, including the pits of the Terracotta Army and the graves of the conscripts who constructed the Mount Li Funerary Garden. (Terracotta Army Museum, Lintong)

ministrative system. A Qin functionary named Dan was buried in grave MI with the tools and products of his work: writing brushes, wooden measuring tools and seven tablets that together composed a map (unique of its type). The map was drawn to scale and shows mountains, passes, bridges, roads, place names, and information on local economic resources. With such organization it was possible for Zheng to administer his new empire under the name Qin Shi Huangdi and to issue the edict in the first year of his reign as emperor (the 26th of his reign as king of Qin) that was made known in every corner of the empire.

At the time, the political conception of the country was *Tian Xia* ('[what lies] beneath Heaven') or the Civilized Universe; it was made civilized by the various laws promulgated by the emperor and the building work of thousands of forced laborers. Examples of large projects include digging irrigation canals, like the Zhengguo canal (dug before unification, making thousands of acres of land on the north side of the Wei valley fertile); construction of the Great Wall under General Meng Tian, who used 300,000 men over a decade to create a wall ca. 2,500 miles long (not yet verified archaeologically); and the building of roads, like the *Zhi Dao* (Straight Road). This ran for I,800 *li* (about 500 miles) from the emperor's summer residence in Yuyang, just north of Xianyang, across the Ordos region to Jiuyuan in Inner Mongolia. Numerous stretches of this road, which was not completed on the death of the First Emperor in 210 BC, have been identified. In mountain

areas it was about 16 feet wide but exceeded 65 feet on flat land. *Qi dao* (fast roads) fanned out from Xianyang for a total of about 4,200 miles, roughly 600 miles more than the 3,720 miles of roads that covered the Roman empire in 150 AD, and some of which in Sichuan were made using planking supported by poles projecting from rock walls.

Forced labor was also used in the construction of the First August Sovereign's two largest works: his capital Xianyang (of which little remains because of the River Wei's shift north) and the emperor's Funerary Garden by Mount Li. Here the three large pits of the Terracotta Army are just a tiny representation of the conception of power that had developed in the Middle Kingdom during the Warring States period. The attention of archaeologists and, with them, that of the general public cannot but focus on these works that lay at the center of Qin power.

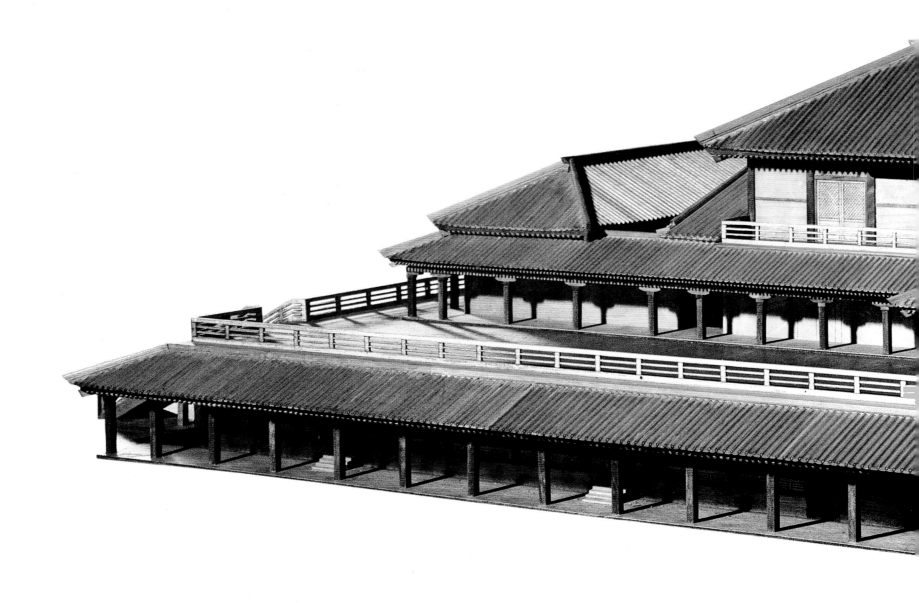

THE IMPERIAL CITY OF XIANYANG

Under the six previous kings Xianyang had grown on the south bank of the river Wei, which was wider and flatter than the north bank, which was dominated by the large plateau. The city was laid out anew by the First August Sovereign on a grandiose political design similar to the concept used by Louis XIV at Versailles.

'Rich, powerful families from across the empire, 120,000 families, were relocated to Xianyang. The ancestral temples, the Zhang-tai Palace and Shanglin Park were south of the River Wei. Each time that Qin conquered one of the feudal states, copies of their palaces and pavilions were rebuilt north of Xianyang facing south toward the Wei. … palaces, raised passages, protected pavilions stood one after the other filled with beautiful women, bells and drums that Qin had taken from the feudal lords….'

Once again, these are the words of Sima Qian describing the greatness of Xianyang.

Archaeological research has concentrated in one of the many palace and temple areas (which covered 8 square miles) scattered across the countryside around Xi'an with their large terraces on pressed earth foundations. Excavation, particularly in the 1970s, has uncovered a large area of kilns used to fire clay architectural elements, and the remains of three buildings (Palaces 1, 2 and 3), of which Palaces 1 and 3 were part of a monumental complex.

The remains of the foundations of the complex on the north bank of the Wei stand on a platform about 20 feet high, 66 yards long east-west and 49 deep north-south. The palace is composed of pavilions on terraces and seems originally to have had two symmetrical wings that crossed a torrent. A pyramid of pressed earth three steps high formed each wing. All around the earth core were rooms with beams decorated with bronze finishings, and floors and walls plastered and painted red and white. More than 440 fragments of polychrome plaster decorations have been found in the ruins of Palace 1, and decorated walls up to 3 feet high have been found still standing in Palace 3. The paintings are of carriages drawn by teams of four horses, ritual processions, buildings, plants, and anthropomorphic figures.

The rooms were connected by a series of portals, corridors, stairways and covered passages, all paved with river pebbles and in some cases with large hollow bricks decorated with phoenixes, dragons and geometric patterns. On the second and third terraces projecting sections in the shape of pavilions enlivened the profile of the building; on the ground floor an arcade with tall, pebbled columns helped to create an effect of monumentality. The entire building was served by an efficient drainage and sewage system that used down-pipes, collection wells, siphons and clay pipes of various diameters. The monumentality of the building, and its three orders of tiled roofs with round antefixes initially suggested it had been built during the reign of Qin Shi Huangdi, but later it was noticed that the structure had

been repeatedly repaired and enlarged, and that the original nucleus was from the Warring States period and had later been integrated into an imperial construction. Some experts think that the building is the Jique Palace built by Shang Yang as a symbol of Qin regality and used by Qin Shi Huangdi as the seat of imperial power.

Traces of a fire in the two palaces might provide evidence of an extraordinary claim made by Sima Qian: 'Xiang Yu set fire to the palaces in Xianyang; for three months the fire did not go out.'

The reproduction in Xianyang of buildings typical of the six conquered feudal kingdoms – as groups of tiles in the style of the different states seem to indicate – was a symbol of personal power but also of the unity of the new state. This was made unique by a single administrative, legislative and economic system while also being a symbol of the 'civilized universe' with which the empire of Qin Shi Huangdi identified.

Sima Qian reported that in 212 BC work began on a new palace on the south bank of the Wei in the area of Shanglin Park that was to contain the largest throne room China had ever seen. Construction may have begun as early as 246 BC but it is probable that this referred only to the erection of the huge terrace made from layers of packed earth on which the palace itself was to be built. The choice of site opposite the palaces of Xianyang was a careful one as, not far from that zone, the first two 'capitals' of the Western Zhou had been built: Feng and Hao. The new palace was never given a name, perhaps because it remained uncompleted on the death of the emperor, and it is known to us by the traditional name *A'fang* or *E'pang* ('next to' [the palaces of Xianyang]). Sima Qian gave the dimensions of the palace: 500 double Qin paces from east to west by 500 Qin feet from south to north, in other words 740 x 122 yards. The palace was built so large because it was designed to receive 10,000 people at a time, and flagpoles 66 feet high were to stand on the base of the highest platform.

Perhaps the measurements given were inexact and the number 10,000 was synonymous with 'very many,' as often occurs in ancient Chinese texts. The only bits to remain of this palace, which was burned down at the end of the Qin dynasty, are hundreds of fragments of tiles, bronze architectural elements, and iron reinforcers and nails that were completely deformed by the heat. Rain, wind and the action of man have slowly worn away the immense terrace on which villages and fields now exist, but the layers of earth so carefully accumulated and pressed by the conscripts who built it are still visible.

After the defeat of the feudal states and their unification in 221 BC, the armies of the emperor did not rest on their laurels. Having brought all the civilized world to heel under a single power, Qin Shi Huangdi began to expand it further, imposing his civilization wherever possible: in river and lake valleys, in the hills and plains, and anywhere that agriculture was possible.

For ten years General Meng Tian remained camped beyond the large bend of the Huanghe to build roads, and trace out and erect the Great Wall that marked the border between the agricultural and pastoral worlds and curbed expansion into the southern grazing lands of Ordos, Shanxi and Gansu provinces. In the meantime, the armies marched up the river valleys that south of the Yangzi lead to the highlands of the southwest (where the sophisticated cultures of the Dian and Yelang flourished around the lakes in Yunnan) and towards the fertile valleys and low hills to the southeast where three prefec-

tures were established in what today are the provinces of Guangxi, Guangdong and Fujian. Here strategy and military engineering produced civil works without precedence: for instance, around 219 BC the *Lingqu* canal (Magical Transport Canal) was dug in record time. As the Dujiayan irrigation system in Chengdu plain in Sichuan, it has remained in use until the present day. The canal joined a southern tributary of the Yangzi to a northern tributary of the Sijiang, thus allowing goods and food supplies to be transported from the middle Yangzi valley to the region of Canton along a water system 1,200 miles

❖

Little of the earliest Chinese architecture has survived, for it featured buildings with wooden frames and beaten-earth outer and dividing walls that never had a load-bearing function. However, traces remain of monumental architecture — chiefly for ceremonial use — in the form of the high platforms composed of layers of beaten earth, upon which the buildings were constructed, and clay roof tiles, which have survived the ravages of time. These architectural elements, and the discovery of the prints left by the bases of columns and beams, enable us to devise possible virtual reconstructions that help us to imagine the shape and spacing of the components of the two monumental gates, as in these two perspective views. They show a city gate, flanked by tall defensive watchtowers, and an inner gate that allowed access to the innermost part of a palace area.

long. In addition to armed soldiers, Qin Shi Huangdi used those equipped with spades to create his empire. In 219 BC 30,000 families were moved into the southern region of the Shandong peninsula to cultivate virgin land; in return for their service, they were given twelve years exemption from participation in public works. In 214 an unknown number of individuals was sent to fight and settle in the three new southern prefectures of Guilin, Xiang and Nanhai; these settlers received no compensation as they were servants, shopkeepers and 'fugitives' (perhaps dissidents or people who had gone into hiding to avoid convict labor). In the same year people generically called 'convicts' were sent to the thirty-four new districts created in the newly conquered northern territories. In 213 BC, functionaries who had not performed their offices well were punished by transferral, some to work on the Great Wall and some to till the soil in the southern region of Yue, which lies between Guangdong and the northern tip of Vietnam. This compulsory transfer may have had something to do with the episode that made the emperor so disliked by the Confucians and history: the history, that is, written by Confucians.

122 top *The decorative motif on this end section of gray clay guttering is a recurrent feature of Qin artifacts and is probably a symbolic representation of the heavens marked by the circular path of the constellation of Ursa Major. (Terracotta Army Museum, Lintong)*

122 bottom and 123 top *The end section of these tiles features two motifs belonging to the same symbolic category: spiral-shaped elements in the outer ring, which appear to "revolve" in the opposite direction to those in the central sphere. It could be a solar symbol or an allusion to the two cosmic principles, yin and yang. (Terracotta Army Museum, Lintong)*

123 center *The geometric decoration on this end section of a tile, from one of the palace or temple buildings of the Yong capital, can be divided into two perfectly symmetrical halves. Here too, the opposition of the two elements may have a symbolic value associated with yin and yang. (Xianyang, Municipal Museum)*

123 bottom *Two horses, each surmounted by a bird, are tied to a central tree in a clear reference to the axis mundi. The theme and composition are among the most evocative of those depicted on Qin tiles and draw on the decorative syntax of the art of the steppes, testifying to the close bond between the Qin culture and those that flourished in the north. (Xianyang, Municipal Museum)*

❖

124 top Although the decorative motifs on these two tiles are very different, they appear to be ascribable to the same symbolic universe that characterizes all types of decorated tiles of the Qin period: that of the cyclical change of position of the celestial bodies — centrally dominated by the most luminous star — whose transit from one celestial house to another one marks the passage of time.

❖

124 bottom Small bronze or jade fish appear in the grave goods of the aristocracy from at least the Western Zhou period. Those shown here were found in Qin tombs dating from the time of the Warring States These objects, which belonged to pendants or were stitched onto funerary robes, were clearly associated with the aquatic realm and thus probably symbolized the netherworld, which was known as the Yellow Springs.

❖

125 In the monumental architecture of the Warring States period, it appears that the symbolic significance of buildings was chiefly expressed in the decorations that adorned the gutter tiles, which were inspired by well-defined regional symbolic and stylistic languages. In the case of Qin tiles such as those shown here, the recurrent designs are related to cosmogonic symbology, the regular division of space and the depiction of the movements of the celestial bodies by means of spiral and S-shaped elements, also known as "cloud" motifs.

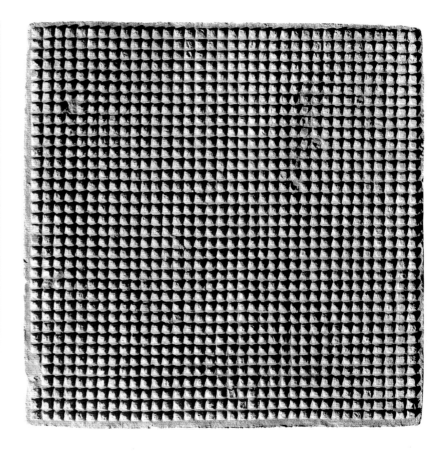

*126 and 127 top These three clay tiles with various
kinds of geometric patterns were found among the
remains of the imperial palaces in Xianyang.
According to the Chinese archaeologists, they may have
been used on both walls and floors. It also seems as
though the decorations of the tiles were originally
enhanced with polychrome pigments of the same kind
that were used for painting on plaster.
(Xianyang, Municipal Museum)*

*127 bottom Although only a few fragments remain of the
frescoes that once decorated Qin Shi Huangdi's palaces, many
of the architectural decorations made from clay have survived.
The photograph shows a large gray clay hollow brick that was
fired at a high temperature and perhaps used as the base of a
balustrade. The five visible faces of the brick are decorated with
an elegant printed motif that was originally emphasized with
colored pigments. This type of decoration was very fashionable
during the Qin dynasty. (Xianyang, Municipal Museum)*

This bronze apotropaic mask adorned a wooden door of Imperial Palace No. 1 in Xianyang. Its hooked nose once held a ring that served as a knocker and handle. The origins of the fantastic figure depicted in the mask, known as Taotie, lie in the symbolic language devised during the Neolithic Age.

129 top *The tolerance between the eyelets of these two gilded bronze hinges, used for some kind of door in the imperial palaces of Xianyang, is extremely precise, testifying to the exceptional technical skills of the Qin casters.*

129 bottom *The depiction of moving bodies was a refinement that characterized much Chinese art produced between the 5th and 1st centuries BC, which incorporated, and in turn influenced, stylistic elements of the art of the steppes. This theme is clearly visible in this bronze piece shaped like a fantastic feline creature, from the ruins of a Qin imperial palace, which once adorned the corner of a piece of wooden furniture.*

THE BURNING OF THE BOOKS AND EXECUTION OF THE MEN OF LETTERS

The origin of the event was convivial at least as the emperor had invited seventy or so men of letters to drink to his health in the palace in Xianyang. Each toast was accompanied by a small speech by the person who raised his glass to the emperor, as is still the custom today. The archery official spoke suitably flattering words, but the learned Chunyu Yue of Qi (a state notoriously filled with Confucians) felt it his duty to pronounce his point of view. He asked, how was it possible for the emperor to maintain control of such a huge country without the vigilant support of his own family members? In short, how was it possible without setting up the feudal model that existed under the early Zhou, which was the Confucians' ideal of good government? This discourse went directly against Qin policy and provoked the angry reaction of Li Si, who was a convinced supporter of the centralized state and the independence of institutions from feudal ties. Consequently, Li Si asked to put a drastic end to dissidence by cutting off its very root: in other words, by destroying the chronicles of the feudal states (with the exception of Qin), the Classic of Poetry and the Historical Records, works that contained and passed on the ideals of Zhou feudality. Everything was to be burned and no-one would have the right to retain a copy of either the chronicles or books. Only the central Qin archive could keep a copy of everything. The emperor welcomed the request and issued the required edict.

The following year — 212 BC according to Sima Qian — the emperor showed an unstable side of his character. For some years he had been financing costly expeditions in search of Penglai, the land of the immortals, with the hope of obtaining the elixir of immortality. In the same period the August Sovereign began to come under the baleful influence of a certain Master Lu, who introduced the emperor to esoteric practices to achieve a state of imperturbability that was the prelude to immortality. The emperor's behavior aroused a good deal of criticism at court, which reached the First August Sovereign's ears. So he asked Li Si to conduct an inquiry among the 'academics.' These individuals were not famous for their courage and began to accuse one another in order to save their own skins. It turned out that 460 of them, for one reason or another, had violated the prohibitions placed on them by the emperor for which they were sentenced to death. This episode was a warning to the whole empire.

These 460 men of letters were not all Confucians and were not, as is widely thought, buried alive for having defended their ideas. The word used by Sima Qian was *keng*, literally 'put to death,' and only in rare cases does *keng* mean 'bury alive.' However, it is clear that many Confucian commentators took the second interpretation and by doing so championed the 460 'martyrs' so that they might denigrate, once more, the hated Qin Shi Huangdi. In any case, the burning of the books and the execution of the men of letters were not directly related.

A substantial increase in work on the A'-fang Palace and his tomb near Mount Li marked the last two years of the emperor's life. Thirty thousand families were relocated to Mount Li, probably to populate the villages of those involved in the funerary rites, in return for which they were exempted from taxes and corvée for ten years. The emperor also made ritual pilgrimages to the sacred mountains in the empire. There he erected stelae inscribed with his edicts, took possession of the *Tian Xia* and symbolically brought order there, placing everything in its right place in the balanced order of the Universe and giving every word its correct meaning. It was during one of these pilgrimages in the seventh month of the 37th year of his reign (210 BC) that Qin Shi Huangdi died. His departure left the country at a time of enormous economic commitment due to the huge works he had commissioned and to his campaigns of expansion and colonization which, despite being of enormous potential, had not yet yielded their harvest.

Who was capable of continuing his policies?

Shortly before his death, the emperor had designated his eldest son as heir but, this fact remained unknown to the boy as he had been sent on a mission in 212 BC to General Meng Tian in the north to meditate on his 'Confucian' sympathies. Exactly because he feared such sympathies, Li Si falsified the emperor's will and brought back the emperor's dead body to Xianyang in a cart of dried fish to mask the smell. He then engineered a plot to force the suicide of the legitimate heir and thus place the younger son, Hu Hai, of whom Li Si was the tutor, on the throne. He came to the throne as Er Shi Huangdi, the Second August Emperor, but was only to reign for three years.

❖

The photograph shows the model of the area of the "Mortuary Garden of Mount Li" as seen from the north. The background is dominated by the three peaks of the "Black Horse Mountain" (Mount Li or Lishan) with the deep ditches that convey the torrential waters towards the tributaries of the Wei River during the rainy season. In the foreground are the Lishan Lingyuan enclosures, with the burial mound set in an eccentric position. The roofing structures covering the three pits of the Terracotta Army are visible to the left of the enclosures (to the east) and the large vaulted building facing the two cubic buildings.

LISHAN LINGYUAN:
THE FUNERARY GARDEN OF MOUNT LI

'In the 9th month the First August Sovereign was buried at Mount Li. As soon as he ascended the throne [246 BC] the First August Sovereign had begun to excavate and model Mount Li, when he unified the world, he had 700,000 people brought from all across the country. They dug as far as the Three [subterranean] Springs, then cast the bronze to make the outer sarcophagus. Models of palaces, towers and the hundreds functionaries together with wonderful and rare things were accumulated in the tomb. Craftsmen were ordered to make crossbows and darts, ready to strike if someone dug in to violate [the tomb]. With quicksilver they made the hundred rivers, the Yangzi, the Huanghe and the oceans, so that they seemed to flow. Above, the entire Sky was represented, below, the Earth. The lamps were filled with 'man-fish' oil so that they would burn forever.

The Second August Sovereign said, 'It is not right that the childless widows of the previous Sovereign should go elsewhere.' He decreed that they should accompany the deceased and a multitude of them died.

When the funeral was over, someone said that the craftsmen who had built the tomb knew of its treasures, and that if they had mentioned these treasures the consequence would be serious. Once the placement of the treasures had been completed, the middle door was closed, the outer door was lowered and all the craftsmen were closed inside unable to get out.

Trees and bushes were planted on the mound so that it seemed like a mountain.'

This was Sima Qian's description of the emperor's burial. He mentions the pomp, the use of whale oil for the lamps ('man-fish' is an unmistakable term for marine mammals), the exception made to the old decree that abolished sacrificial victims (in this case the emperor's childless widows), the clear allusion to tomb robbers and the consequent cruel killing of the craftsmen who knew the secrets of the tomb. But beyond all that Sima Qian does not go, except to say that the following year the Second August Sovereign decreed an increase in the sacrifices in temples for the cult of the First Emperor. Sima Qian either remains silent on or was ignorant of the pits containing funerary offerings and the sacrificial pits that, two thousand years later, the Chinese proudly called 'the Eighth Wonder of the World.' In some way, the sacrifice of the craftsmen was successful in keeping the secret of the buried treasures. Everyone forgot and the miniature reproduction of the *Tian Xia* ([what lies] beneath Heaven), i.e., the civilized universe, became an underground universe.

The different parts of Qin Shi Huangdi's tomb lie about twenty-two miles east of modern Xi'an. Work began on them as soon as the emperor mounted the throne and it was completed in 208 BC, two years after his death. The different parts cover a surface area of 22 square miles on terraces on the slopes of Lishan (Mount of the Black Horse), the largest of which is entirely occupied by the *lingyuan* (funerary garden). All the secondary structures of the *lingyuan* (accompanying graves and sacrificial pits) seem to lie to the north and east of the funerary garden.

Evidently the geomancers considered the area to be propitious. In fact, it was protected to the south by the power of the earth (Lishan) and to the north by the power of water (the River Wei), and it was crossed by a north-south axis around which the entire mausoleum lies, i.e., one which joined Lishan in the south to the temples of the old capital, Yueyang, in the north. To the west the repose of the emperor was protected by the power of the Qinling mountains and by the power of the ancestors worshiped in the ancestral temples to which the tomb was connected by an avenue twenty miles long. To the east were the passes that led to the Great Central Plain, the lands that Qin had subjected and to the lands of its enemies. How could the sleep of the emperor be protected on that side?

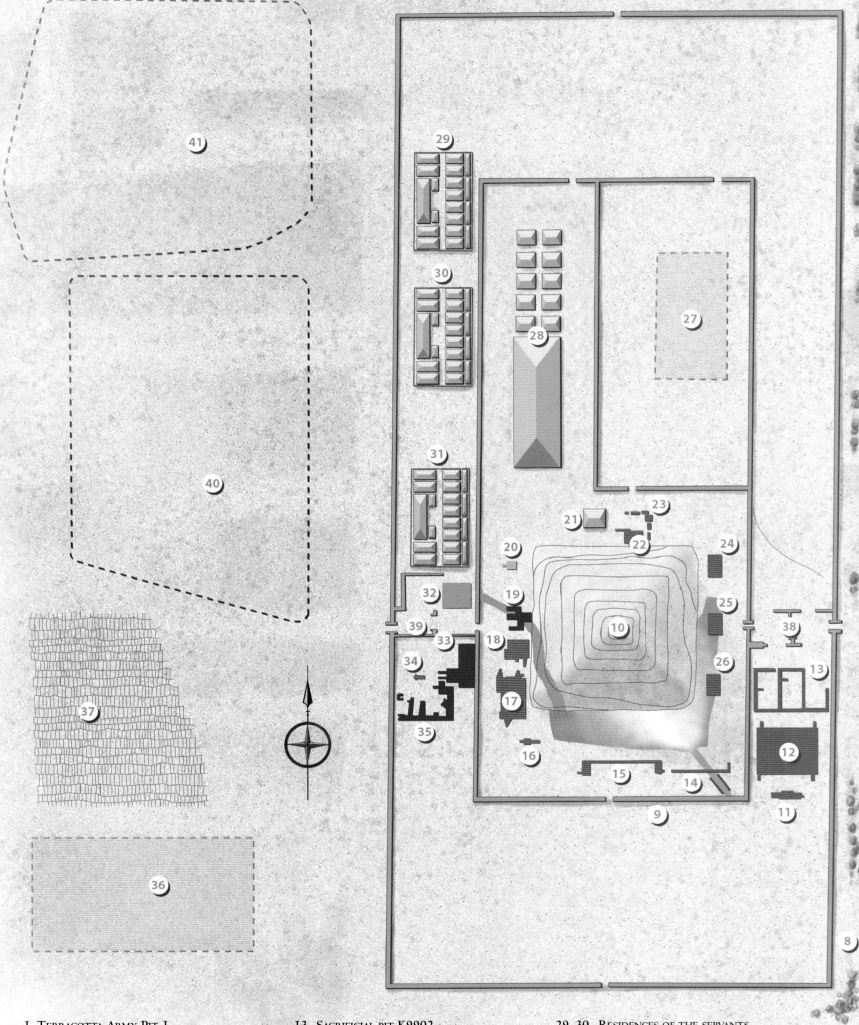

1 TERRACOTTA ARMY PIT 1
2 TERRACOTTA ARMY PIT 2
3 TERRACOTTA ARMY PIT 3
4 TERRACOTTA ARMY PIT 4
5 LARGE GRAVE OF ACCOMPANIMENT
6 AREA OF THE PITS OF THE EAST STABLES
7, 32 SATELLITE TOMBS (LARGER) AND GRAVES
OF ACCOMPANIMENT
8 FIRST ENCLOSURE
9 SECOND ENCLOSURE
10 BURIAL MOUND
11 SACRIFICIAL PIT K9901
12 SACRIFICIAL PIT K9801

13 SACRIFICIAL PIT K9902
14 SACRIFICIAL PIT K0001
15 SACRIFICIAL PIT K0002
16 SACRIFICIAL PIT K0006
17 SACRIFICIAL PIT K0003
18, 22, 23, 24, 25, 26 GRAVE GOOD
BURIAL SITES, ALSO KNOWN AS
SACRIFICIAL PITS
19 PIT OF THE BRONZE CHARIOTS
20, 27, 36 SATELLITE TOMBS
21 ROOM OF REST
27 NECROPOLIS OF THE CONCUBINES
28 AREA OF THE SIDE ROOM

29, 30 RESIDENCES OF THE SERVANTS
OF THE "FUNERARY GARDEN"
31 BANQUETING ROOM
33 "PITS OF THE MENAGERIE"
34 SACRIFICIAL PIT K0005
35 PIT OF THE "WEST STABLES"
36 NECROPOLIS OF THE *LISHAN*
37 CONSCRIPTS' CEMETERY
38, 39 SERVICE STRUCTURES FOR THE MONUMENTAL GATES
40 AREA OF THE FUNERARY GARDEN FOR THE
MANUFACTURE AND FIRING OF TILES AND BRICKS
41 AREA OF THE CRAFTSMEN'S HOMES
AND WORKSHOPS

SHAHE RIVER

WULING DAM

The focus of the funerary garden is the eccentrically positioned burial mound in the inner of two large enclosures bounded by high, pressed earth walls protected nearby to the southeast by a large earthwork, the one-mile-long Wuling barrier. This was built on a southwest-northeast axis to deviate the Shahe torrent that runs down from Mount Li toward the River Wei on the east side of the funerary complex.

The height of the tomb, which was built as a tall pyramid with two four-sided platforms, is now lower than its original height. According to the latest measurements, some say the current height is 182'7", according to others it is 115 feet high at its lowest point and 285 feet at its highest. The base measures 383 yards north-south by 377 east-west, but with such discordant data it is difficult to estimate what the original measurements were. Confusion is also created by a source from the late 3rd century AD that claimed the mound was originally between 380–394 feet high but not all Chinese specialists have faith in this claim.

If the mound has lost height, the loss may have been caused because at a certain point the layers of mallet-tamped earth were created more hurriedly. Perhaps the laborers had gone missing or there was a lack of direction by the *Shaofu*, the Qin department of administration, whose express job it was to build the Mount Li funerary garden. Consequently, the poorly packed earth would have begun to crumble and slip down the sides to form a heap around the bottom between 3 and 10 feet thick.

Currently we do not know if excavations have been made inside the mound, though rumor has it that various soundings have confirmed the presence of bronze, clay and wooden objects. But we do know that surveys carried out between 1998 and 2000 discovered an impressive drainage system 1,425 yards long and at points 130 feet deep, which runs along the base of the mound and was clearly planned to protect the burial chamber from underground water. The channel, its wells and vents are connected to a long discharge channel 574 yards long in a section already surveyed.

We also know that in 1981–82 the Geological Institute of the Chinese Academy of Sciences conducted various surveys around the base of the mound that revealed the presence of mercury ten times greater than in the surrounding area. Once more Sima Qian was correct, the 'quicksilver' could have been the residue of what was used to make the flowing rivers and seas in the August Sovereign's burial chamber.

❖

135 top This piece of corded, pentagonal gray clay pipe was part of the underground drainage system of the Mount Li Funerary Garden. It is of the same type as the pipes that crossed the beaten earth walls that mark off the two main enclosures.
(Terracotta Army Museum, Lintong)

❖

135 bottom The double-pitched roofs of the temples in the Mount Li Funerary Garden were covered with semi-cylindrical gray clay tiles. Those forming the last row, the gutter tiles, featured a round end section (measuring around 6 inches across), whose visible face was decorated with printed, incised or excised motifs, generally with a well-wishing symbolic meaning. The round face was practical as well as decorative, for these tiles covered and protected the final part of the underlying rafters that supported the weight of the roof. In this case the zoomorphic motif modeled on the end section of the tile is composed of a bird with a showy crest depicted beneath a branch of a tree. According to the symbology of the cardinal points, the bird (known as the Scarlet Bird) is the symbol of the south, thus the tile probably belonged to one of the southern religious buildings.
(Terracotta Army Museum, Lintong)

The Structures of the Funeral Cult

The mound was surrounded by two rectangular, concentric walls around the nucleus of the funerary constructions. The outer enclosure measured 2,393 yards north-south by 1062 east-west; it had three monumental gateways on the east, west and south sides and guard towers at the four corners. The east and west gates stood about one third of the way along the wall in line with those in the inner enclosure and with the central east-west axis of the mound in the southern half of the inner enclosure. Recent investigations have confirmed the absence of the north gate in the outer enclosure and have established the width of some of the monumental gates. The east gate of the inner enclosure is 84 yards wide and 25 deep (east-west), and the corresponding gate in the outer enclosure has the same width but is 24.5 yards deep; on the south side the outer gate is 74 yards wide and 16.8 yards deep (north-south) but the inner gate is narrower at 71.5 yards wide and deeper at 20.3 yards.

In the space between the two walls, on a level with the east and west gates, the remains of two tripartite towers (*que*) have been found at the sides of the avenue that passes through the gates. The east tower stood north of the avenue and measured 50.2 yards long and ranged from 5–16 yards wide. The west tower that stood south of the avenue was 48.2 yards long and between 5.5 and 17 yards wide. Investigations carried out in 2000 revealed that porticoed corridors ran along the wall of the inner enclosure (1,460 x 634 yards) on both the interior and exterior sides. The corridors were roofed with decorated tiles, and the walls were made of plastered earth decorated with polychrome motifs. A third space in the

136-137 *This virtual bird's-eye view from the southeast shows the burial mound of Qin Shi Huang Di and two large enclosed spaces to the north of it. The westernmost space contains the religious buildings with the houses of the priests, while the easternmost one had no elevated structures because it was destined for the graves of accompaniment of the emperor's concubines.*

northeast quadrant of the inner enclosure measured 760 x 361 yards, was lined by a wall on the north and east sides, and seems to have been reserved for the burial of elite members of society who would be accompanied by servants and other individuals. The other enclosed areas lie north of the mound and were occupied by temples dedicated to the cult of the August Sovereign and the residential quarters of those who served in the temples. A sewer system made from corded, pentagonal clay pipes served the entire funerary complex.

QINDIAN, THE ROOM OF REST

A four-sided structure on a pressed earth platform with a surface area of 4.23 square yards has been found a little over 17 feet from the mound, almost in line with the north-south enclosure wall that lines the northeast quadrant. The structure was originally ringed by arches and had a gate 16.4 yards wide on the east side. The gate was reached by a stairway roughly a yard long that led from the main body of the building. Chinese archaeologists have uncovered a series of construction materials: fragments of large hollow bricks decorated with geometric motifs, semi-cylindrical guttering with stamped end sections, flat roofing tiles, parts of walls, fragments of plaster made from clay mixed with straw, and lumps of burned earth mixed with burned objects. Clearly the building had been destroyed by fire, as had occurred to many of the monuments in the funerary complex.

This structure was the *Qindian*, the Room of Rest, i.e., the main 'temple' for the cult of the dead August Sovereign. Several historical sources mention that before Qin Shi Huangdi, sacrifices made for the dead were only officiated in the *Zongmiao*, the temple of the ancestors, which was situated inside the city, as at Yong. Usually the temple was divided into front and rear rooms along a north-south axis. The front section of the temple (*miao*) was the cult room proper where the tablet of the deceased (a sort of small stele that bore the name of the dead person) and those of people associated with the cult were kept, and to whom the ancestral sacrifices were made four times a day. The north part of the *Zongmiao* was the *Qindian*, the Room of Rest or Room of the Sarcophagus, where *mingqi* (articles that represented the deceased's assets in real life), personal effects, a staff and burial clothes were kept. Some sources state that it was in this room that the sarcophagus for the ruling sovereign was stored and that each year it was painted with a new coat of lacquer. Also that it was in this room that the body of the dead sovereign 'rested' before being sealed in his sarcophagus and being transported from the *Qindian* to the far end of the burial chamber. According to some, it was Qin Shi Huangdi who altered the funeral ritual with the shift of the *Qindian* from the city to the place of burial. It was used to hold the ruler's personal effects that would be used in the burial ceremony, and also as

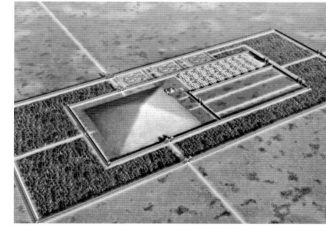

the main place of cult worship of the deceased after burial.

If the First August Sovereign was responsible for this change in custom, the *Qindian* must have been one of the first buildings to be constructed at the Lishan lingyuan around 246 BC.

The association between the *Qindian* and the burial mound remained a constant feature of imperial funerary architecture even after the Qin dynasty had fallen.

137 right *This is what the huge burial pit would have looked like when almost completed, in a bird's-eye view from the northeast. The conjectured virtual reconstruction clearly shows the complexity and number of architectural structures, which resembled a little funerary city that would have satisfied the ceremonial needs of the daily worship rituals performed in honor of the deceased emperor.*

BIANDIAN, THE SIDE ROOM

The name of this ritual structure derived from the fact that its prescribed position was facing the *Qindian*.

A raised area measuring 569 x 241 yards in the northwest quadrant of the inner enclosure was the platform for various buildings. Stratigraphic investigation in 1973 revealed a group of foundation levels, one of which was divided into four blocks by supporting walls made of pressed earth between 4' 6" and 21' 4" feet thick.

The floors in the blocks were made either from beaten earth or stone slabs. Sections of pebbled roads ran between the walls, and roofing tiles, ridge tiles and gutter tiles were found. One of the gutter tiles had a semi-circular face 24 inches in diameter decorated with a mirror-image of an obliquely rendered 'dragon.'

The profile of foundation platform 2 is quite well conserved in one of the four blocks and it has been possible to work out that it supported a rectangular building oriented south-north, 62' long by 11'2" wide. There was a door on the west side reached up four stone steps. Inside the door a stone 'threshold' divided the building into two sections, each of which had passageways with stone floors.

These finds are suggestive of a monumental building whose principal function was to store the more valuable liturgical objects used in the cults practiced in the *Qindian* and the building itself.

LISHAN SHIGONG, THE MOUNT LI BANQUETING ROOM

A large rectangular structure measuring 218.7 x 184.4 yards was excavated in 1981–82 in the area between the west walls of the two enclosures on the west side of the funerary garden, close to the avenue that runs through the west gates. The investigation concentrated on the south side of the structure where an area measuring 2,687 square yards was opened. Six bases of foundations for six rectangular buildings were found. The best preserved, Base I, runs south-north, measures 27.3 x 8.75 yards and is punctuated by five pillars. The structure had a leveled and very hard earth floor, a series of arches at the front and an area of broken and pressed shards of tiles that was probably used to prevent rainwater from reaching the building.

The area examined was filled with clay construction elements, such as different types of tiles, sewage pipes, filled and hollow bricks, and cylinders used to line wells. In addition to these were many tools (broken and whole), some made of glazed clay, and others of iron and bronze. The most important objects were those with inscriptions that allowed the name and function of the entire structure to be identified, in particular an elliptical bronze bell with decorations in gold and silver and the characters *Yue Fu* (Department of Music), weights inscribed with the edict from the 26th year of King Zheng's rule (i.e., the year of unification of the empire and the standardization of weights, etc.) and also weights inscribed with the same edict reissued by the Second August Sovereign. These and other weights were also engraved with short but eloquent inscriptions such as *Lishan Shigong* (Mount Li Banqueting Room), the *Lishan Shigong Shi* (Mount Li Banqueting Room Stone) and the *Lishan Shigong Zuo* (Mount Li Left Banqueting Room). Together these buildings formed the Banqueting Palace in the Mount Li Funerary Garden – but which banquets were they used for?

We know that the funeral ritual used for the August Sovereign was adopted with little change by the emperors of the following Han dynasty. Various chapters in the *Hou Han Shu* (Chronicle of the later Han, i.e. the Eastern Han) give a succinct account of the many and complex rites used. The daily sacrificial ceremonies were officiated in the Room of Rest, the weekly ones in the Side Room and the monthly ones in the Ancestral Temple (*Miao*).

Once a month the clothes and cap of the deceased held in the *Qindian* were changed, while food and drink were offered to the spirit of the emperor four times a day in the Banqueting Palace. This latter building also provided the meals for the people who worked in and administered the whole funeral complex.

THE RESIDENCES OF THE FUNCTIONARIES

The complex construction of the immense funerary garden lasted thirty-seven years and, according to Sima Qian, made use of 720,000 conscripts between the years 221 and 208 BC. The no less complex liturgy of the rites performed once the August Sovereign had been buried implies the existence of a large and skilled organization of administrators, construction foremen, geomancers, 'priests,' cooks, guards and ladies-in-waiting. All these functionaries attached to the tomb resided and worked *in loco* in the offices and residential quarters that lay to the north of the Banqueting Palace. A large area measuring 219 x 196 yards (which has only been partly investigated) contains a series of foundation platforms of pressed earth covered by the usual layer of broken clay items, including many sections of guttering decorated at the top with 'cloud' motifs.

All the above were visible and were probably in the form of rectangular pavilions, with columns, wooden trusses and architraves, walls plastered with earth or clay and straw, and covered with sloping roofs adorned with decorated ridge tiles and gutters that were probably also painted. Standing on platforms or terraces of different height, reached by flights of steps, the pavilions were given an air of stateliness and monumentality. Unfortunately, all the buildings so far examined were weakened by fire and subsequently collapsed.

However, this visible monumentality was minimal when compared to the magical but hidden universe that surrounded the last resting place of the First August Sovereign for over nine miles in all directions, and of which it is believed we know only a small part. The most recent estimate (July 2002) of the number of pits inside the two enclosures is 180.

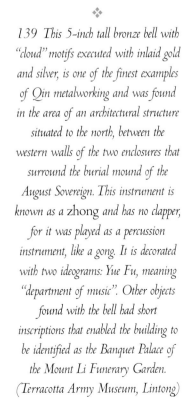

THE UNDERGROUND STRUCTURES:
AN UNDERGROUND PALACE, SACRIFICIAL PITS AND GRAVES OF ACCOMPANIMENT

The tomb of the August Sovereign — with its bronze sky perhaps studded with gems as stars, with rivers and oceans of mercury, automatons, traps and treasures — lies beneath the burial mound, however, no archaeologist has yet had the opportunity to gaze upon its mysteries. Nonetheless, do we really know nothing of this last resting place?

It should be remembered that during the Warring States period, particularly in the regions of the southern kingdom of Chu, the custom arose of dividing the burial chamber (or the external sarcophagus, the *guo*) with boxes or narrow compartments arranged around or on three sides of the inner sarcophagus. These new spaces contained the grave goods. The fact that the objects were set out in functional groups and the presence of short inscriptions suggest that the spaces represented the public life, ritual activities and private life of the deceased. This translation of the deceased's living space into his burial space is made explicit in the exceptionally undisturbed and rich grave of Yi, the Marquis of Zeng, a small fief in the modern province of Hubei. The tomb consisted of four wooden chambers with walls more than thirteen feet high that were originally covered

with material. Their functions were clearly represented by the objects found inside each one. Probably the number of rooms followed from the rank of the deceased, as the tomb of King You of Chu (ruled 237–238 BC), a contemporary of the First Emperor, had nine rooms within the burial space. In other Chu tombs, recognition of the function of the spaces has in many cases been made possible by the inventories of grave goods written on bamboo tablets that specify the goods in each chamber.

Another important feature of these tombs that clearly states the symbolic and ritual function of the division of the burial space is the presence of small painted apertures or doors on the partition walls; these apertures were supposed to facilitate the mobility of the ethereal spirit (*po*) of the deceased. It was believed that each individual was endowed with two spirits: one (the *hun*) was volatile and left the body at the moment of death; the other (the *po*) remained with the body inside the tomb and it was for the *po* that the various tools, books, food, drink, clothes, medicinal herbs and even instruments of pleasure were left. An example of the latter was two bronze phalluses joined at

❖

140 left This type of three-footed yan *(steamer) appeared during the late Spring and Autumn period and was produced throughout the Warring States period (to which this example belongs). This* yan *may have reached the area of the Qin capital as plunder, ending up in the grave goods of a veteran of the southern campaigns. (Municipal Museum, Xianyang)*

❖

140 right This type of ritual ding *tripod, which appeared at the end of the Spring and Autumn period, became widespread during the Warring States period, to which this example belongs, and remained in use throughout the Qin and Western Han dynasties, with slight variations. This is a sign of great ritual continuity, despite the cultural mix achieved by the Qin. (Municipal Museum, Xianyang)*

141 top This bronze vase belonging to the fang hu, or fang, family was part of the grave goods of a Qin burial discovered in 1984 at the Renjiacui site about three miles east of Xianyang. It is one of the most important Qin graves of the middle Warring States period and yielded the dismembered skeleton of a young sacrificial victim covered with a red substance, a pigment that had never been found in any of the other graves. (Municipal Museum, Renjiazui, Xianyang)

❖

141 bottom This perfectly proportioned hu jar for alcoholic beverages, typical of the Qin bronzes of the 3rd century BC, was to remain in use with slight variations until the first centuries of the Common Era, also as an important component of aristocratic grave goods.

the base in a V shape that was found in the tomb of Prince Liu Sheng, who died in 113 BC during the dynasty of the Western Han. Liu Sheng's grave example is not inappropriate as the dual nature of the spirit and the division of the tomb into chambers was mantained for the entire period of the Han dynasty. The use of multi-chambered graves became a distinctive feature of the tombs of the nobility with the result that they came to be known as 'underground palaces.' It therefore seems more than reasonable not only to consider that the concept of the duality of the spirit was shared by the First Emperor and that this was in some way reflected in the duality of the ritual layout of the Funerary Garden (visible/invisible structures, rites for the *hun* spirit and rites for the *po* spirit, etc.), but also that the space in which the fabulous treasures were placed was divided into chambers with specialized functions. This is particularly the case if we consider the extreme precision of the Qin administration, which would never have been guilty of a lack of order, and even less would have made an exception to the rules relating to the last resting place of the greatest of the *po* spirits that the Middle Kingdom had ever known.

According to one of the greatest experts of Qin archaeology, Wang Xueli, who has access to scientific tests not yet completely published, the Underground Palace of the First August Sovereign lies about 165 feet below the burial mound, at the bottom of a pit in the shape of an upturned truncated pyramid. The burial chamber seems to be bounded by a wall 4–5 yards thick and high, made from pressed earth and strengthened by unbaked clay bricks. The dimensions of the entire rectangular palace are 500 yards north-south by 425 yards east-west. Bearing in mind that the diggers of the pit had to reach the 'Three springs,' as Sima Qian says, at the depth at which the sarcophagus lies in the burial chamber, we can expect that the ac-

tion of the water from the underground fault (the 'Three springs') may have seriously damaged the various chambers in the tomb. Having said that, it is to be hoped that the drainage system mentioned previously and the bronze lining referred to by the Great Historian have protected the individual chambers sufficiently to allow further investigations.

On the north side of the wall identified so far there are two openings: the first is 26 feet wide and stands roughly 30 inches from the northwest corner; it looks onto a ramp covered with tree trunks that led from the surface to the interior of the tomb; the second opening is almost 60 feet wide, lies about 104 yards from the first and gave access to the sacrificial pits on the north side of the mound. Like the earlier tombs of the Qin kings, that of the First Emperor had large ramps on each of the four sides. Chinese archaeologists have made preliminary investigations of these but no information has been forthcoming on the ramp on the south side because that is the area of the greatest accumulation of earth that has been eroded from the mound above.

Evidence of five ramps has been gathered on the east side; the central one (65 yards long and between 14 and 22 yards wide) was the most important and was flanked by two service ramps. There is a clear resemblance to the 'royal avenues' in the capital in which a wide central carriageway reserved for use by the sovereign was flanked by two narrower roads for use by commoners.

A series of 'entrances' to underground galleries at a depth of 13 to 16 feet on the north side has been investigated. These are laid out in two rows: the first has 20 'entrances' and the second, roughly 12 yards north of the first, has 14 each about 16 feet wide. They seem to lead into corridors or tunnels separated by pressed earth walls and sealed by unfired bricks.

143 left Ding *tripods such as this are frequently found among the grave goods of aristocrats. This one was discovered in a Qin tomb from the Warring States period. The decoration may have some cosmological symbolic meaning (due to the three circular registers) or a shamanistic significance (if the animals depicted were the representation of the spirit/animal that guided the officiant/shaman toward the netherworld). The vase could have reached Qin territory as a gift or plunder, or it could have been produced there in imitation of the fine products of Wei. (Municipal Museum, Xianyang)*

In 1973 a pit was examined that was partially covered by the edge of the mound, about 44 yards from the west gate in the wall of the inner enclosure. Its layout was quite complex though it was all contained within a square 55 yards long on each side. The underground structure was composed of a corridor from the burial chamber and the part that was examined; free from the accumulation of earth on the west side of the mound, this area was between 13 and 25 yards wide and roughly 55 yards long. The corridor seems to lead to a rectangular bay that runs east-west and communicates via a narrow passage with a second parallel bay to the north. These two bays were probably store rooms for some of the grave goods. On the south side of the corridor, about halfway along the examined section, a small opening leads into a rectangular bay measuring about 16 yards east-west and 22 north-south. In the southwest corner of this bay there is a narrow passageway or closet area that runs parallel to the two bays that lie to the north. In this passageway, a rectangular structure has been detected divided by earth partitions into five parallel north-south bays. During November and December 1980, a stratigraphic excavation was made of the northernmost of these partitions (measuring 22'4" x 6'10"). Two incomparable works of bronze art were discovered from the late ancient Chinese era and one of the most important discoveries in the history of archaeology: the First Emperor's two bronze chariots.

THE PIT OF THE BRONZE CHARIOTS

The storage space was originally lined with wooden planks and covered by tree trunks. Inside, standing one behind the other and both facing west, there were two single-shaft chariots, each unique of their kind, made to be drawn by four horses. Each chariot was driven by a bronze charioteer. Even the dimensions of the chariots were unusual in that they were both exactly half-size.

The two chariots lay on their right sides and had been badly damaged by the collapse of the ceiling following the disintegration of the tree trunks. The chariot found at the front is referred to as Chariot 1; the one behind as Chariot 2. The hooves of the horses of Chariot 1 were broken in several pieces; the charioteer was in relatively good condition but the structure of the chariot itself had been broken into thousands of pieces. The hooves of the horses in Chariot 2 were also broken but the fragments of the chariot frame and roof were not so minutely broken; even so, there were still 1,555 pieces.

Restoration of the two chariots began immediately using relatively simple methods and technically limited means, and are an excellent demonstration of the skill of the Chinese restorers. Just three years later, in 1982, Chariot 2 was exhibited to the public, and in 1988 the newfound beauty of Chariot 1 was also displayed.

There is much to admire about the chariots. Foremost was the skill of the bronze casters: Chariot 2 alone used 1.2 tons of metal which had been cast in clay molds to create 1,742 components of bronze, 988 of silver and 732 of gold. The various pieces ranged from chains made of links just 7/100ths of an inch thick to the roofing of the chariot 24.75 square feet in surface area and between 7 and 15/100ths of an inch thick.

Equally impressive was the elegance of the proportions, the chromatic contrast between the white of the horses and the blue of their tassels, and the different colors of the walls of the chariot cabin that perfectly imitated damask. However, the most outstanding feature of the models is the knowledge they provide of the actual chariots used in ancient China.

Many real chariots and horses had been found in the graves of the nobility prior to this discovery but they had all been reduced to decomposed pieces of wood, oxidized bronze finishings, and lifeless and colorless horse skeletons that lacked the cut of their manes, the setting of their tails, leather straps, bridles, rope collars, plumes or the padding on their harness. We knew that a parasol or canopy was used from inscriptions on ritual vases from the era of the Western Zhou, as in the inscription of the *Mao Gong Ding* (*ding* tripod belonging to Duke Mao now displayed in the National Palace Museum in Taipei) that mentions '... a tigerskin parasol lined with red material....'

The oldest example we have comes from pit M1100 in the ducal necropolis in the state of Yin, near Liulihe (Hebei province), also from the period of the Western Zhou, but it is only the bronze components of the frame so we are unable to know if it was made from material or hide, and whether it was decorated or not, sewn or tied. A Qin poem in the Classic of Poetry tells us that chariots drawn by four horses were driven using eight reins, of which six were held by the charioteer: 'The four horses as black as iron are at their best, the six reins held in the hand...'

However, we did not know how the reins were tied to the bit, how they passed into the bridle, how thick they were, if they lay along the flank of the horses or over the withers, how they reached the chariot and how the charioteer held them. Nor were we aware how the charioteer was dressed or armed or where he stood on the chariot, if the car of the chariot was lined with leather, or if the balustrade was decorated. How could the charioteer guide the horses at the gallop and prevent the external ones, which were not harnessed, from knocking detrimentally against the internal ones that were harnessed? To all these queries and many others the bronze models provided an answer, but what type of chariots were they and what was their function?

The first chariot (this weighs slightly over 1 ton and measures 8'5" from the horses' noses to the end of the chariot body) is a reproduction of a light war chariot. This is demonstrated by the fact that the charioteer carries a long Qin sword on his back, a crossbow with twelve darts in his quiver, and a shield in a silver support. Chariots of this type are referred to by historical sources as *gao che* (high chariots), perhaps because of the high parasol or the standing position of the charioteer. The forward position of the war chariot suggests that it may have been the escort for the second, which was used for pleasure and called an *an che* (chariot of tranquility) in ancient texts.

Chariot 2 measures 10'5" long and 5'4" high and is divided into two functionally separate parts: the front section used by the charioteer and the rear formed by the

In 1978, the Archaeological Group of the Mausoleum of Qin Shi Huangdi pinpointed a vast sacrificial pit in the western part of the imperial tomb. Located between the burial mound and the door of the west wall, it is divided into different chambers. One of them, just 22.3 x 6.9 feet in size, yielded two incomparable masterpieces of the late-ancient Chinese Bronze Age, as well as one of the most important discoveries in the history of archaeology: two single-shaft bronze chariots designed to be drawn by a team of four horses. These chariots — unique specimens — were set one behind the other facing west. Each was driven by a charioteer, also made of bronze, and everything was half natural size. (Terracotta Army Museum, Lintong)

cab and elliptical roof that covered the entire body.

Who traveled in this chariot? Where was the small convoy heading on its journey west? Until the entire pit is excavated we cannot know for certain, but we can hazard a guess. It is a pleasing thought that this sumptuous chariot and its escort were waiting for a high-ranking passenger – the *po* spirit of the First Emperor – to make an inspection tour or to go out hunting in his invisible estates. Another reason for the exceptional importance of the discovery is that it documents the type of horse used in archaic China.

It was a Mongol breed known as the Tarpan, which was probably domesticated by the breeders on the northern steppes.

Not far from the chariots, some unusual sacrificial pits were found that do not seem connected with the hunt in any way.

CHARIOT NO. 1

The westernmost, or front, chariot of the pair found in 1978 is referred to as Chariot No. 1. The charioteer was in relatively good condition but the entire structure of the actual chariot had been broken into thousands of pieces. Following restoration, Chariot No. 1 was finally displayed in its newfound beauty in 1988. The model is a meticulous reproduction of a type of vehicle known as a gao, (high chariot), which was used in battle or for the inspection tours made by the highest imperial officials. The group composed of chariot, horses and charioteer, depicted wearing the clothes and headdress of an army officer, weighs 1.17 tons and is composed of hundreds of mobile pieces that have enabled extremely detailed study to be made of an ancient war chariot. The prevalent color of the painted decorations is white, symbolizing the west, the direction in which the two chariots originally faced. This has led to the hypothesis that the two vehicles were positioned in this way to await the soul of the August Sovereign and accompany it on an inspection tour of his western possessions in the world beyond the grave. (Terracotta Army Museum, Lintong)

148 This ribbed bronze cylinder, decorated with what are commonly known as "cloud" motifs, features inlaid gold and silver. It was part of the shaft supporting the canopy covering the charioteer of Chariot No. 1.

148-149 The photograph shows several details of Chariot No. 1 that not only bear witness to the perfection of the craftsmanship technique, but also to the sublime harmony of the proportions of the entire work. It illustrates the long sword typical of the Qin period that, prior to the Lintong excavations, was only known from texts. The accurate depiction of the folds of the charioteer's garment and the position of the heads of the two horses clearly reveal the conscious quest for a compositional model conveying both stateliness and movement.

❖

150 top and 151 These details of the charioteer of Chariot No. 1 clearly show that he held six of the eight reins that controlled the team of four horses. The reins of the inner side of the central pair were fastened to the chariot rail, where the deadly crossbow was also housed, close at hand, while the quiver holding the darts was positioned on the side of the chariot body.

❖

150 bottom This streamlined bronze shield decorated with polychrome "cloud" motifs was positioned on the right side of the charioteer of Chariot No. 1 and held by a dedicated support. The shield has an armband for carrying and reproduces a lacquered wood shield. It has provided important evidence about systems of personal defense in archaic China. Indeed, the presence of decomposed wooden shields had often been noted in Qin graves belonging to the Spring and Autumn and Warring States periods, but all that remained of them were imprints, which did not allow the reconstruction of their form or decoration. Nevertheless, no traces of defensive objects were found in the pits of the Terracotta Army: the only defense of those soldiers was their courage.

152-153 This evocative front view of Chariot No. 1 illustrates both the complexity of the harnesses of the four horses — the outer pair of which were responsible for directing the team — and the radial system of ribs of the parasol, which was extremely similar to a modern umbrella.

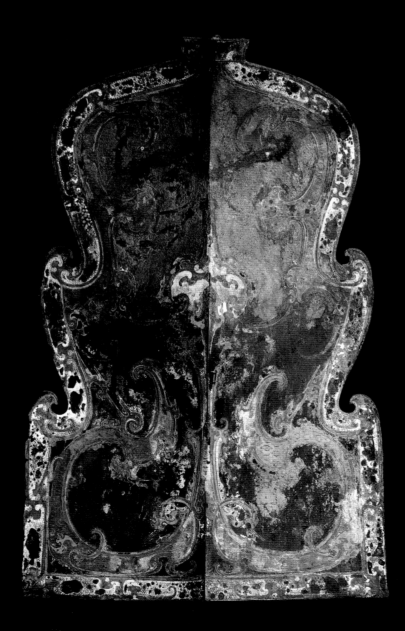

Upon discovery in 1978, the hooves of the white horses of Chariot No. 1 were broken in several pieces. Today they can be admired in their full splendor. The detailed, attentive and calculated rendering of the horses makes it obvious that we are looking at an authentic work of art that successfully strove to reproduce reality.

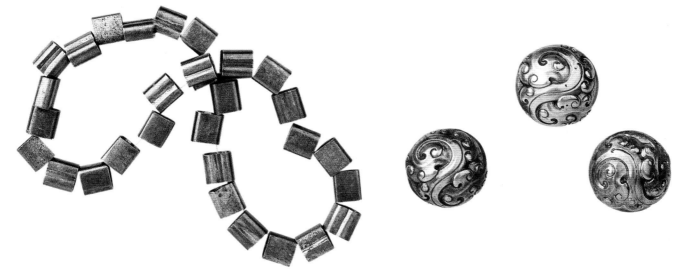

Chariot No. 2

❖

156 and 157 top These gold and silver crownpiece harnesses are from one of the horses of Chariot No. 2, discovered in 1978 in a chamber that forms part of a pit with sacrificial offerings on the western side of the August Emperor's burial mound. In the centre is a leaf-shaped frontlet, with rings on the back for fastening the cords made from alternating gold and silver tubular beads that were used to secure the bit. The five hemispherical studs — two gold and three silver — decorated with a sinuous dragon turning upon itself, were used to fasten the cords at the points in which they crossed.

❖

156-157 bottom The body of Chariot No. 2 is almost trapezoidal in shape and is divided into two parts: a front area for the charioteer, formed by the box and the connection with the shaft, and a rear part, with a cabin protected by a high mudguard, fastened to the shaft and the axle of the high wheels. Note how the charioteer is kneeling on his heels, in a traditional posture shared by many Far Eastern cultures.

158 This bronze box (7.5" tall) was found in the cabin of Chariot No. 2. It probably reproduces a leather box covered with fabric or a bag of lacquered fabric. Various hypotheses have been advanced regarding the use of this object depicted in miniature: some have suggested that it could have been a box used to contain axle grease or the seals of a geomancer, others that it was a bag for jewelry, or even a cloth bag for personal possessions.

158-159 The picture clearly shows the complex system used to harness the four steeds: the drawing pair in the center were harnessed to the yoke by means of a "reversed-V" collar held by cords that hung down onto their chests. The yoke was in turn fastened to the shaft, which ran along the entire length of the chariot body and then curved upwards until reaching the horses' withers. A strap, covered with gold and silver beads, connected the yoke of the inner pair of horses to the collar of their respective outer companions and prevented the outer pair — which contributed traction by means of a harness — from diverging from the trajectory followed by those on the inside. The collar of the two outer horses (30.5" long) shows exquisite workmanship. It is made of 42 gold plates and 42 silver plates that were welded together.

160-161 This photograph lets us admire the painted "lozenge" and "cloud" motifs embellishing Chariot No. 2. A frame of tiny floral patterns surrounds the sinuous "cloud" motifs that cover the entire wall of the cabin, imitating a silky damask fabric. The picture also clearly shows the delicacy of the facial features, garment folds and position of the charioteer.

The Pit of the Functionaries

Identification of the outline of a pit is made quite straightforward by the contrast in color of the local yellow soil against the brown of the soil used to fill the pit. After a pit has been found, if its contents are 'sampled' with a series of vertical probes, the archaeologists involved (usually the 'Archaeological Team of the Mausoleum of Qin Shi Huang') establish the priorities of the stratigraphic excavations to be made. In the case of pit K0006 (490 square yards), which lies halfway between the southwest corner of the mound and the southwest corner of the inner enclosure, the work carried out was rapid (July–December 2000) but also complex as the objects found received restoration treatment while the dig progressed. This undertaking was made possible as a result of improvements in the techniques of excavation and restoration and by the fact that the pit had not suffered from either tomb robbers or fire.

The pit is an irregular rectangle in shape that lies on an east-west axis and has a long access ramp (49'3" x 9'9"- max. 23'7") on the west side. The internal space is bounded by a thick bank of pressed earth and divided into two distinct sections of which the wooden flooring, walls and roof (on which a layer of decomposed matting was found) remained almost intact. The first section was rectangular (34'9" x 13'4") and had a service bay (12'6" x 9'6") on the south side. The second was also rectangular (67'7" x 12'6") but greatly set back from the first. The skeletons of horses without harness were found in the back bay; studies have not been completed but the estimate is that twenty or so were buried, at least eight of which were adult males. In the front room, at the beginning of the access ramp, the remains of a completely decomposed, single-shaft wooden chariot have been found close to four horse skulls.

In the center of the room, an unprecedented discovery was made of twelve clay statues that stand between 6' and 6'4" tall (like the Terra-cotta Army) of individuals that bear no resemblance to any of the thousands of statues so far seen in the area of the funerary garden. The clothing, outstretched arms and half-closed hands of four of the statues have identified them as charioteers; the other eight, the flesh of some of which are still colored, all seem to be waiting in dignified silence; their hands are crossed over their bellies and tucked into the wide sleeves of their garments, and they wear a small hat tied beneath the chin with a bow. Identification of the figures as functionaries is made possible by the 'tools of their trade' that hang from their waists, i.e., a short, slightly curved knife with a handle in the form of a large ring, and the whetstone to sharpen it. In addition to brushes and ink, this type of knife was one of the scribes' most important tools as the blade was used to smooth the wooden or bamboo tablets and to erase unwanted or poorly written characters.

So now we know the appearance of the dozens of Qin functionaries whose tombs have been excavated in various regions of China, for example, Mr Xi in Tomb II at Yunmeng and Mr Dan in Tomb I at Fangmatan.

But there is more: next to the east part of the service bay were aligned four large bronze axes with wooden handles. What were these axes used for and who used them? It was noted that at least two of the charioteers did not seem to be grasping reins and their hands were positioned as though they were holding a rectangular object. Could it have been the handle of one of the axes? If that were the case, then a quotation from the text *Guo Yu* (The Songs of the Kingdoms) would help us to establish the rank and office of the functionaries: 'The high [functionaries] of punishment use armor and arms, the low [functionaries] of punishment use axes.' In other words, the statues were of low-grade functionaries who worked in the legal and penal department.

The group of statues in Pit K0006 appeared like this to the excavators at the end of 2000, as though a gigantic hand
had pushed them over, facedown into the mud. Following the discovery of thousands of statues of soldiers in the three
pits housing the army, this pit revealed the other side of the emperor's power: his functionaries.

164 left and center The Chinese archaeologists had little trouble identifying the 12 standing figures aligned in Pit K0006, as they all carried the tools of their trade on their right side, hanging from their belt. A whetstone and knife with ring handle are clearly visible in Statue 1 (left) and Statue 8 (center), whose entire complexion has been preserved. The iron knife had to be very sharp in order to enable the scribes to smooth the wooden tablets on which they wrote the documents with brush and ink, and the same knife was also used to erase any spelling mistakes.

❖

164 right As in the statues of the soldiers, the volumes of the figures of the functionaries — of which the eleventh of the row is shown here — have been constructed to depict still, rather than moving, figures.

❖

165 This photograph, depicting functionary 12 from the front and functionary 9 in a three-quarter view, allows full appreciation of the skill of the Qin master modelers in depicting the gravity of the figures awaiting imperial orders by means of an ingeniously natural posture, enhanced by that typically Chinese way of hiding joined hands in wide sleeves as protection from the piercingly cold wind of the steppes.

❖

166 and 167 These two close-ups of the head of young functionary 9 clearly reveal the great attention paid to texture in molding the clay. The full and rounded forms of the garment, moulded with a wooden tool — as clearly revealed by the traces on the left shoulder and the front of the scarf — or with the fingers alone, in the rear part of the bow, contrast with the angular forms of the hairstyle and face, which were achieved with cutting and pointed tools.

THE PITS OF THE MENAGERIE AND OF THE WEST STABLES

The large number of underground structures discovered has meant that not all of them have been excavated completely or in depth. This is the case of the 31 pits that lie north-south in three rows 87 yards long. They were found in 1977–78 in the area between the inner and outer enclosures just south of the west gate. Only some of the pits have been excavated but the findings have explained their nature. Each of the 14 pits in the two outer rows (8 on the west side and 6 on the east side) seem to contain a small statue of a servant kneeling on his heels in the traditional posture of many Far Eastern cultures. Each statue faces east toward the burial mound. In the first of the two cases investigated, the figure has no grave goods, and in the second the figure has a clay basin and a bronze crossbow dart. Four statues of this type were found between 1932 and 1964 in various points around the mound; they are of servants or maids, with removable hands and heads.

The 18 pits in the central row, however, contained a surprise. Each pit seemed to contain the skeleton of a wild animal or bird that was sometimes placed inside a clay sarcophagus. This was accompanied by a bronze ring and a trough made from a clay basin. A preliminary analysis of the skeletons showed that the animals were herbivores, probably deer, and that the birds were of different species. The most accredited interpretation of these pits is that they symbolized either the hunting grounds of the August Sovereign or his menagerie.

In his 'History of the Qin Material Culture,' Wang Xueli reports that two pits were found to the south of the 'menagerie.' They were briefly examined immediately after discovery. Wang Xueli hypothesizes that these may have represented stables. The first pit measures 694 square yards, is rectangular, and has a double access ramp. The second lies to the south of the first and its rectangular pit and access ramp together form an L shape measuring 2,033 square yards. Both pits contain horse skeletons, with the hundred or so estimated to lie in the L-shaped pit being divided among three wooden enclosures. Wang Xueli also reports that eleven clay standing statues between 5'11" and 6'2" tall were found with the horses. Some of these are shown with their hands hidden in their sleeves over their bellies while others seem to be brandishing long weapons. The former are low-ranking officials and the latter the guardians of the stables.

Wang Xueli's interpretation that these pits represented stables may yet be subject to change as his description of the skeletons and statues seems to resemble closely what was uncovered in Pit K0006, the Pit of the Functionaries.

The detail of the face of this young "servant" effectively shows the care with which anatomical details, such as moustaches and hairstyles, were fashioned in the clay statues discovered in Lintong. In this case the centrally parted hair is gathered in a knot at the nape of the neck, in typical Qin style. The neckerchief worn beneath the tunic still has part of the original pigment that originally covered it. (Lintong, Terracotta Army Museum)

Sacrificial Pit K9901 is rectangular and covers an area of 835 square yards, with access ramps
on the short sides. It is divided into three parallel corridors with wooden floors, walls and ceilings.
The fragments of 11 terracotta statues were found in an area measuring just 10 square yards
in Corridor 3. The statues are of male figures in various poses, either life-size or slightly larger,
which the Chinese archaeologists believe to be "acrobats."

THE PIT OF THE 'ACROBATS'

A sacrificial pit (Pit K9901) in the area between the southeast corner of the inner enclosure and the outer defensive wall was excavated in 1999. It was more or less rectangular with an access ramp on each of the short sides (east and west), pressed earth walls forming three parallel corridors, wooden flooring, walls and ceiling, and a structure that resembles the one in Pit I of the Terracotta Army. Archaeologists at the Shaanxi Province Institute of Archaeology and the Archaeological Team of the Tomb of Qin Shi Huang have conducted an exploratory investigation of this pit (which measures roughly 340 square yards) by digging a trench of 80 or so square yards (approx. 4 x 20). The items found were restored as the dig progressed.

The results of this small test, published at the start of 2001, showed that this pit too was of extraordinary importance. A large bronze ritual tripod (weighing 467 pounds), was found in the upper section of the filling soil; its style shows it was made either in Jin (southeast of Shanxi province) or the kingdom of the Eastern Zhou around the modern city of Luoyang (Henan province). The tripod was probably made around the end of the 4th century BC or the start of the 3rd, which was the period in which the Qin conquered Jin and what remained of the Zhou kingdoms. It is therefore probable that the tripod was an important item of war booty and may have been placed in the palaces or ancestral temple of the Qin before being added to the August Sovereign's grave goods. In addition to this tripod, which is in itself of historical importance, fragments of eleven terracotta statues were also found in an area measuring just 10 square yards in Corridor 3. The statues are of male figures in various standing poses, either life-size or slightly larger. Sadly, the statues were in very poor condition as a result of the roof collapsing following a fire.

❖

This large bronze ritual tripod (weighing 467 pounds), was found in the upper section of the filling soil of the "Pit of the Acrobats". Its style and decoration shows it was cast around 300 BC in a foundry of the kingdom of Jin or that of the Eastern Zhou, just before the two areas fell under Qin rule. It is therefore probable that the tripod was an important item of war booty and may have been housed in the palaces or ancestral temple of the Qin before being added to the August Sovereign's grave goods.

These figures do not seem to be soldiers, nor do they wear tunics or armor, just a short skirt decorated by motifs that imitate the embroidery on silks found in coeval graves in the area that had once been part of the kingdom of Chu. Unlike the soldiers in the three pits of the Terracotta Army or the functionaries in Pit K0006, these statues, though made following the same technique, are not compact. Portrayed free of their heavy clothes, they are seen to have solid bodies with the mass of the stomach and the muscles of the chest, arms and calves clearly defined and modeled. The bodies are more dynamic, as though caught in the act of assuming a resting position. In short, the approach taken seems almost the opposite of the style used to portray the Terracotta Army and one that we would never have expected to see in Qin art.

Who are these people? The Chinese ar-chaeologists have called them 'acrobats,' however, other finds have been made in the pit that do not seem to relate to acrobats: the hooves of a bronze horse (the body of which is probably still covered by the collapsed roof), a horse's harness and the ornamentation of a chariot, arrow tips, crossbow darts and armor plaques. The clothing and dynamic postures of the figures and their association with arms and armor perhaps permit different interpretations to be made. These statues resemble figures painted on a roll found in Grave 3 at Mawangdui (at Changsha in Hunan province) dated to 168 BC. Entitled *Dao Yin Tu*, the work can be described as an illustrated manual of gymnastic and breathing exercises. The figures found in Pit K9901, therefore, may not be acrobats but gymnasts or wrestlers ready to begin an exercise of martial arts. Excavations now in progress will clarify this mystery.

❖

172 *These two views of statue 5, the tallest (approx. 6.5 feet) of those found in the "Pit of the Acrobats," clearly show the skilled art of the master modelers at the emperor's service. Here the musculature of the human body, which is only just perceptible beneath the clothes of the soldiers or functionaries, is realistically explicit, full and powerful, despite not being anatomically accurate.*

❖

173 *This photograph shows the young body of statue 1, standing steady on powerful legs, with the right hand gripping the left wrist. It is an unusual gesture, like those made by his ten companions. The nudity of the figures, which are wearing only short skirts, and their unusual gestures led the Chinese archaeologists to believe that they may be acrobats.*

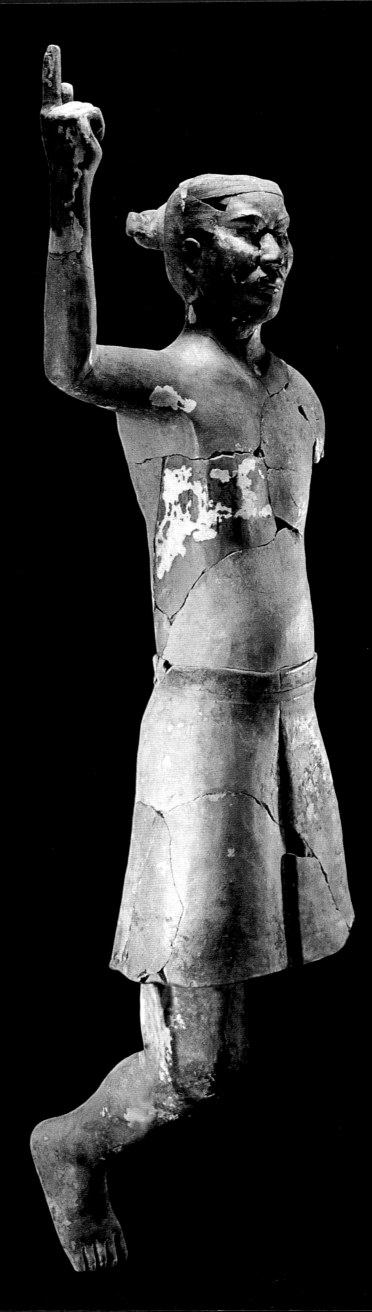

174 *Statue 2 depicts a figure that seems to be making the clearest movement of all the 11 statues so far excavated from the "Pit of the Acrobats." Sadly the loss of the left leg and arm do not enable us to be absolutely sure what sort of gesture the young man was making, although it seems likely that it was an acrobatic or gymnastic movement*

❖

175 *In this side view of statues 3 (left) and 6 (right), it is clear that the figures are making wide arm movements as they walk. The clothing and postures of both these statues and the other nine found in the "Pit of the Acrobats" can be compared with the figures depicted in a sort of illustrated manual of gymnastic and breathing exercises found among the extensive grave goods of princely grave 3 in Mawangdui, which dates back to 168 BC. This parallel enables us to conjecture that the "acrobats" may actually be gymnasts or wrestlers shown performing a martial arts exercise.*

The only one of the 11 painted terracotta statues in the "Pit of the Acrobats" not to have suffered damage to the head is statue 2, which is shown here in two close-ups. It depicts a young man with a very well-groomed appearance, which must have been enhanced by the polychrome pigments of which traces still remain on the face and shoulders. In the right-hand picture, note the inscription partly covered by traces of color, which was probably a technical note left by the master modeler for the helpers responsible for assembling the head on the body. Indeed, the eleven statues of the "acrobats" are the only ones of the thousands uncovered in the Funerary Gardens whose heads are fixed directly to the bodies and not housed in the hollows that were usually hidden by the scarf.

The Pit of Stone Armor

Between September and December 1998 five trenches in Pit K9801 were sampled, about 45 yards north of the Pit of the 'Acrobats.' K9801 is the largest of the pits found so far inside the walls of the funerary garden. Rectangular on an east-west axis, it has two short ramps at the ends of the two longer sides. The pit covers a surface area of 16,372 square yards. The five stratigraphic test trenches to be opened (covering 183 square yards overall) have revealed once again a perimeter bank of pressed earth around a space divided into corridors and lined with wooden planks and beams on the floor, walls and ceilings. In this pit too the structure had suffered a ruinous fire. The surprise discovered in three of the five pits was represented by a layer of thousands of small burned limestone plaques lying on the floor as though they were tiles in an enormous game of dominoes. Only at the end of the investigation was understood that the mass of tiles came from 150 suits of armor and more than 50 helmets.

The use of armor and helmets was one of the greatest innovations in military technology during the period of Warring States, the warfare of which saw the growing importance of large masses of infantry. Armor and helmets were essential elements for heavy infantry to resist their attackers or to provide the shockwave after the first attack by the vanguard armed with lances. The use of distinctive visible elements like brightly colored ribbons or strips of leather enhanced the visibility of the officers during battle. Usually helmets and armor were made of leather squares

sewn together to provide protection but allow flexibility. Others used small iron plaques, like the helmet found at Xiadu, the secondary capital in the kingdom of Yan. Only the frontal opening differs the style of this helmet from those found in Pit K9801, though the latter also have convex plaques to protect the throat.

What was decidedly unexpected — and unique — was a set of armor made using diamond-shaped plaques measuring 2.5 by 5.5 inches. This set, however, was not made to be worn by a soldier but by a horse. The find is unique: at the time of the discovery, ancient sources made no references to the use of armored horse trappings until the Eastern Han (25–220 AD) era. The find not only brought forward the use of armored horses in China by almost half a millennium but also questions the hypothesis that it was the Sarmatians of the Eurasian borderlands who first used them in the third century BC and that horse armor was slowly imitated, in whole or in part, by first the Parthians, then the Romans and then the Germans, before being adopted by the nomads of the eastern steppes who introduced it to China.

In any case, the helmets and armor found in K9801 — made from limestone probably quarried in mountains about 40 miles north of the site — were too fragile and heavy (on average the armor weighed 40 pounds and the helmets 7 pounds) for actual use. Once again they were made purely for funerary use and were another of the marvels of the underground empire built for the spirit of the First August Sovereign.

When Pit K9801 was discovered in 1998, the plaques were no longer held together by metal and formed a layer of thousands of burnt pieces scattered on the floor, like a giant game of dominoes, representing a true nightmare for excavators.

Each plaque found in Pit K9801 is engraved with numbers, which obviously guided the craftsmen who originally stitched the various plates together, and which also proved useful to the restorers.

180 top and 181 The photographs show 2 of the 150 suits of armor found in 1988. That on the left belongs to the kind without shoulder plates, while the form of that on the right is the same as that worn by several of the soldiers of the Terracotta Army, consisting of a cuirass, shoulder plates and apron. The introduction of armor and helmets was one of the greatest innovations in military technology during the period of Warring States, which was increasingly based on the use of large masses of infantry.

180 bottom Discovered in 1998 in Pit K9801, this helmet is made of limestone plates that overlap like "fish scales" and is one of the most important finds in the area of the pits for sacrificial offerings that surround the burial mound. The helmet was part of an offering composed of 150 suits of armor and over 50 helmets, of which this was the first to have been reconstructed by the restorers of the Terracotta Army Museum. Its function was probably exclusively funerary, but it is a faithful reproduction of a leather or iron prototype, such as that found at Xiadu, the secondary capital in the kingdom of Yan. Only the frontal opening is different from the helmet shown here, although this also has convex plaques to protect the throat.

THE PIT OF THE BRONZE BIRDS

The more recent and lesser-known finds made outside the burial mound enclosures include those from the "F"-shaped Pit K0007. This pit has an access ramp on one of the short sides and a main trench on an east-west axis to which two shorter ones are joined at right angles (Trenches I and II). The pit, situated in the area northeast of the outer enclosure (approximately 3300 yards from the northern side of the burial mound), covers an area of 1,170 square yards, and was extensively excavated between September 2001 and March 2003. The internal structure of the pit consists of corridors lined with jointed wooden planks and beams that form a complex system with dividing walls, supporting beams, pillars, thresholds and double walls on the north and south sides. During the 2001 excavations ten life-sized bronze waterbirds were unearthed in Trench I (covering an area of just 29 square yards), fixed on rectangular bases (18.5 x 14 inches), some of which have two sides decorated with openwork. A further 33 birds were subsequently discovered. There are 20 swans, both swimming and standing in various positions as they scrutinize the water, 6 cranes, including one shown raising its long "S"-shaped neck after having plucked a worm from the mud with its beak, and 20 wild ducks depicted very naturally as they swim, fish or flap about in groups. During the excavation of this trench, numerous prints of hands and feet were discovered that were probably left by the people who caused the destruction of the pit. The prints were stratigraphically distinct from the footprints left by the shoes of the workmen who had constructed the pit. Originally, it must have been very damp in the pit as the prints

were left on wet ground, and the 46 birds were placed in and on either side of a small channel through which water very probably ran. As the birds are undoubtedly aquatic species, the hypothesis suggested by the excavators may well be correct; it is their opinion that the pit housed a reconstruction of a marsh or a watercourse. Could this have been a symbolic reproduction of one of the rivers of China to which Sima Qian referred? We may find an answer to this question as soon as we are able to formulate a convincing hypothesis to explain the most recent discovery made in Trench II. This consists of a group of 15 terracotta statues, again life-sized, with their hair covered by caps and wearing trousers and heavy surcoats, which feature the typical flap on the right and are belted at the waist with a small rectangular bag hanging from the belt. Eight of these statues are depicted sitting with their legs stretched out and their upper body leaning forward. The position of their hands, which are almost touching their feet, can be interpreted in different ways, one of which suggests that they could be men depicted "paddling," but in that case, where is their boat? The other seven statues are instead shown kneeling, with their left arms reaching out and their right arms raised as they appear to grip a tool with a cylindrical handle. Their heads are bent, as though they were carefully watching something below. Could they be fishermen waiting to hurl their harpoons? It is difficult to say for sure and the discoveries made in the largest trench (III) have not yet provided any clues: so far the only finds have been another bronze crane and the skeletal remains of various animals (unfortunately, we do not yet know to which species they belong).

❖

The contents of Pit K0007 initially seemed the most mysterious of all the wonders buried near the emperor's grave. The photograph above shows the sight that appeared before the excavators' eyes: a small channel flanked by wooden banks, which were originally adorned with bronze statuettes of waterfowl, including the goose and perhaps the crane shown here during excavations (left) and after restoration (right). Various clues enabled the archaeologists to realize that it was a reconstruction of a marshy area, possibly one of the Chinese rivers that the historian Sima Qian believed was located inside the burial pit.

THE PITS OF THE IMPERIAL STABLES

Shortly before the discovery that focused the world's attention on the small town of Lintong, archaeologists at the local District Museum had begun an investigation into a group of 93 sacrificial pits (98 according to another source) about 380 yards east of the outer wall of the *ling yuan* near the village of Shangjiao. Five were excavated in 1972–73 and another 46 over the following three years. The diamond-shaped pits either held a statue or had a statue in another pit that lay in front of it. The figures were of the same type as those found in the Pit of the Menagerie; they were shown looking east while kneeling in front of the skeleton of a horse that faced the burial mound. The bodies of the horses were probably placed in the pits after being sacrificed in another place. The statues (between 25 and 28 inches tall) and skeletons were accompanied by a variety of grave goods: close to the animals' faces a lamp on a high clay pedestal was usually placed, and a jar or bowl, in some cases containing grains of millet or oats. In front of the kneeling figures – evidently stableboys or grooms – there were clay water jars, clay or high-pedestalled iron lamps, and the iron implements used by a shoeingsmith. The function of these unusual sacrificial pits was explained by inscriptions on some of the articles found in the pits, for example, *gong gai* (palace stable), *zuo gai* (left stable), *xiao gai* (small stable) and *zhong gai* (middle stable). In other words, these pits symbolized the imperial stables.

❖

This statuette shows a "footman", with mobile head and hands and part of the original pigment, and was found in one of the sacrificial pits near the village of Shangjiao, approximately 380 yards east of the outer wall of the Funerary Garden. Inside the pit, the figure was kneeling and facing east in front of the skeleton of a horse, which was probably laid here after having been sacrificed elsewhere. The inscriptions on some of the artifacts revealed the function of these unusual sacrificial pits, which symbolized the imperial stables.

THE PITS OF THE TERRACOTTA ARMY

As is now widely known, Pit I of the Terracotta Army was discovered by accident by peasants digging a well, and Pits 2, 3 and 4 were discovered during archaeological investigations in the summer of 1976. The site of the four pits lies three quarters of a mile east of the outer enclosure of the burial mound, immediately north of the avenue that sets out from the east gate.

More than ten years of study of this area has led to the plan of each pit being established, their internal structures verified and a sample of their contents being removed. Overall, the four pits cover almost 7.5 acres and are estimated to contain (except for Pit 4, which is empty) at least 7,000 terracotta statues of warriors of different type, more than 600 terracotta horses, more than 100 wooden war chariots and innumerable real bronze weapons. The warriors and horses are not life-size but a few inches larger than the animals and men on which they were modeled. This expedient was evidently adopted to increase the monumentality and sense of power that the army gave, whether observed by an enemy of flesh or of spirit.

❖

This photographs show two soldiers of the heavy infantry. The hair of one is gathered in a side knot, whereas that of the other is tightly divided into sections that form a flat braid at his nape. One of the soldiers has a square, narrow chin, while that of the other is wider and rounder. Although experts in Qin art have not yet reached any agreement on the meaning of the various somatic differences of the faces of the soldiers of the Terracotta Army, many claim that they may be attributable to different ethnic origins.

Pit 1

*'The attack of a victorious army is like the sudden surge of a body of water
enclosed in a pool one hundred fathoms deep.'*
Sunzi. *The Art of War* (4.19)

The rectangular pit, which has been covered by a gigantic hangar since shortly after the start of excavation work, measures 252 yards east-west by 68 yards north-south. The level of the brick floor lay just over 16 feet beneath the ground level of the time. The space within the pit is divided up by ten large pressed-earth partitions that run parallel through the entire length of the pit to create nine central corridors 11'4" wide and a narrower perimeter corridor. Five ramps on both the east and west sides starting in the 2nd, 4th, 6th, 7th and 10th corridors gave access to the pit. Five ramps at regular distances on each of the long sides provided supplementary entries.

When the soldiers, chariots and horses had been arranged in the corridors, the entire structure was covered by a ceiling of large tree trunks that rested on partitions and outer rims reinforced by planks and wooden pillars. A layer of matting and another of earth were spread over the tree trunks, then the entire pit was sealed by various levels of pressed earth. This construction technique was used in all the large pits so far been found.

Although excavation of the entire pit has not yet been completed, we know that the troops were arranged in the strategic 'rectangular formation.' The archers stand at the front facing east in three rows; behind them platoons of light infantry provide support at the head of the formations of heavy infantry. The latter are led by officers on command chariots, which are wider than their combat counterparts as they had to carry not just the officer and charioteer but also the bell and drum that were used to give orders during the battle.

The infantry are without the command chariots in only the 3rd, 5th and 7th corridors. The distribution of the troops — defended at the sides and rear by archers and crossbowmen looking outwards from the main body — is based on flexibility and power. The right and left wings are arranged symmetrically, ready to fan out or come together in a pincer movement. Command chariots alternate with bodies of heavy infantry in corridors 1 and 10, while in both corridors 2 and 8 a squadron of heavy infantry is led by a single command chariot that probably also directed the armored warriors in corridors 3 and 7. In the center (corridors 4 and 6), two formations of chariots served by platoons of light infantry and one of heavy infantry (corridor 5) provided the main thrust of the attack.

This exceptional view of Pit 1 (measuring 17,055 square yards) gives us an immediate understanding of the immensity of the work, its rational layout and the breathtaking number of statues depicting the strength of Qin Shi Huangdi's buried army. The picture also reveals that the army was not designed for human eyes: the wide earthen banks of the corridors clearly show the traces of the tree trunks that supported the heavy beaten-earth roof.

❖

190-191 The arrangement of the front squadrons of the Terracotta Army in Pit 1, as shown in this drawing, illustrates a type of deployment described as a "rectangular formation" in the texts of military strategy of the period. The archers stand at the front facing east in three rows, with two noncommissioned officers, who can be distinguished by their armor; behind them platoons of light infantry provide support to the formations of heavy infantry, each of which is commanded by an officer, who rides in the chariot drawn by four horses, along with the charioteer and the man responsible for communicating the orders (the three figures behind each chariot). This arrangement — defended by archers and crossbowmen looking outwards — reveals a strategy based on the flexibility and power of attack.

❖

191 top These four details, showing the shoulder plate of a suit of plate armor, a soldier's face, an archer's hand and a horse's muzzle, clearly illustrate the main characteristic of the plastic art of the Qin craftsmen, which was the highly naturalistic depiction of details.

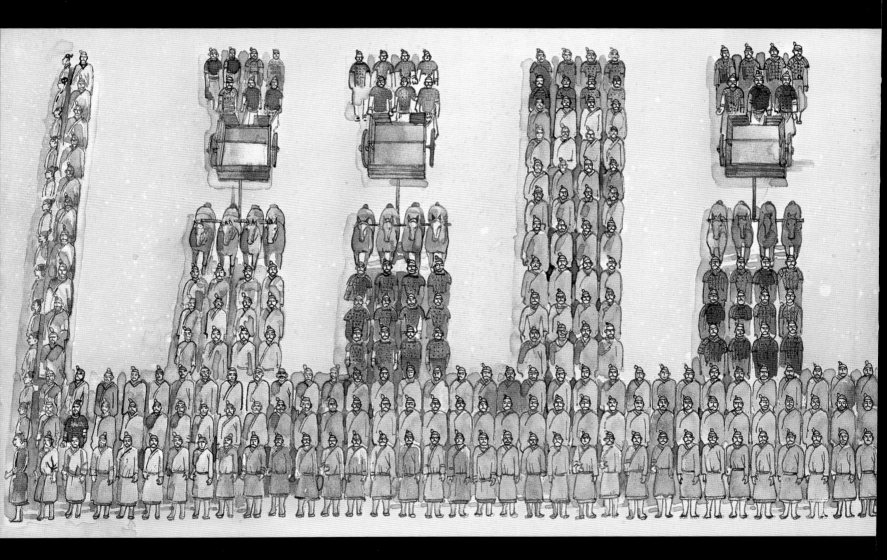

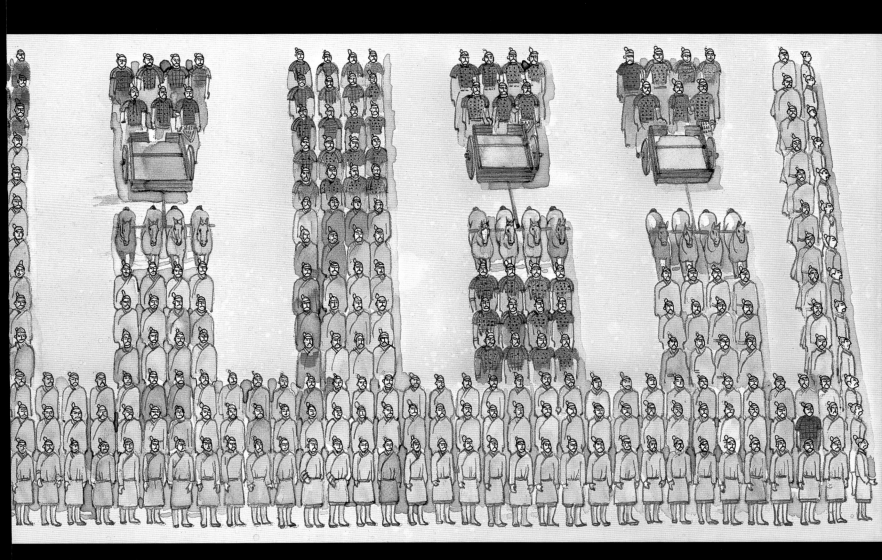

192-193 *This photograph shows a platoon of armored infantry, commanded by the officer in the foreground, who is distinguished by his curious "tablet" headdress (similar to those of the functionaries and perhaps made of lacquered fabric in reality). The closely ranked men wear plate armor of the same type found in Pit K9801 and their hair is knotted on the sides of their heads, and generally covered with a sort of cap. According to several scholars, those statues without a cap or with a knotted handkerchief represent various grades among the ranks of noncommissioned officers. A parallel corridor where the statues are still being excavated can be seen in the background.*

194 and 195 *One of the aspects that makes the Terracotta Army unrivalled in the history of human creativity is the fact that no two faces are the same. This claim of the Chinese scholars appears to be true if we look at these archers (large photograph) in the vanguard of the troops arrayed in Pit 1; their function in the crude reality of battle was to launch the attack, showering the enemy with arrows. The bulk of the army would have moved in immediately after. Here we can see the right wing (top). The empty space behind the first platoon has been left by the decomposed wooden structures of the command chariot.*

❖

196 *The foreground of the photograph shows the completely decomposed command chariot of the first squadron of the right wing. None of the chariots of the Terracotta Army have survived, due to the natural decomposition of the wood, or to the damage suffered when the pit was set on fire, presumably during the rebellions that broke out at the fall of the Qin dynasty. Note how the entire structure was paved with solid bricks, while the traces of the vertical poles that supported the beams of the roof can be seen in the narrow corridor housing the soldiers defending the wings.*

❖

197 *The three foot soldiers shown in the photograph to the side wear the typical wide plate armor of the heavy infantry and, given their position and number, can be identified as the squadron that defended the command chariot, of which two of the horses' heads can be seen here. The head of the horse in the foreground, characterized by a powerful and unnatural jaw, perfectly exemplifies the evocative qualities of a mature plastic art, modeled in molds and by hand, which was based on the respect of proportions and the realistic fashioning of an abstract model rather than the faithful reproduction of a real one.*

198 *The photograph shows the three rows of archers in the vanguard of the army in Pit 1. Both the typical surcoats — which may have been padded and were fastened by a leather belt with a hook buckle — and the square-toed, shoes, possibly made of felt in reality, are clearly visible.*

199 *These four statues also depict archers, as revealed by the position of their right hands that would originally have held the typical Qin longbow. Note the similarity of the profile of these four figures, which confirms the fact that they were modeled in molds. The differences between the individuals were achieved by means of subtle expedients, particularly that of using a wooden tool to fashion the anatomical details of the faces, the shape of the moustaches and the hairstyles.*

❖

*We know that during the Warring
States period military ranks were
marked by clearly recognizable
features, such as hair accessories,
bows, colored ribbons and particular
kinds of clothing. This photograph,
showing a platoon of armored
infantry in which no two soldiers
are alike due to variations in
hairstyles and types of armor, makes
us realize both how much
information has been lost to us by to
the disappearance of the original
colors, and the great efforts made by
the Chinese archaeologists to achieve
at least a general understanding of
the military hierarchies of the
Terracotta Army.*

202 The soldiers of the light infantry platoon shown in the picture above were armed with real bronze spears with long wooden shafts, which were equally suited to throwing and stabbing attacks. It is believed that many of these spears were stolen from the imposing Terracotta Army during the rebellions that lead to the fall of the Qin dynasty.

203 The position of the right hands of these three heavy infantrymen reveals that they too were armed with spears. However, the statues shown in this photograph also reveal another of the "tricks of the trade" used by the Qin master modelers to give the figures an individual character, for their heads are bent at different angles, giving an almost natural sense of movement when viewed together.

204-205 This photograph shows the men of one of the most feared specialties of the Qin army: the crossbowmen. The Qin army did not adopt this deadly weapon, which originated in the Chu region along the middle Yangzi valley, until a fairly late stage. However, when they did, the Qin crossbowmen became much-feared masters of the art among the armies of the Warring States. The picture also shows the details of the complex hairstyle of these soldiers: two long sections of hair from each temple formed a pair of braids that were joined at the nape of the neck, acting like a headband to secure the rest of the hair that was tied on the top.

PIT 2

'In battle there are only two methods of attack: direct and indirect. But these two used together offer an infinite series of combainations.'
Sunzi. *The Art of War* (5.10)

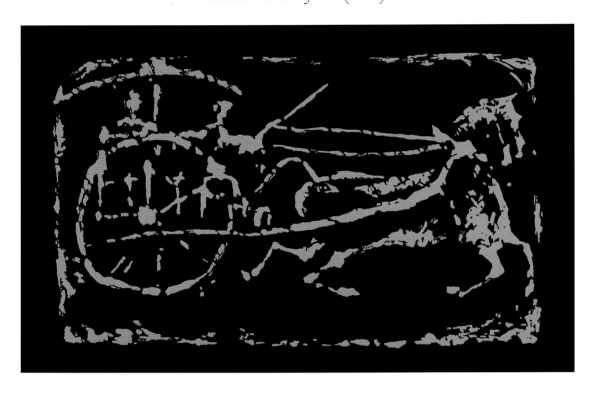

Lying about 22 yards north of the large rectangular pit is Pit 2, whose L shape is formed by a rectangular space and, on the south side, an irregular four-sided area to cover an overall area of 7,175 square yards. It is clear that the shape of the pit was designed specifically to accommodate a particular tactical formation of a part of the Qin army. There are four main blocks of troops: the forward section of the north rectangle contains a square formation of 332 men. These include unarmored archers that surround a body of kneeling, armored crossbowmen, both of which are supported by platoons of foot soldiers armed with long lances.

Behind these troops are two parallel blocks: in each of the three corridors to the north is a pair of fast light chariots, separated by a platoon of horsemen. Behind the chariots is a squadron of 108 horsemen armed with crossbows; they stand composedly holding the reins of their saddled horses as they wait for the battle order.

In three corridors to the south of this formation are 25 heavy support chariots followed by platoons of heavy infantry each ranging between 11 and 32 men. Each chariot carries a charioteer and two soldiers wearing armor and armed with long weapons.

In the four-sided area to the south, divided into eight corridors, stands the squadron of 64 light war chariots, eight in each corridor.

Overall there are about 1,000 soldiers, 89 chariots and 400 horses in this pit set out in a flexible formation that allows each unit to fight individually or as part of a single body. This formation was called by the battle strategists of the era 'Concentric Deployment.'

❖

206 The photograph shows the decoration of a brick from a tomb, manufactured shortly after the fall of the Qin dynasty, which illustrates the structure of a pleasure carriage, with large wheels and a wide canopy, of a lighter kind than the war chariots in Pit 2.

❖

207 The statues of the horses of the Terracotta Army, such as this one found in Pit 2, have enabled us to discover many details of the art of horse breeding, in particular regarding the tending of manes and tails. In this case the mane is partially shorn on the upper part of the neck only, in order to avoid the hairs from obstructing the horse's sight when galloping.

Of the huge amount of information provided by the statues in this pit, one of the most important aspects regards the faithful representation of the use of cavalry. Unlike the infantry and charioteers that wear a long tunic over large leggings, the horsemen wear a short tunic, not unlike that worn by the 'acrobats' in Pit K9901, over tight trousers. Their armor is lighter and they wear a cap to protect the head. The caps were probably made from leather for the actual troops. The horses do not have stirrups, which were yet to be invented, but wear a small saddle held in place by straps and a girth. The actual Qin saddles would have been made of wood padded with material or leather.

Various Chinese sources suggest that it was around the middle of the first millennium BC that the horse began to be used by the nobles of the Middle Kingdom for riding (like the horse breeders of the north) rather than just to pull carts and chariots. Traditionally it was King Wuling of Zhao (northern half of Shanxi province and the southern part of Hebei province) who first made use of mounted archers in 307 BC. Like the horsemen in Pit 2, they wore trousers and a cloak, as was the custom among the Hu peoples settled along the northern borders of Zhao in what is now part of Inner Mongolia.

The adoption of a cavalry by almost all the Warring States (475–221 BC) brought a growing need for horses, which were for the most part supplied by the Di peoples, herders who had settled on the plains inside the large bend of the Huanghe River (Ordos region) as far as the Taiyuan plain in Shanxi. However, until the Qin dynasty (221–206 BC), the cavalry was only of secondary importance as it was used to support the foot soldiers or to conduct ambushes and rapid raids behind enemy lines. The horsemen in Pit 2 are all set out on the left wing, slightly back from the attack forces of chariots and infantry, ready to intervene in the battle wherever necessary. We still do not know, though, the role of the armored horses, which we know to have existed from the contents of the Pit of Stone Armor.

208 left The lamps used by the archaeologists in the earthquake-proof cement structure covering Pit 2 create evocative views of the sea of tree trunks cut from the sample trenches excavated by the teams of archaeologists. This is the covering layer of the pit, but only an illusion of the original trunks remains because the almost completely decomposed wood has been replaced by the soil that has assumed its features, like a fossil.

208 right The formation in Pit 2 features part of the army arranged in four blocks: a squad of archers surrounding a group of crossbowmen is arrayed to the north. Behind, two light chariots are followed by a squad of horsemen and a platoon of cavalry in two parallel blocks in each of the three corridors. The heavy chariots, followed by platoons of infantry, are arrayed to the south, in three corridors. The squadron of light war chariots is arranged in the four-sided area to the

south. A total of 1,000 warriors, 89 chariots and 400 horses are arrayed in the flexible formation that the battle strategists of the period called "Concentric Deployment."

209 The photograph shows several of the crossbowmen, who originally held real notched crossbows and belonged to the square formation composed of 332 men in the northern forward section of Pit 2.

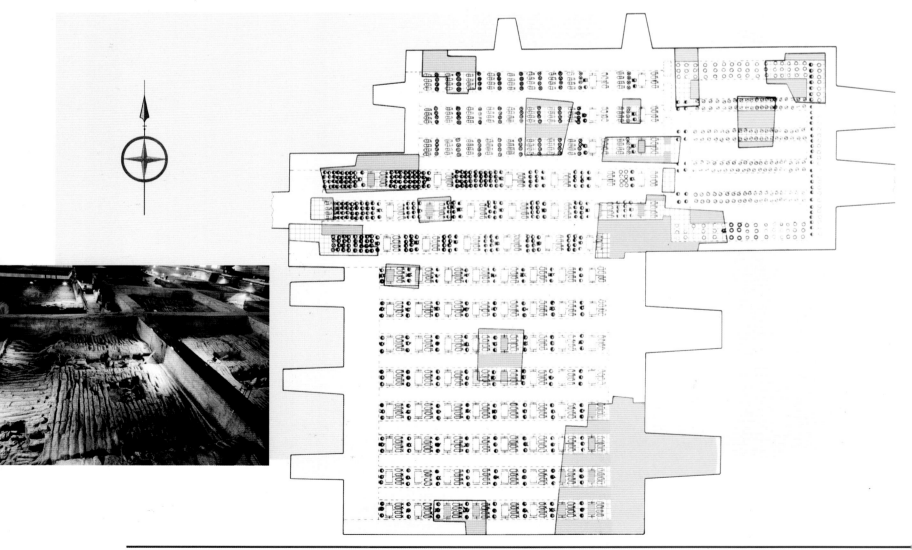

210 and 211 A simple saddle without stirrups — which had yet to be invented — and a sturdy bronze bit can be seen in this photograph of a saddled horse with fine bronze harness, like its 107 companions in Pit 2. The formation of the cavalry platoon in Pit 2 features the cavalrymen (in the center) standing next to the heads of their horses, whose reins they hold in one hand, while the foot soldiers of the support platoons of the 25 heavy chariots (right) were arrayed in three corridors in the southern section of Pit 2.

212 and 213 These close-ups of an armored foot soldier reveal the complexity of his hairstyle. Several scholars claim to have identified symbolic meanings in the structure of the Terracotta Army and in certain details such as hairstyles or the position of hands. In the case of this particular hairstyle, it has been conjectured that the sections of the braid dividing the head into four sections represent the uneven quadrants of the solar wind radiated towards the Earth by the sun and that the braid itself represents a phallus bearing the cross of the sun. According to this hypothesis, the various types of hairstyle connect the warriors to the sun and its associations with fertility.

The photograph shows a group of draft and saddle horses from Pit 2 during restoration, and thus not in their original position. It is clear that the stocky, large-boned animals belonging to this group have no substantial anatomical differences, demonstrating that they had not been subject to selection. It is still not absolutely certain which breed of horse was used in the regions along the Yellow River valley as draft animals from the 13th century BC and subsequently as mounts, from around the 4th century BC. However, it seems very likely that it may have been closely related to the small wild horse of the steppe, better known as Przewalski's horse, after the Russian naturalist Nikolai Mikhailovich Przewalski, who rediscovered the breed in 1879 on the steppe between China and Mongolia.

PIT 3

'Fighting at the head of a large army is the same as fighting at the head of a small one: all that is required is to establish signs and signals.'
Sunzi. *The Art of War* (5.2)

The subterranean, U-shaped Pit 3 lies east of Pit 2. It covers an area of 622 square yards and faces west. Due to its small size, it is the only one of the four pits to have been excavated entirely. Inside there were only 68 men and a single large command chariot with its four horses. The purpose of the face-to-face formation of the warriors in this pit seems to have been to protect the high-ranking officer next to the chariot that stands centrally in front of the ramp. Besides the remains of a deer, perhaps a propitiatory sacrifice before the battle, the north arm of the U contains 22 warriors in two parallel rows. The arrangement in the south arm is more elaborate even though it is clear that the aim is to create a corridor from the chariot to a platoon of 24 closely packed lancers. This formation is probably the one called *Jin Mu* (curtain formation) in the texts of military strategy of the period. It is clear that the warriors, all non-commissioned officers, provided protection to the chariot on which the high-ranking officer would climb to go into battle. The ribbons (originally painted in bright colors) tied to his armor and headgear indicate his importance; he may, in fact, have been the commander in charge of the entire army. His troops' bravery is made clear by their refusal to wear any sort of personal protection apart from their armor; no shield or helmet has been found in any of the three pits. In this pit, however, bronze cylinders with a pyramidal tip known as *shu* have been discovered, which were mounted on rods about 3 feet long, the purpose of which was to unhorse enemy cavalry or blunt the attack of their chariots. The hypothesis that these rods may have been simply parade weapons seems to have little to support it in this context.

The last of the pits found in this area of the tomb – the rectangular Pit 4 – lies between Pits 2 and 3 but did not contain anything. It is another indication that the work involved in preparing the sacrificial pits had not been completed in 208 BC when the Second August Sovereign caused the beginning of the revolt that led to the end of his dynasty when he accelerated the work on the A'fang Palace and Mount Li Funerary Garden.

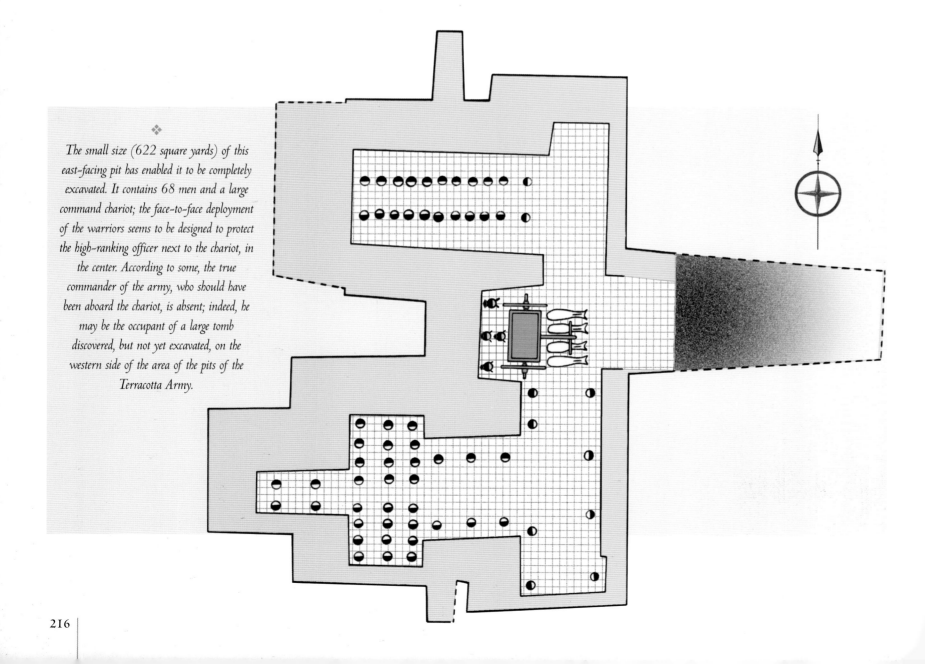

The small size (622 square yards) of this east-facing pit has enabled it to be completely excavated. It contains 68 men and a large command chariot; the face-to-face deployment of the warriors seems to be designed to protect the high-ranking officer next to the chariot, in the center. According to some, the true commander of the army, who should have been aboard the chariot, is absent; indeed, he may be the occupant of a large tomb discovered, but not yet excavated, on the western side of the area of the pits of the Terracotta Army.

217 top left This photograph shows the face-to-face deployment of the soldiers, all wearing armor, along the perimeter of the westernmost bay of Pit 3. It supports the interpretation that claims that they represent a squad of chosen guards, positioned to form a sort of protective corridor for a high-ranking official - though we have no way of knowing if this figure is present or not.

217 top right This view from the east shows the formation of 24 guards protecting the passage leading from the southern bay to the command chariot. The defensive function of these soldiers has been supported by the discovery in Pit 3 of bronze cylinders with a pyramidal tip known as shu, mounted on sturdy rods, whose purpose was to unhorse enemy cavalry or blunt the attack of their chariots.

217 bottom left The great wooden chariot was positioned in the center of Pit 3, although only its imprint has remained for the archaeologists, and was followed by four high-ranking officials, identified by the bows on their armor.

217 bottom right The mass of ceramic fragments in the foreground, lying as it appeared to the archaeologists who unearthed it, belongs to 22 warriors arranged in two parallel rows. The photograph reveals how the restoration work must necessarily be conducted in stages. The remains of a real stag were also discovered in this bay of Pit 3, the tangible evidence of a propitiatory sacrifice performed before battle. Although this practice is described in the ancient military treatises, it had never before found archaeological confirmation.

THE ART OF WAR

'It must be recognized that the general who understands the nature of war has in his hands the fate of the people and the state.'
Sunzi. The Art of War (2.20)

One of the many confirmations provided by the Terracotta Army to hypotheses prompted by inconclusive historical or archaeological data is that of the infantry as the main instrument of war during the period of the Warring States. It is difficult to know, however, whether the Terracotta Army was a true representation of the thousands of troops drafted across the territory or just of the elite body that formed the core of the army under the personal command of the sovereign. Expert troops of this nature, belonging in this case to Duke Hui of Wei, are described in the *Xunzi*. They were trained to march 100 *li* a day while wearing heavy armor and a helmet, carrying a crossbow and fifty darts slung over the shoulder, a pike across their shoulders, a sword at the side and provisions for three days. It was warriors of this sort and the availability of non-specialized troops that allowed the Qin to change the concept of war in the 3rd century BC. Instead of individual battles that had the purpose of confronting the strength of one army against another, the Qin indulged in military campaigns aimed at conquering territory.

In this climate of growing military specialization, a new intellectual discipline based on the development and discussion of the technical and theoretical art of war came into being during the Warring States period. These principles were debated in numerous treatises by generals and thinkers whose names formed the title of their works, for example, Sunzi. Their works provided the basis of the knowledge that allowed Qin generals to become highly successful, for instance, Shang Yang, Bo Qi, Wang Jian and members of the Meng family.

❖

These two armored foot soldiers reveal how the armor was worn directly over a tunic, whose sleeves emerged from beneath the shoulder plates. The type of pants and footwear varied according to role.

With this new type of army formed by drafted soldiers and specialized career troops under the command of a high-ranking officer, which were camped hundreds, perhaps even thousands of miles away from the capital where the supreme head of the army – the sovereign – resided, the legitimacy of the orders for mobilization or movement of troops was a major problem. It was brilliantly solved by the Qin strategists with the adoption of a special bronze tool known as *hu fu* in the form of a tiger. The object was formed by two symmetrical pieces on which gold inscriptions explained and legitimized its function: the sovereign kept one half, the local commander the other half. Only when the commander received the half sent to him by the sovereign, thereby recreating the symbol of authority, was he authorized to move the troops in his charge. The inscription on the *hu fu* found in 1953 at Zhouzhi (Shaanxi province) says, '*Fu* of the armed troops: the left half to the sovereign; the right half to the *jun* [commander] of the East.'

It is clear that the orders issued down the command chain during battles in which thousands of troops specialized in different forms of combat were involved had to be acknowledged by the troops, as Sunzi explains.

'22. … on the battlefield shouted orders do not travel far enough; therefore gongs and drums are needed. Nor can ordinary objects be seen clearly enough; therefore standards and flags are needed.

23. Gongs and drums, standards and flags: these are the means by which the ears and eyes of the soldiers are attracted to a particular point.'

[Sunzi. *The Art of War* (7)].

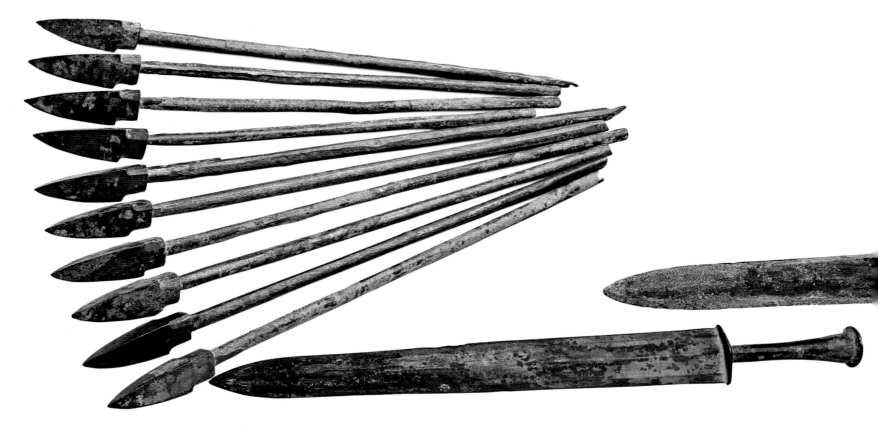

That these were the means by which orders were transmitted in the Qin army is demonstrated by bronze 'bells' without a clapper that were struck like the gongs found in Pit I near command chariots, and by the brightly colored scarves and ribbons reproduced on the statues of officers in the Terracotta Army. The visual signals were clearly seen by the troops, whose weapons and uniforms supplied by the state arsenal are widely documented in the three pits.

Generally speaking, the small section so far excavated of the three pits has provided very valuable information on military procedures and the high quality of production techniques, which until the discovery of the Terracotta Army had never been substantiat-ed directly. Consider, for example, the variety of types of armor, which differed according to the wearer's role: a heavy suit with gauntlets, arm guards, a tunic, apron and collar for the charioteers; a light, tightly fitting suit for the horsemen; a 'long tunic' with sleeves and shoulder straps for certain officers, whilst others had only a chest plate held in place by wide straps that crossed at the back; a short tunic and skirt for crossbowmen as they required flexibility to draw their bows while kneeling on the ground; and a skirt-like garment for the cavalry.

The precision of the reproductions of the various forms of clothing and hairstyles of the thousands of statues provides an exceptional opportunity for study of Qin ma-terial culture. Likewise for the shapes of the chariots, the size of the chassis, and the ornamentation, which are exactly like the originals.

The more than ten thousand weapons found so far flourished by the terracotta troops are real, but before the discovery of the Army, scholars' knowledge of them was based on only a few literary references. This was the case for the *pi* and the 'Wu sickle.' *Pi* were hexagonal blades about 12 inches long, with a long tang inserted into staffs up to 10 feet in length; the 'sickles' were heavy strike weapons with a blunt point and cylindrical handles that were developed in Wu. Nor were the bronze *shu* points found in Pit 3 known of previously.

We were aware of the Qin swords, which vary in length from 32 to 37 inches and were usually carried slung over the back, as shown, for example, by the charioteer in chariot 1 in the Pit of the Bronze Chariots. We also knew of the pike in which a long staff has a blade that sticks out at right angles and a lance point at the top. Extraordinarily, these weapons, especially the swords, had maintained their cutting edge after 2,200 years and were still able to cut a human hair or through 19 sheets of paper, nor did they show any sign of oxidation. Analysis of these superb examples of Qin metallurgy revealed that the swords had a tin component of 21.3%, a quantity that hardened the metal almost to the degree of tempered steel.

220 top center and right The short bronze sword (jian) was one of the principal innovations in battle technique of the Spring and Autumn period. That in the center, with a flat hexagonal blade, dates back to the end of the Spring and Autumn period or the beginning of the successive one. That on the right, with two raised ribs in the center of the hilt, belongs to a characteristic type of the Warring States period. The presence of swords in grave goods from the 7th century BC testifies to the birth of the infantry and the importance of hand-to-hand combat.

220 bottom left This sort of bronze gong or zhong is of the same type as those found in Pit 1. It is decorated with an intricate intertwined dragon motif (pan chi) and was used by officers aboard chariots to summon the attention of foot soldiers or to transmit orders.

220 bottom right This bronze halberd blade (ge) belongs to the type used between the late Spring and Autumn period until the end of the Warring States period. The blade is still attached the bronze cylinder that fastened it to the long shaft.

220-221 The three pits have yielded important finds for the study of Qin military art. Prior to this discovery certain weapons were only known from literary sources. One of these is the "Wu sickle," a strike weapon with a blunt point and cylindrical handle developed in the kingdom of Wu.

221 Discovered in 1976-77 in Pit 2 (trench 4), this statue (77 inches tall) portrays a gongcheng (an officer of the 8th rank — the highest) in the heavy infantry, lined up behind a battalion of archers armed with crossbows. It was possible to identify the officer by his height — for he is slightly taller than the rank and file — as well as his very elaborate hairstyle and the ribbons and bows decorating his long apron-type armor without arm guards.

220 top left These 10 bronze crossbow bolts are part of the 41,000 arrowheads found in the three pits of the Terracotta Army. The arrowheads differ both in shape (in this case a short pyramid with an equal-sided triangular base) and in the length of the shaft, according to the different shooting and target requirements. They clearly testify to the level of specialization of one of the deadliest weapons of antiquity.

❖

222 left This noncommissioned officer, probably of middle-low rank, is depicted wearing a tunic under a short suit of armor with shoulder plates and the characteristic rectangular "tablet" headdress.

❖

222 right This warrior with a calm but resolute expression was of a much higher rank, undoubtedly a general. This is revealed by his two overlapping tunics covered by a short pointed surcoat reinforced with lightweight armor, which is composed of small plates arranged like fish scales, instead of the sturdy plaques worn by the lower-ranking officers. His long, wide pants reach down to touch his shoes, with square, slightly upturned toes.

❖

223 The task of the greatly feared Qin archers — several of whom are depicted kneeling and others standing, like these — was to open the battle and disorient the enemy, showering them with arrows.

❖

224 left This 73-inch statue was one of
the first to be discovered in 1974, in Pit
1. The figure is wearing tunic armor with
shoulder plates and arm guards above a
knee-length garment, revealing puffed
pants. Based on the type of headdress, this
figure is likely to represent a
noncommissioned officer from the middle-
low ranks, probably a taifu (5th rank
on an ascending scale of 1 to 8) in the
heavy infantry.

❖

224 center The armor of this soldier
still shows clear traces of the red pigment
that emphasized the points in which the
laces are marked. The sole personal
protection of the fearless soldiers of the
Qin army was their armor, whose
complexity and protectiveness varied
according to rank and function. Indeed,
the three pits have yielded no
accompanying shields for the protection of
these fearful terracotta warriors.

❖

224 right and 225 This charioteer –
of whom we also see a rear view showing
his complex hairstyle – held the reins
used to steer the chariot. He was protected
by sleeveless armor, which enabled him to
move freely, and wears a tall and rigid
headdress reminiscent of that of certain
officers. A very high degree of
professionalism was demanded of
charioteers, for their skill could be decisive
for the outcome of a battle.

❖

226 This general — whose back, also shown in the photograph, is rendered as attentively as his front — wears the characteristic headdress corresponding to his rank and known as a he, *from the name of a pheasant renowned for fighting to the death.*

❖

227 This noncommissioned officer with scarf and flat rectangular headdress probably held a long weapon in his right hand while brandishing a shorter one in his left hand, in a posture typical of the subalterns.

❖

228 and 229 The decorations on the shoulders and chest of this general with exceptionally refined features were originally emphasized with bright colors, enabling his subordinates to identify him during battle. However, this high degree of visibility needed to be matched by an equal amount of courage, for it made officers an easy target for the enemy forces.

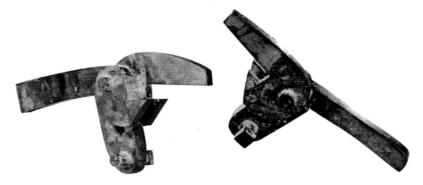

The real surprise, however, was provided by the investigation into the origin of the shiny, blackish patina on all the best preserved weapons. The results of the various scientific analyses performed on a crossbow dart disclosed the secret that had maintained this weapon almost intact – the bronze was composed of the following metals: copper (85.14%), tin (11.39%), lead (1.95%) and chrome (approx. 2%). The chrome had formed a protective film 10–15 microns thick and prevented oxidizing agents from attacking the metal beneath. Chinese specialists of archaeo-metallurgy rightly claim that this use of chrome was not simply fortuitous, but the result of a chemical process controlled by the Qin armorers. In the West, the chromium plating technique was discovered just eighty years ago.

The most fearsome of the Qin weapons was the crossbow. This was the most important technological innovation in warfare during the Warring States period. Like the long sword, and perhaps the use of massed infantry, the crossbow seems to have been invented in Chu but from the start of the 4th century BC, the rest of the Warring States were quickly adopting it. The impact and range of this weapon depended on the flexibility and endurance of the short, thick, strong bow, and on the resistance of the string, which, at the moment of firing, must have caused a strong vibration to run throughout the bowman's body. Soldiers who used this weapon were specially chosen for their physical strength as they had to be able to load the crossbow by holding the cord with one hand and pushing the wooden bow away from them with their feet, as seen in certain low reliefs from the Han era. They also needed to be strong enough to hold the weapon still during firing as it had no butt to help maintain stability. Examples of the deadly bronze darts show that they were cast with a perfectly equilateral pyramidal tip. Obviously the trigger spring that released the string was a fundamental component. The bronze springs found in the pits of the Terracotta Army and certain Qin graves are formed by four parts: two jaws, the cock that engaged the string, and the trigger. The parts subject to most wear were the jaws in the lacquered wood body of the weapon; their function was to move the pin that grips and rotates the trigger, and the cocking pin into position. To prevent sudden breakage of a pin during the battle, the faces of each jaw were symmetrical so that one could quickly be exchanged for the other. Once fired, the dart could travel over 850 yards with a force that could easily penetrate a shield or suit of armor.

It is reasonable to ask whether the deployment of the army to defend the only side of the imperial tomb not protected by natural magical forces reflects the tactics of warfare that we know of through the treatises on military art written during the period of Warring States. Specialists believe that it is, with at least three interpretations.

Under the theory of the 'Three Armies,' the troops in Pit 1 represent the Army on the Right, those in Pit 2 the Army on the Left, those missing in Pit 4 would have been the Army in the Center, and those in Pit 3 represent the army's high command. Moreover, some experts believe that a large four-sided tomb with a single access ramp (as identified

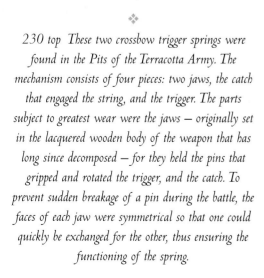

230 top These two crossbow trigger springs were found in the Pits of the Terracotta Army. The mechanism consists of four pieces: two jaws, the catch that engaged the string, and the trigger. The parts subject to greatest wear were the jaws — originally set in the lacquered wooden body of the weapon that has long since decomposed — for they held the pins that gripped and rotated the trigger, and the catch. To prevent sudden breakage of a pin during the battle, the faces of each jaw were symmetrical so that one could quickly be exchanged for the other, thus ensuring the functioning of the spring.

west of Pit 4) could have been the actual grave of the general of the Qin army.

The second interpretation considers that the deployment of the troops represents the main body of the army, the reserve troops, the rear guard and the general staff. Pit 1 would contain the bulk of the army in the battle formation referred to as 'like a shoal of fish' during the Spring and Autumn and Warring States periods. Pit 2 represents the support troops which, being positioned to one side of the main army, could provide reinforcements or be sent unexpectedly into attack from the flank. The rearguard would have been buried in Pit 4, ready to give the *coup de grâce* to the enemy or to lead an improbable retreat; and Pit 3 was built as the headquarters where the strategists and *bu zhang* (specialists who used sacrifices and divination to decide the right moment to attack) operated.

The third and perhaps most accredited interpretation reflects the description of the troops given above and their formation. However, some critics of this interpretation point out that the rectangular Pit 4, aligned north-south, might have symbolized the battlefield and therefore that it was intentionally left empty. Though not wholly without foundation, this hypothesis needs to be considered with caution.

❖

230 bottom and 231 The garments of the crossbowmen had to ensure them complete freedom of movement, as they had to shoot with their knee resting on the ground and hold the bow still with their feet while cocking the string. They thus wore short suits of armor and short skirts. These two soldiers, with their hair gathered in a high knot and a steady forward gaze, show the pure determination that was required of these chosen troops, along with accuracy and physical strength. Indeed, at the moment of shooting, the string sent a violent vibration throughout the body of the archer, who had to be capable of keeping himself steady.

So far the discussion has embraced the finds in the immense underground world, their layout and their probable symbolism of the world that the First August Sovereign held in his absolute power. But what place in the art of the day had those terracotta statues of functionaries, general and soldiers, and the bronze chariots with their metal drivers? To my mind there is no doubt that these objects represented an element of continuity with the art of the period of Warring States, particularly in the treatment of the human figure for the function they had, i.e., as a symbolic presence at the service of the *po* spirit of the dead emperor.

Stylistically, in relation to the treatment of the human body's volumes, these statues follow in the art of the fairly infrequent anthropomorphic figures from the late Zhou period, particularly those cast in bronze. Yet they also represent a move forward from the Warring States period, particularly in that the representation of the human figure is no longer simply evocative as, for example, in the art of Chu, but tends to show the physical and psychological reality of the subject in question. In the case of the stable boys, soldiers of the Terracotta Army or the functionaries in Pit K0006, the figures are built as solid volumes that hide the body under heavy clothing, though where the clothing is absent (as in the 'acrobats'), the anatomical study is clear in the rendition of the musculature. But the artistic development

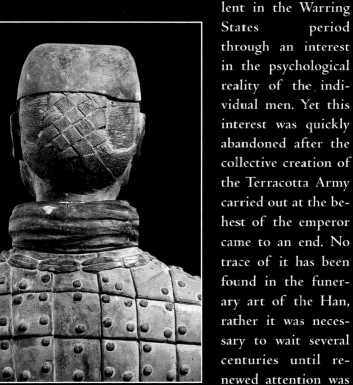

epitomized by these statues lies less in their physical rendition than in the attempt to represent the psychological individuality of the character portrayed, making each face a work in itself through careful reproduction of individual features, and the different styles of the soldiers' mutton-chop whiskers, beards, goatees and hairstyles. The makers of these statues did not produce just empty dolls but were artists who attempted to recreate the shadow of a smile, a slight breath, a modest lowering of the eyes, or dignity in the face of death. On the other hand, their object was not the representation of physical or spiritual beauty, nor a perfect balance in the physical proportions. Their aim was to give form to the models of ethical and moral perfection that were to serve the August Sovereign in the afterlife. The attempt was to reproduce the spiritual reality of the individual subject and it did not much matter if the faces resembled those of the real Qin soldiers or not. What was important was the desire to break away from a symbolic stereotype of funerary art prevalent in the Warring States period through an interest in the psychological reality of the individual men. Yet this interest was quickly abandoned after the collective creation of the Terracotta Army carried out at the behest of the emperor came to an end. No trace of it has been found in the funerary art of the Han, rather it was necessary to wait several centuries until renewed attention was

❖

The rear view of this figure shows several characteristic details of the horsemen's clothing: the lightweight cuirass armor, which enabled relatively free movement, and the unmistakable cap, probably made of leather, which fastened beneath the chin with a sort of strap.

paid to the physical reality and consciousness of the human figure in the art of the Tang dynasty (618–907).

Manufacture of the Army was a collective work but, for the first time in the art of ancient China, we are able to identify individual artists. During restoration of the statues inscriptions were discovered in hidden corners of the figures, either incised or brushed in with red or black ink. These inscriptions can be thought of as a sort of certification or mark of quality control; what is sensational is that these marks have torn aside the veil of anonymity to reveal the names of eighty-five different *gong shi* (master craftsmen). For the first time, the inscriptions have also provided us with a few sparing details of their lives. Thus we now know that some of the artists were employed by state workshops (referred to by the term *gong*, 'palace') run by central government; for instance, Gongjiang, Gongde, Gongpo, Gongkai and Gongchao. Other artists were employed by non-governmental workshops like those in Xianyang, Linjin, Yueyang and Anyi, or by district workshops such as Xianyangci, Xianyangwu, Linjinzhong and Yueyangge. We have also learnt that each *gong shi* was aided by eighteen assistants (*cheng*), from which we deduce that there were a full 1,530 craftsmen working for the 85 masters whose names we know.

The inscriptions usually give the name of the workshop where the statue was produced, the name of the master involved, the name of the office supervisor and the year of the reign of Qin Shi Huangdi. In addition, they have also provided definitive confirmation of the writing style used in Qin that was developed, on the First Emperor's wishes, as a standardized form to be used throughout the empire. The graphical variants of the inscriptions found on the statues also provide evidence that the 'eight forms' of official writing were being developed. These later matured into the stylistic variants of Chinese calligraphy.

Attentive examination of the terracotta figures that form this silent army has revealed that the Chinese craftsmen emerged from anonymity for the first time on this project, signing their work, probably for reasons of quality control. Indeed, inscriptions can be found on the hidden parts of the statues — either engraved or written with brush and black or red ink — detailing the names of the 85 masters, or gong shi, *who employed a plethora of assistants.*

234 *This elegantly modeled statue, of which we can see a profile and rear view, depicts a general commanding the rows of troops discovered in Pit 2. The face is framed by the hairstyle and sideburns and has a square profile; a solid block softened by a few incised lines that emphasize the lips and catlike eyes. The intention of the master modeler was obviously to convey the calmness and determination of this man aware of danger, an officer ready to die bravely and fearlessly. This courage and fearlessness of the Qin soldiers, exalted in the ancient historical texts, is evoked in the explicit reference to the fighting spirit of the* he *pheasant, from which the characteristic headdress of the generals — clearly visible in both photographs — took its name.*

235 *This figure of a general clearly shows the distinctive marks of authority: a high and complex hairstyle, bows, and armor almost completely devoid of plaques, which was thus relatively lightweight. Indeed, a commander had to be ready to move unhindered in battle and, above all, did not need to have his back protected because the possibility that he could retreat was simply inconceivable.*

236 top left The greatness of the craftsmen who modeled these statues lay in their ability to give each one of them a character and bearing consonant with the role of the figure represented. The generals, for example, can be recognized by both the stateliness of the figures and their refined dress, but above all by the sensation of steadfastness and imperturbable boldness that they emanate.

236 center and bottom left Precision, composure and determination — along with considerable strength and physical resistance — were the qualities required of these lethal shooters, the Qin crossbowmen. All these virtues are apparent in the face of this soldier. The finely modeled head reveals the complexity of the hairstyle. The hair is gathered in a high knot in an intricate interwoven design.

236 right The hu fu, a small tiger-shaped bronze object with gold inscriptions composed of two halves, was devised to ensure security in the transmission of orders: one half was given to the officer in charge of the contingent deployed in a certain location, while the other was kept by the sovereign, who would send it to the commander in the case of mobilization or attack.

237 The sword represented the sole form of personal protection for the generals: they were not required to participate physically in the attack, but to direct the unit under their command with expertise. The harsh code of behavior of the period did not permit any kind of surrender and the idea that a commander could turn his back on danger was unconceivable.

This particularly well-finished statue of a soldier dressed in a simple tunic, from Pit 1, enables us to observe several details of the modeling that could escape our notice at a cursory glance of the troops deployed in the pits. The anatomical details of the face, the moustache and the hairstyle — with central parting and a high knot — have been formed with great care. The same is true for the details of the clothing, such as the neckerchief visible above the neckline of the tunic, or the simple belt that fastens the garment.

❖

*The introduction of armor during the Warring States period was one of the chief innovations of the military technology of the
time. Enormous masses of infantry were increasingly often deployed on the battlefield and were also used as a striking force
after the vanguards, armed with lances, had launched the first attack. In the case of armored infantry in particular, the use of
helmets and cuirasses was indispensable to protect the soldiers from the impact of enemy attacks. Most of the armor was
composed of leather or iron plates, tied together to allow a certain degree of flexibility, as well as the necessary protection.
Particular care was paid to the vulnerable areas of the back and chest, where it was necessary to ensure that the plates would
not separate if the armor were struck with a pointed weapon, but form a solid barrier.*

❖

242 and 243 *This photograph shows the full and deeply wrinkled face of an adult man, a low-ranking official in the armored infantry arrayed in Pit 1. The treatment of the anatomical details of this well-proportioned face — the carefully tended, almost handlebar moustache, the unusual three-pointed beard, the wrinkles, the arch of the eyebrows and the shape of the eyes — reveal the hand of a skilled master modeler, perhaps one of the gong shi, of whom 85 are currently known. We possess a few biographical facts about these craftsmen: their name and district of origin, or the workshop to which the various masters and their over 1,500 assistants belonged — which was often state-owned.*

❖

244-245 *Solid masses and powerful builds can be discerned beneath the heavy clothes and armor of the soldiers, almost contrasting with the psychological lightness and refinement with which the Qin craftsmen have attempted to express the single individuals, as though each figure were a work unto itself, a clear model of ethical and moral perfection, regardless of rank or role. This evident effort explains the great diversity of somatic traits, the vast array of hairstyles, moustaches, beards and goatees that contribute to giving the faces personality, and the incredible variety of the gazes and expressions that are depicted beneath a veil of apparent uniformity.*

246 *This warrior has highly prominent facial features, very different from those of his fellow soldiers: there is certainly no risk of boredom when contemplating the Terracotta Army. In an attempt to systematize this infinite sequence of human types, several scholars have proposed a classification articulated in 30 or so categories, while others have conjectured another narrower one based on the analogy between the shape of the various faces and that of 10 fairly simple and schematic Chinese characters.*

247 *It is possible that this crossbowman originally held a real notched weapon. Indeed, according to Sima Qian (145?-89? BC), the great historian of the Han dynasty, the emperor's tomb was defended by crossbows ready to shoot their bolts at whoever might attempt to violate it. This type of weapon, invented in the southern kingdom of Chu, but immediately adopted by all the Warring States from the beginning of the 4th century BC, represents the most important innovation in military technology of the Warring States period.*

The Conservation and Restoration of the Terracotta Army

The First August Sovereign of the Qin dynasty had been dead only a short time when his empire began to falter, and even his last resting place felt the effects. It has already been mentioned that when the dynasty fell, rebels and thieves entered his tomb and set it on fire. Archaeologists discovered that many statues had been decapitated and deliberately broken, and many of the weapons stolen.

The fire started when the Qin dynasty fell charred most of the wooden structures built to protect and cover the underground chambers, and the great heat refired many of the terracotta figures, turning them from gray to red and deforming many of the fragments. As the wooden structures collapsed, the figures beneath were knocked over.

More than two thousand years passed before the funerary pits accompanying the tomb were discovered. During this period the pressure exerted by the weight of the earth and various floods had put the resistance of the materials to a severe test. The sediments deposited by the water and the earth above had filled every empty space inside the pits, including the hollow interiors of the broken statues. The partition walls of pressed earth that separated the rows of soldiers and supported the wooden coverings were worn away by the water to a level beneath that of the heads of the soldiers, therefore placing even more pressure on them.

These factors explain why not even a single statue was found complete. Many of the figures were broken into seventy or so parts, some even two hundred. Most of the statues, therefore, were incomplete and often the individual pieces no longer fitted together perfectly. Many of the bronze objects were also broken, deformed or deteriorated; the slabs of calcareous stone rock in the 'Armor Pit' were chemically bonded to the deposit of loess (crumbly, yellow soil) and wooden items were either carbonized splinters or simply impressions in the earth that crumbled on contact with air.

From the beginning of excavation in 1975, Chinese restorers and archaeologists had to tackle enormous problems of conservation, some of which presented themselves immediately, while others appeared after objects had been removed from the earth. In the sections of the tomb that had been broken into in ca. 206 BC, the fragments of the individual statues were scattered across a vast area and mixed, and those fragments subjected to the heat of the fire can no longer be fitted back together. Breakage is not the only problem: once removed from the damp soil and exposed to the air outside, the compact layer of colors on the surface of the statues wrinkles and becomes detached in a few minutes. To preserve the layer of colors long enough to give a more long lasting treatment, the figures have to be conserved in a very damp atmosphere, but this in turn is conducive to the formation of mildew and similar micro-biological aggressors which must be dealt with without placing the delicate surface of the painted terracotta at risk. The atmosphere in which the statues were found, and to which they were returned after restoration, also suffers from exposure to air: the partition walls of pressed earth crack and the earthy imprints of the

❖

Chinese archaeologists during the excavation of a terracotta chariot in Xi'an in 1977: the surrounding earth is roughly the same color as the terracotta, making the field researchers' task even more difficult, for they were forced to work in cramped and dimly lit conditions.

wood quickly turns to dust. The high number of visitors causes a continual change in the micro-climate inside the large pavilions that cover the pits, and the considerable quantity of micro-organisms and dust brought in from the external environment damage both the figures and the internal environment.

Many solutions have been tested during thirty or so years of research but their durability and validity have not yet been demonstrated. Meanwhile other questions wait to be answered. For this reason, excavation has — wisely — been slowed since 1989. Of the presumed seven thousand soldiers, only two thousand have been disinterred and the few statues that are still excavated in Pits 1 and 2 are used first and foremost for research on the conservation of the colors. Only Pit 3, the smallest, has been explored completely. Surveys of the area immediately surrounding the burial mound of Qin Shi Huangdi led to the discovery of many other pits that

contain objects made from stone and bronze, and other terracotta figures. Removal of items from the ground has only occurred where a precise program of conservation and restoration techniques exists, as in the case of the statues of the 'acrobats' and the functionaries. Other places, like the burial chamber that covers the real tomb, have not been opened, so as to avoid exposing the finds to the risk of irremediable deterioration. Since 1999, work has proceeded slowly on the armor made of small calcareous stone tiles; the work is made difficult by their number and condition, as they are made of a material the exact nature of which is not precisely known.

Although research into restoration and long-term conservation has not yet produced definitive results, great progress has been made in the analysis of materials originally used for the manufacture of these works. Before establishing a treatment program, it was necessary to know how and of what material they are made. By now the manner in which the terracotta statues were modeled and assembled is well understood: with regard to the definition of pigments, collaboration between conservators, archaeologists, chemists, geologists and physicists has led to satisfactory results. Consider, for example, the discovery of the color called 'Han purple,' a complex artificial pigment that was previously almost unknown. Since 1992 the Chinese team's research on the color has been assisted by experts from the Monument Protection Office in Bavaria, thanks to a Sino-German scientific program. Together the two countries have diagnosed that the base preparation for the painted layer was a thin coat of lacquer. For a decade now, Chinese and German researchers have been testing different methods to increase the resistance of the lacquer to climatic changes and to enhance the adhesion to this organic material to the terracotta. Since 1998, the German conservators have also been part of the studies attempting to find new ways to assemble the fragments of terracotta. Thanks to the cooperation between various disciplines, research makes use of scientific and other methods, in an attempt to discover permanent but reversible, repeatable, controllable and economically feasible methods of conservation on a large scale.

❖

The work of the experts proceeds gradually, with the aid of spatulas and brushes. All progress must be documented: sketches or photographs of details and certain groups prevent the loss of information during the reconstruction of the statues. The excavation proceeds from the top down, in order to preserve the totality of the bodies as long as possible.

The statues are perfunctorily cleaned of the earth that has enveloped them for over 2,000 years in the field. However, due to the detailed rendering designed to reproduce the tiniest details of each part of the armor and give the hands and faces a realistic appearance, scrupulous and painstaking cleaning is necessary, which can only be performed in better working conditions. Consequently, the process is continued in well-equipped and illuminated laboratories, bearing in mind that materials are easily degradable.

252 top Once the earth above the rows of soldiers has been cleared, the sight is rather discouraging. Much of the destruction was caused by the rebels who attacked the capital and the tomb of the First August Sovereign several decades after his death: they threw down and decapitated numerous warriors, plundering many of their precious bronze weapons.

252-253 The remains of the side structures, built to support the wooden beams that covered the rows of warriors, can be seen in the background of the photograph. Earth was spread on top of the wooden covering structures, thus burying the entire army. The rebels set these structures on fire, causing them to collapse and destroy the bodies below.

253 top *The arbitrary destruction of the terracotta statues has resulted in unusual combinations: in this case three fragments of head have met and fused into a single block.*

253 bottom *This photograph provides a very clear view of the beaten earth dividing wall, which shows the traces of the wooden supporting beams. It is possible to reconstruct the appearance and color of the wooden parts from the earth that enveloped them for many years, for although the wood has decomposed, the surrounding earth has preserved the imprint.*

254-255 *As the fragments were disseminated over a very wide area, missing pieces are sometimes found many feet from the discovery of the main body.*

RECONSTRUCTION OF THE TERRACOTTA STATUES

Restoration of the statues of the Terracotta Army's soldiers and horses has been – and will be for many years to come – one of the most impressive undertakings in the history of conservation in the entire world. The work of the restorers has consisted not only of the difficult recomposition of the fragments, but also and above all in the resolution of a problem that at the start of the enterprise seemed extremely problematical: the separation of the earth from the ceramic fragments without harming the colored pigments.

However, the damage was also beneficial in certain way: the fractures in the terracotta figures provided important information on the techniques of manufacture and on the exposure of the parts to pressure and forces. The parts of the statues tend to break at the points in which the elements of which they are composed – modeled separately while the clay was still damp – were bonded together using very wet clay. This is clear in the joints between the bust and the arms, the legs and the trunk and along the sutures between sheets of clay rolled around the molds for the hands and head. And the thicker the clay, the greater the risk of breakage: a leg made from solid clay breaks more easily than a hollow leg created using a rolled sheet of clay. Legs, and in particular the join between the legs that supports the weight of the entire statue, is more at risk than the 'humerus' that only supports the weight of the forearm and hand. To overcome the risks of breakage, a glass resin pin was inserted at the points of major strain. The pins are inserted in the cavities of the torso and the inner side of the seams of the legs, thereby reducing the excess mechanical stress. And to connect the fragments that suffer greater internal pressures, metal strips have been used. Both methods, however, have recently been abandoned; the first because with time the initially rigid glass resin becomes more apt to crack, and the second because the insertion of metal strips creates new tensions that expose the clay to the risk of unexpected breakage.

The projecting parts of the statues have suffered fractures for other reasons: hands, forearms and heads have suffered from the collapse of the wooden ceilings and, later, from the pressure of the deposits of loess that invaded the fosse. Moreover, Xiang Yu's insurgents decapitated many statues.

The working conditions in the pits make reconstruction of the statues on the spot very difficult: there is little room or light and no water or electricity is available. To reduce the possibility of further breakages during transportation, the rear section of Pit I, which has not yet been excavated, has been fitted out as a restoration laboratory. The fragments from a single figure are kept together while those not yet identified (often minute) are spread out on large sheets of plastic. The procedure is then rather like completing a giant jigsaw puzzle. The fragments that fit together are temporarily fixed with plaster that will later be removed when the statue is reconstructed properly. To rebuild the 'chariots,' it is necessary first to clean the edges fractured by the earth and dust and remove all grease with alcohol. 'Pre-assembly' without a binder is performed to understand the exact positions of the fragments, on which lines are drawn and numbers added so as to be able to reconstruct them accurately.

In the assembly itself, the binder must be reliable and manageable. Strongly adhesive resins have been added to with agents to delay hardening so that the restorers have sufficient time (no more than 24 hours) to rebuild, piece by piece, the body of the statue. Recomposition begins with the neck or, more frequently, the base, taking the largest pieces of the load-bearing parts. Limited numbers of fragments can be dried on sand beds whereas the load-bearing sections must be dried vertically with the help of wooden supports, bandages and drops of plaster that hold the pieces firmly until the glue has dried. So as to deal with a complete statue quickly, as soon as it is possible the structure is stood up and the arms, hands and head attached last.

However, even the most careful restoration is unable to return the statue to its original state, and there is always an incomplete part or some empty space to be filled. Usually the color and more sophisticated exterior ornamentation have disappeared forever and missing hands, arms and heads are irremediably lost, but the gaps in the surfaces of the body can be filled using the information provided by the surrounding pieces. Initially the gaps were filled using white plaster touched up with a mixture of plaster, pigments, ink and earthy dust. A visitor to the pits who sees the rows of soldiers from a distance is unaware of the extensive repairs, in the same way that he cannot see the dark marks that the binder has often left along the edge of the sutures. This type of restoration therefore creates the illusion of completeness that in reality no longer exists.

Today, the tendency is not to hide the damage completely. The statues of 'acrobats' and functionaries that have undergone restoration in recent years were treated using this criterion. Fragments, even tiny ones, have been repositioned without using heavily invasive techniques, like the insertion of metal pins; the resin-based glue is colorless and all trace of it is meticulously erased on the outside of the sutures, but, above all, the missing parts have not been rebuilt and the sutures between the fragments have intentionally been left apparent.

Several procedures have been adapted to the widest held theories of conservation at international level but the solution to some problems remains provisory. For example, new methods of gluing are being tested because chemical process of the resin being used is irreversible; the resin is also very hard and its degree of cohesiveness is higher than that of the clay. That makes it impossible to add missing parts found after gaps have been filled with plaster. Furthermore, the tension created by the glue tends to break the clay in new places. After restoration, the statues are replaced, with the aid of a winch, exactly where they had previously been in the row of the soldiers.

The formation of the army already unearthed lies beneath the gaze of the visitor as not even the First August Emperor may have seen it. The wooden structures that covered the walls and supported the ceiling of the galleries were installed before the statues were moved in. The current display is certainly very attractive but it creates difficulties that an ordinary museum would not suffer: the statues stand very close together and deterioration in the materials of individual figures is hard to notice. And an earthquake, however small, could rock the statues enough to create a domino effect that would knock them all over. To prevent such an occurrence, the heads of the statues, which were originally fitted into the collars of the torso without any other form of attachment, are now fastened to the trunk with artificial resins or plaster. The statues are not fixed to the ground as this would require operations that would damage the terracotta.

Contact with the soil — where only a layer of bricks separates the statues from the ground — creates continual exposure of the clay to seasonal atmospheric changes. The winter climate dries them out and therefore makes them very fragile, while the summer humidity in the ground rises through the legs of the statues, encouraging the growth of mildew and depositing salts that make the terracotta porous. Consequently, the environment inside the display area is monitored continuously and water sprayed during the winter; this also helps to close the cracks that form in the partition walls between the galleries. In summer the attack of micro-organisms is resisted using ventilation and bio-acids.

257 The statues are normally reconstructed from the base upward, in order not to lose sight of their unity. It is necessary to bear in mind the center of gravity of the terracotta figures in the process, thus avoiding the risk of a precarious equilibrium.

THE POLYCHROME OF THE TERRACOTTA SOLDIERS

Only tiny traces remain of the realistic colors with which the soldiers were painted because the layers of color stuck to the earth that had covered them for two thousand years when the soil was removed. As the organic binder of the pigments had either dissolved or penetrated the loess, every attempt to separate the color from the earth led to the destruction of the polychrome decorations. Some of the more sophisticated decorations were saved by immersing the turf that had absorbed the colors in beds of plaster, thus preserving them from immediate pulverization; however, even in cases where the statues had preserved their coloring, after initial separation from the wet soil the layers of pigment inevitably became detached during excavation. After years of research, Chinese and German scientists have discovered the cause: a preparation of lacquer (a natural resin obtained from the lacquer tree, *toxicodendron vernicifluum*) had been applied between the color and the terracotta. This resin usually resists variations in atmospheric conditions well so the researchers assume that in this case organic components no longer traceable were added, perhaps to increase the material's capacity of absorption and ductility. They might also have been added, more simply, for reasons of economy, given that the amount of lacquer used to cover the seven thousand statues required the production of between 150–200,000 trees. In any case, the water in the soil penetrated this preparation and became an integral part of it. The loss of humidity due to exposure to the air causes a reduction in the volume of the lacquer's surface, which then develops a network of cracks and, within a few minutes, the lacquer arches and flakes off. To save the polychrome, it is necessary to begin with the lacquer: this must be prevented from reacting to the changes in the climate and therefore increasing or contracting in volume. Therefore a method to fix it solidly to the terracotta was required. The resin does not react to common solvents so the conservators were obliged to test alternative methods to improve the cohesion and adhesion of the lacquer, which, it was later discovered, had been applied in two coats. Given its sensitivity to the minimum loss of internal humidity, conservation and preliminary cleaning of the fragments, plus the application and drying of the consolidating agent of the colored layers, are implemented in an environment saturated with humidity. Immediately after excavation, the fragments with polychrome are closed in plastic bags and stored in cabinets in which 100% humidity is maintained. Two special containers very similar to incubators have been constructed in Munich; they have transparent walls and a controlled environment and are used to clean the clay fragments. The containers are closed within a perforated plastic sheet that allows the restorers to insert gloved hands to remove – with the aid of a microscope – the earth using wooden spatulas and soft brushes. If the earth is stuck solid to the layer of paint, the restorer is obliged to choose between lifting off all the earth, which will also remove the colored particles, or leaving a certain layer of earth on the pigments.

❖

258 The lacquer used as a base for the colors flakes off the terracotta statues easily, while the mineral pigment sticks to the surrounding soil. These samples of soil placed on a bed of plaster have been subjected to a conservative treatment to provide evidence of the multicolored pigments with which the warriors were originally covered.

❖

259 This photograph shows one of the six archers of Pit 2 that were restored in situ. As the excavation gradually proceeded, the cleaned part was subjected to a conservative treatment. The damp atmosphere and dim lighting contribute to preventing significant alteration of the microclimate before the stabilization of the lacquer and pigments

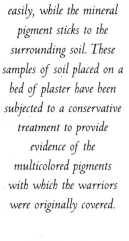
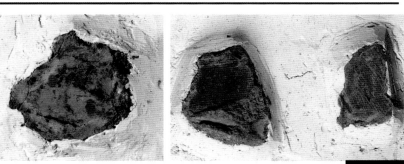

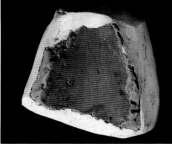

First attempts at drying out the materials, after cleaning, in a microwave oven or, on the contrary, to freeze them produced negative results. So the scientists concentrated on searching for a chemical fixative that would not alter the appearance or tonality of the colors, and which would remain elastic and not preclude later interventions. The consolidating agent had to be sufficiently fine to filter into the lacquer's molecular structure and to substitute the water contained there, and then to dry in conditions of maximum humidity. The first efforts using solutions of glycerin or sugar — both of which have a suitable molecular structure — were unsuccessful. Better results were obtained with polyethylene glycol (PEG or PEG2000), an alcoholic solution widely used in industry and for conserving archaeological objects. Starting with a combination of PEG and polyurethane (a plastic material used as a binder in the preparation of paints and adhesives), in 1996 the researchers succeeded in developing a procedure that was subsequently perfected and put into practice on a wide scale. In this process soft cotton compresses were soaked in a solution of PEG and polyurethane and applied on the colored fragments. An initial concentration of the consolidating agent that was too high led to the emptying of the water from the pores of the lacquer without leaving enough time for the new solution to replace it, and thus causing cracks to appear. However, the impregnation with the new solution occurred in three phases of growing concentration of the fixative. Thin rice paper or a film of perforated plastic separated the compress from the pigments which otherwise would have become attached too easily. When the lacquer is saturated, the compress is lifted off and the excess solution on the polychrome surface removed. The lacquer impregnated in this manner is less sensitive to changes in humidity and adheres well to the terracotta base.

Following further indispensable improvements, this method was applied for the first time on a wide scale in 1999 on six kneeling archers found in Pit 2. Their entire suits of armor had been covered with two thick coats of lacquer and lined with red in the points where the ties were marked; heads and hands were painted over the lacquer with flesh-tone pigments. With the exception of the heads, which are removable, the conservators treated the statues on the spot, leaving the backs, which remained in the ground, untreated. The removal of the earth had to be carried out as quickly as possible and without the usual aids: electricity, diffused light and a microscope. Before applying the compresses with the stabilizing solution, the statues were repeatedly sprayed with water until the layer of lacquer was saturated so that the water could be replaced by the consolidating agent without the lacquer changing its volume. After treatment, the aesthetic result and the stability of the lacquer were satisfactory, but three of the statues, after being removed from their locations, began to crack and peel a few months later. In addition, signs of the cleaning that took place *in loco* and excess polyurethane became very evident, the latter seemingly in greasy patches. The heads, however, having been cleaned and handled in the laboratory, were much better preserved, one in particular, referred to as 'green face' for the curious pale green color of the flesh.

Only a minimal part of the soft layer of lacquer and pigment on the 'acrobats' was preserved, but the small areas treated in 1999 with PEG and polyurethane have remained unaltered until today. The polychrome on the statues of the functionaries was thinner and applied less carefully than that of the soldiers so, in this case, the colored surface of the fragments was consolidated before reconstruction of the statues began. No cracks appeared after the treatment but the overall appearance of the figures has been altered by the wet, greasy look of some fragments caused by the accumulation of residual consolidating agent on the surface.

❖

The black pigment applied to the eyes and eyebrows and around the mouth of this ruddy-faced, functionary discovered in Pit K0006, gives personality to his expression and emphasizes the uniqueness of his features.

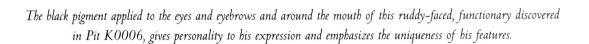

❖

262 The colors used for the complexions help to characterize the individual warriors: the tones of the faces and hands vary from the palest shades of yellow-green to deep brick red.

❖

263 The photograph shows a completely restored archer. Despite the application of conservative measures, the color of three of the six archers has started to crack following the removal of the statues from the site of discovery. This is because the lacquer — which imitated the real appearance of the lacquered leather armor and also served as a base for the colored pigments — is extremely sensitive to climatic changes.

As the procedure is not without defect, alternative methods of saving the color layer are being tested, still based on the stabilization of the two layers of lacquer. Since 1997 a group of German and Chinese chemists have been working on acrylic monomers with the restorers; these are small, simple molecules able to filter into both the lacquer and the terracotta. A commercial product, known as HEMA or Plex, used to make flexible contact lenses, seems suitable for use as a consolidating agent as it does not seal the surface and is able to absorb large quantities of water without liquefying. The application of this product is similar to that in the first procedure; the simple Plex molecules remain liquid until they are stimulated to form solid macromolecules and create a dense network inside the lacquer structure, and between the lacquer and the terracotta. This process, called polymerization, is artificially induced through the electronic radiation of the terracotta piece for roughly a week in an aerated environment. As polymerization occurs in an environment devoid of oxygen, only the molecules that penetrate deepest combine, so that the surface monomers can be removed without alteration of the color.

This second procedure has a better visual effect than the first because the color seems dry and remains clear. The radiation given to polymerize the Plex also destroys the mildew, thus removing the need to check for micro-biological infestation. If, however, the Plex is not applied carefully, cracks form during consolidation and the colored layer can lose its cohesion.

A more devastating effect only becomes visible after a longer period: many of the fragments treated over the last few years are today stained in what at first looks like patches of diluted color, but later they tend to burst and form small craters. The reason is not yet understood but it certainly depends on the type of pigment seeing that the green and violet are particularly vulnerable. Moreover, the instrument used for the radiation is not sufficiently large to contain entire statues and is not easily transportable to the site of the Terracotta Army. For these reasons, the conservators at present prefer to stick to the PEG and polyurethane treatment while waiting for better results in the research on lacquer consolidation.

Thirty restorers have worked for eight years on the two bronze chariots discovered in 1978 in more than three thousand pieces. To ensure the maximum care was paid when removing the earth that covered it and in the recovery of the pieces, the half-covered remains were taken together with the soil beneath them in a single gigantic block that weighed more than eight tons. In the laboratory the block was cut into four parts: two contained the horses and two the chariots. While extracting the fragments, the conservators numbered them individually so that they could be placed temporarily in the same position in which they were found.

The next phase of analysis, before deciding how to proceed with the restoration, was to decide what the materials were and their state of conservation. The bronze alloy of the chariots is composed of copper, tin and a low percentage of lead. The moving elements (for instance, the bridles and wheel bosses) are, like the exterior of the chariot, partially inlaid with gold and silver, whereas the principal decoration consists of a doughy layer of polychrome paint applied directly on top of the bronze. After being broken into pieces, the fragments of bronze were deformed, oxidized and corroded, unlike the precious metals that have been conserved beneath their blackened patina. The paint surface is dominated by the white, which is composed mainly of lime. The other prevalent colors are blue, green, red, violet and black. As the paint layer had reacted with cracks and flaking to the change in environmental climate after excavation, a synthetic consolidating agent was immediately used to stabilize it without altering the appearance of the colors.

A special vise was used in an attempt to return each piece to its original shape. The correct curvature of the large 'parasol' on Chariot 2 was recreated by reducing the degree of arc resulting from the curve of the individual fragments: a model and a plaster mold were used to remodel the finds in accordance with the reduced curvature, then the fragments were fixed directly on the original parasol rods.

Before gluing the fragments, it was necessary to clean the edges by removing the earth, the parts made crumbly by corrosion, and the oxidation patina as much as was possible. Aluminum powder was added to an artificial resin to prevent contraction of the volume during drying. The adhesive force of the glue was increased by heating the pieces to 60–80°C for several hours but it has its limits; the parts that supported the greatest weight of the chariots were reinforced with welding; depending on the weight to be supported and the state of oxidation of the alloy, the conservators decided on a case-by-case basis the temperature and the metal to be used. In some invisible load-bearing parts plates, pins or sturdy metal wire was used for reinforcement. The bronze rods that converge into a disk beneath the parasol on Chariot I, which rests on a solid central stem inlaid with gold, were in an advanced state of corrosion, so for this it was decided to use stainless steel rods which, not being visible, ran beside the original rods and met in a thin disk above the bronze disk. The central stem is now supported by a parallel rod and stands on a more solid base.

During restoration of the individual elements, the conservators carefully examined the apparatus by which the chariot moved and the manner in which the horses were harnessed. During final assembly, they realized that the chariots were a faithful imitation of reality though they were only half life-size. No-one would ever have thought of attempting to move the chariots, but it was necessary to reassemble them to respect their operability, with the wheels mobile, the bridles attached and the couplings practicable. The last touches hid the traces of the welding and glue: chariots, horses and charioteers now appear to the observer whole and with large sections painted.

264 The chariots were found one behind the other. The wooden beams protecting them had rotted and collapsed due to the pressure of the earth and the attacks of microorganisms, shattering the chariots in over 3,000 pieces. The wood had decomposed and the remains of the more resistant materials were found lying where they had fallen.

265 The decorations of the harness studs, the central shaft of the parasol and certain details of the chariots, such as the axle boxes, have all been preserved incredibly well because they were damascened in gold and silver. It is sufficient to clean these precious metals to restore them, although it is necessary to reconstruct the parts in which they were inserted.

To the observer kneeling on the holes excavated to a depth of 13 to 16 feet, the sight is enigmatic and fascinating: plaques made from calcareous stone feebly tied by corroded copper wire no longer have the profiles of suits of armor or helmets, but create bizarre new shapes like fantastic reptiles. Before touching the enormous mass of small stone plaques, the archaeologists tried to recompose their original forms 'virtually,' marking the pieces that perhaps belonged to the same garment numerically. In the pilot restoration, the pieces that seemed to come from a single set of armor were recovered, and those of a helmet with a neckpiece that tied beneath the chin. The plaques were massed in indivisible conglomerates of stone and earth. Chemical analysis revealed that the calcareous stone had developed a thin layer of chemical fusion with the loess around it where it was in contact with the soil. It was not sufficient simply to separate the individual plaques: the surface of each plaque had to be 'recreated' as it had been destroyed over the millennia. This operation was made more difficult by the precarious state of the stones: the pressure

placed on them by the earth above for more than two thousand years, and the mildew created by the organic content of the soil had induced cracks and micro-cracks that sometimes ran parallel to the surface, splitting the plaque into thin layers. Similarly, the corners of the plaques were often broken having been rendered fragile by the reduced thickness of the smoothed stone and by the perforations for the copper wire. Another problem was that the gray calcareous stone had been transformed into white, powdery calcium oxide by the heat of the fire in 206 BC. At the moment of the excavation, the burned sections seemed intact, but on contact with the carbon monoxide in the air they disintegrated in just a few days. Only as the stones became more distant from the heart

of the fire did their undamaged parts increase in number.

After careful cleaning, the fragments of individual plates have been consolidated with strong inorganic glue dissolved in alcohol. The missing parts have been filled in with plaster and colored to be as similar as possible to the stone.

The recovery of the blocks of stone and earth and the reconstruction of the plaques provided enough information for the final assembly. The manner in which the individual plates were overlaid and the methods of tying them at the edges and perforated corners were identified. In the end all the components required to reproduce the original appearance were available. After each plaque had been cleaned, replaced in its original position and stabilized, the restorers prepared for the assembly, which they did by replacing the corroded copper wire that had been made solid with the earth or stones, and which was therefore irrecoverable. The restored plates were tied with new quadrangular bronze wire tied 'horseshoe-shaped' on the chest and back where the

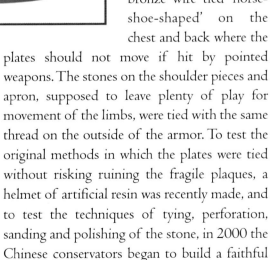

plates should not move if hit by pointed weapons. The stones on the shoulder pieces and apron, supposed to leave plenty of play for movement of the limbs, were tied with the same thread on the outside of the armor. To test the original methods in which the plates were tied without risking ruining the fragile plaques, a helmet of artificial resin was recently made, and to test the techniques of tying, perforation, sanding and polishing of the stone, in 2000 the Chinese conservators began to build a faithful copy of an entire suit of armor.

The challenge to modern techniques and sciences to recover and conserve the contents of the Funerary Garden of the First August Sovereign of the Qin dynasty continues for the benefit of future generations.

266 and 267 bottom *In the first pilot restoration, the pieces that composed a helmet with neckpiece were recovered, along with others that appeared to belong to a single set of armor. Each suit of armor was comprised of breastplate, backplate, shoulderplates, front and rear tasses (a tasse is a series of overlapping plates). The bronze wire that connected the breastplate and backplate was tightly fastened to ensure the rigidity of the plate structure. The shoulderplates and tasses were instead made from knotted bronze wires, twisted on the outside to allow a certain degree of freedom of movement.*

267 top *No fragments have been found of terracotta statues capable of wearing these heavy garments. The armor must thus have been supported in some other manner, possibly by an unknown suspension device, of which no evidence has yet been found.*

THE DECEASED EMPEROR AND HIS RETINUE
EVIDENCE OF THE WORK PERFORMED

Construction of the tomb and statues for the Terracotta Army was an immense project. Just like a manufacturing line, the clay was pounded with quartz, cut into lengths and pressed in molds under the eye of the master modelers to create the component parts of a statue. The head was incised in every tiny detail and was the last piece to be added to the statue. There were greater difficulties in the construction of the horses due to the large hollow volumes of the animal's belly and neck; these were held in shape by a wooden skeleton. We have little information about the workshops or the kilns in which the statues were fired at 900–1,000°C. We do know, though, from the inscriptions the exact location that each figure was assembled and painted after firing: the moustache and hair were painted black, the face pink, and the clothes, armor, ribbons and head-covering in dazzling colors.

The cyclopic construction of the infrastructure of the funerary garden, including the tiles, bricks and piping, must also have required an enormous quantity of clay that is unlikely to have been dug far away. Near Yuchibao (Village of the Small Fish-lake), roughly 1.5 miles north of the funerary garden, is a large depression filled with water from a stream deviated by the Wuling dam that may well have been the source of the clay. The hypothesis is supported by a passage from the *Shui Jing Zhu* (Commentary on the Classic of the Waters) written by Li Daoyuan (466?–527) during the period of the Northern Wei dynasty (386–534). In the section 'Weishui' (River Wei), we read:

'To construct the *lingyuan* Shi Huang quarried earth; so the area was empty and deep. Water collected and formed a small lake called the Small Fish Lake. It lay 5 *li* northeast of Qin Huang Ling and was 4 *li* in circumference.'

Evidently the place name and its origin were well known to Li Daoyuan.

Other evidence of the construction of the tomb was found in 1973 at the site of Zhengzhuang, just under a mile northwest of the outer enclosure of the *lingyuan*. The site was found to contain the remains of various buildings, tools such as hammers and chisels made of iron, handcuffs and collars also of iron, and bronze weapons, earthenware, and fragments of dressed and undressed stone. These finds revealed that the site had been used for dressing stone, of which 975,000 cubic yards had been used in the construction of the tomb, and that the work had been carried out by conscripts (shown by the handcuffs and collars) supervised by functionaries resident in the buildings. Though no trace remains of the functionaries, the existence of the conscripts is confirmed by two huge burial areas to the west of the outer enclosure.

THE CONSCRIPTS' CEMETERIES

Of the 700,000 conscripts, according to Sima Qian, who worked on the construction of the Lishan Lingyuan, hundreds died there, as is revealed by a vast burial area found between the villages of Zhaobeihu and Yaochitou to the west of the mound and explored between 1978 and 1980. In the section of the cemetery in Zhaobeihu, of the 114 graves identified in parallel rows, 32 have been excavated. Some of these were individual graves, others common ones of varying size and form. In total 100 individuals were excavated: with the exception of three adult females and two children, the skeletons were of men generally between the ages of 20 and 30 years of age. Analysis of the skeletons has shown that not all died of natural causes. In Pit M34 (the largest so far excavated at a size of 34'9" x 3'7"), eleven bodies were laid out on three levels: the limbs of the three skeletons on the second level, say the excavators, had been mutilated before burial. However, as the skulls were also separate from the bodies and the bones of each individual neatly piled, we cannot discount the possibility that the dismembered skeletons were reordered when the layer of bodies above was buried. Certainly one of the eight individuals in grave M33 suffered a violent death, as his bones show clear traces of the use of a cutting weapon. These marks are very similar to those on the skull of the individual buried in grave M41. Experts are awaiting with great interest the results of the paleopathological analysis of all these skeletons as they may reveal much about the conditions of life and work of the conscripts. In several cases, we are aware of personal facts regarding the conscripts as in many of the graves the bodies were buried with a large fragment of tile on which the name, provenance, residence and, in some cases, rank and title of the individual were scratched. These unfortunate subjects of the August Sovereign, originally from many of the newly conquered territories, were legally referred to as *juci*, a term that has been explained by one of the legal codices found at Shuihudi. *Juci* were individuals punished with compulsory work for a misdemeanor or to settle a debt owed to the State. Not being true criminals condemned to forced labor, the *juci* were not only allowed some basic rights – like keeping their name and being allowed their own money (bronze *banliang* coins were found in several graves) – but they also retained their rank and title. Nor can it be excluded that the women and children found in the cemetery were family members, in which case this would be evidence of the principle of joint responsibility that underlay the Qin penal code. During the brief reign of the Second August Sovereign, this code was made more severe after the emperor fell victim to the wicked designs of the eunuch Zhao Gao. Zhao Gao became first minister after plotting against Li Si and forced the young emperor to harshen interpretation of the laws and to increase the penalties, in particular with regard to members of the imperial family and Qin aristocracy. A real period of 'Terror' occurred during which many of these unfortunates were put to death.

According to some Chinese scholars, some of the tombs of accompaniment in the area of the Lishan Lingyuan may have belonged to those unlucky members of the imperial family.

These fragments of tiles were discovered in two graves in the in the burial area – found between the villages of Zhaobeihu and Yaochitou to the west of the mound and explored between 1978 and 1980 – that houses the tombs of the conscripts who worked on the construction of the Lishan Lingyuan. Seven hundred thousand conscripts, or juci *– individuals punished with forced labor for an offence or to settle a debt owed to the State – worked on the complex between 221 and 210 BC and hundreds died there. As they were not true criminals condemned to forced labor, the* juci *retained some basic rights, such as keeping their name and being allowed their own money (as testified by the bronze* banliang *coins found in several graves), and sometimes also their rank and title. In the cemetery in Zhaobeihu, 32 of the 114 graves have been excavated and in many of these the bodies were buried with a fragment of tile on which the name, provenance, residence and, in some cases, rank and title of the individual were scratched. The inscription* Dong Wu Bu Geng Suo Ci *on that on the left tells us about the age and origin of the deceased: "Young conscript from Dongwu." (Lintong, Terracotta Army Museum)*

The highest aspirations that a morally upright man had at the time of the First Emperor were to be a useful servant of the sovereign, to work on his behalf with dignity and loyalty, to receive his favors and esteem, and to be a part of the administration or the army. They were the same aspirations that Sima Qian manifested in a heart-rending letter written to his friend Ren An between 93–91 BC. The letter has survived in the Biography of Sima Qian included in the *Han Shu* (History of the Han Dynasty) written by the historian Ban Gu (32–92 AD). It is one of the most beautiful and compassionate pages in all of Chinese literature. Despite the shattering moral pain of having been unjustly punished with castration for a presumed act of insubordination, the Great Historian manifests great sadness at not having succeeded in serving his emperor well.

This was not the case for the army general Huo Qubing, who was so highly regarded by the Han emperor Wu Di (140–87 BC) that he was awarded the honor of being buried next to the Maoling Funerary Garden. In life as in death, the closer one was to the emperor, the greater the honor. This is the explanation of the 'graves of accompaniment' in the funerary gardens of the Chinese emperors starting with the First August Sovereign. Princes and princesses of royal blood, wives and concubines, ministers and generals:

this was the retinue whose duty it was to accompany the spirit of the dead emperor.

So far three main groups of graves of accompaniment have been found in Lishan Funerary Garden, and a few isolated graves like the one near the four pits of the Terracotta Army.

In the area between the inner and outer enclosures of the burial mound, north of the two west gates, a group of 61 graves has been found, each rectangular with one or two access ramps. To date it appears that none of these graves has been excavated, but preliminary soundings have revealed that many of them are inexplicably empty.

This group includes one of the largest graves of accompaniment yet studied; it measures 17 x 16 yards and has a ramp 17.3 yards long. It is highly likely that this was the grave of Prince Gao, one of the many sons of Qin Shi Huangdi. Gao was offered the throne after Er Shi Huangdi, but refused for respect of his dead father and, above all, so as not to lose the right to be buried near to him.

Twenty-eight rectangular tombs with ramps on the north side have been identified inside the walled space that forms the northeast quadrant of the outer enclosure. They are laid out in three rows to cover an overall area of 199,014 square yards, but nor in this case has any one of the graves been excavat-

ed. However, their proximity to the burial mound of the First August Sovereign has suggested that they may be the tombs of his young wives and concubines who, as Sima Qian reported, the Second August Sovereign ordered should follow the First Emperor to the grave at the time of the emperor's burial. Only future examination will support or prove wrong this harrowing, though credible, claim.

About 380 yards east of the outer enclosure, near the village of Shangjiao, a further seventeen graves have been found that lie south-north parallel to the Pits of the Imperial Stables. Eight of the graves were excavated between October 1976 and January 1977. All the burial pits, except one with a ramp facing west, are of two main types, both of which are typically Qin: the first has a deep rectangular pit in the shape of an overturned truncated pyramid, with a niche dug in the north wall (about 7 feet from the mouth) as has often been seen in earlier Qin tombs, or a storage space dug at the end of the south wall of the ramp where some of the grave goods were placed. The second type of grave is composed of a rectangular or diamond-shaped pit, at the base of which, on the east side, is a wide bay where the sarcophagus was laid. In this second type the grave goods were placed either in a bay dug on the north side, or inside the 'burial chamber,' or at the base

These clay models of granaries made to be placed in tombs were a typical feature of Qin funerary ritual from the middle/late Spring and Autumn period: the wish for a plentiful harvest evidently also accompanied the deceased into the afterlife. Their presence in Qin tombs, along with minqi *depicting farm carts drawn by oxen, represents evidence of the new attention to real life in the composition of grave goods.*

of the pit just in front of the entrance to the sarcophagus bay that was usually closed by a door or wall made of planks.

The use of these graves by members of the Qin aristocracy is shown by the size and shape of the pit and by the use of an outer and inner sarcophagus (*guo* and *guan*), both made from tree trunks or large planks. In some cases the inner sarcophagus was divided into two levels: the lower one was where the body was placed, and the upper part contained some of the grave goods, probably the deceased's clothing to judge by silk fragments found.

The discovery of these graves has provided valuable information on the funerary models of the Qin dynasty. The structure of the tombs demonstrates that certain Qin elements (like the side niche) were maintained and that the model of a burial bay with a storage place was becoming more common, though distinct from the 'burial chamber,' which was developing into an area of access to the grave, either with or without a ramp. This concept was further developed during the Han dynasty with the use of T-shaped brick structures consisting of a burial chamber and two side storage areas. It is interesting to note how the structure of the two sarcophagi resembles southern Chinese practices, for example, from the kingdom of Chu; however, this should not be surprising as we know how much the Qin absorbed other cultures into its own.

The eight graves uncovered were all dug for individuals but only in seven cases has it been possible to conduct a preliminary analysis of the bones. The dismembered skeleton of a young woman aged 18–20 was found in M17; a woman about 10 years older was buried in a supine position in M11; and men aged about 30 were buried individually in graves M10, M12, M15 and M16, however in these cases the skeletons were not only dismembered but often spread around their graves, both inside and outside the sarcophagi.

With regard to the grave goods found, some were common objects though exclusive to the Qin people from the start of the Warring States period; examples are the clay *hu* jars with a 'garlic head' rim, the bronze boilers (called *fu*) for steam cooking, and the small clay models of granaries that have a roof made of wooden beams often topped by a small bird. Other goods reveal exchanges with different cultural areas, such as a type of spherical bronze vase (a sort of cooking pot common in the regions of Ba-Shu culture in Sichuan), with two rings of different diameter on the shoulder of the pot on opposite sides; or articles common in type to many of the Warring States but with local characteristics, like thin bronze mirrors or bronze belt hooks in the form of seahorses, goslings and individual or intertwined dragons. Examples of these were faithfully reproduced in belts worn by the terracotta soldiers.

Some of these graves were found to contain unusual grave goods, like the case of a sort of silver handle in the form of a toad inscribed with the characters *Shao Fu* ([belonging to the] Palace of the Young Lord) and the two bronze seals for private use found in graves M11 and M16.

It is the opinion of some Chinese specialists — and the data would seem to back them up — that the eastern group of graves was that of the members of the imperial family and Qin functionaries that Er Shi Huangdi, then dominated by the eunuch Zhao Gao, sentenced to death in spring 208 BC. If what Sima Qian wrote was true, the purges of that year were extreme, with the aim of eliminating any form of opposition in the court. Yet it was not the oppressed palace aristocracy that put an end to the dynasty, but the nebulous world of the conscripts, made up not just of galley slaves, impoverished peasants and 'tax dodgers,' but also functionaries, intellectuals and aristocrats from every part of the empire, right from the period of the First Emperor. This is clear from the inscriptions found in the conscripts' cemetery.

EPILOGUE: A MISTERY SOLVED

In the fourth month of 209 BC, the Second August Sovereign decided that work on the funeral mound of his father was complete, but not that on the A'fang Palace. As the Great Historian reports, the construction of A'fang was restarted at the same time as a new stimulus was given to the military campaigns to conquer the 'barbarians of the four directions.' The strain on the imperial economy was increased further to provide for the troops distributed on the various fronts, those located in the capital (who had been increased by 50,000 crossbowmen called up from various regions) and the conscripts working on A'fang. According to Sima Qian: 'Within a radius of 300 *li* from Xianyang, peasants were prohibited from eating their own grain. Thus the laws and regulations became increasingly severe.'

Although he writes from an ethical and typically Confucian standpoint, in his considerations at the end of the chapter *Qin Shi Huang Ben Ji* (Basic Annals of the First Qin Emperor) Sima Qian is not wrong when he says the reason for the fall of the Qin dynasty was political. He wrote that the kingdom of Qin brought an end to the Warring States and created the empire, but it was unable to recognize the 'technical' difference between the art of conquest and the art of maintaining conquered subjects. The Great Historian did not say that the First August Sovereign was hated for the bizarre aspects of his character or for his vain search for the elixir of immortality, but for having been heedless of the expectations of peace and security that the people harbored after the cruel centuries of the Warring States, and he adds that the dynasty could have been saved if only the Second August Sovereign had been minimally mindful of the needs for peace and stability in the empire. In other words, the Qin dynasty fell due to its loss of popular consensus.

It was an obscure conscript, a certain Chen She, who in the seventh month of 209 BC organized a band of rebels, gave himself the title 'king of Chu' and set off a revolt. After a year, Chen She was killed, but so was the Second Emperor as a result of a palace conspiracy conceived by Zhao Gao. In any case, there were already other revolts taking place and the nomination of Ziying, the son of one of the Second August Sovereign's brothers, as king of Qin made no impression. The imperial title no longer had any meaning as the leaders of the rebels had already recreated the six kingdoms defeated and annexed by Qin Shi Huangdi.

After just forty-six days of rule, the young Ziying surrendered and handed the seal and symbols of the Son of Heaven to the duke of Pei, Liu Bang. Liu Bang was the lieutenant of Xiang Yu, commander of the forces of Chu and, a few years later, the founder of the Han dynasty.

'The duke of Pei entered Xianyang, sealed the palaces and stores, then camped at Banshang. After almost a month had passed, feudal armies arrived of which Xiang Yu was the head. He killed Ziying and all the descendants of the Qin aristocracy. He massacred the people of Xianyang, burned the palaces and took prisoner their staff, both men and women, he confiscated their goods which he distributed among the feudal lords. With Qin defeated, the territory was divided up [between] three [kings] named King of Yong, King of Sai, King of Di, known as the Three Qin. Xiang Yu declared himself the Leader King of Chu of the West, with solemn proclamations he divided the world up between the feudal lords so that Qin no longer existed. After five years had passed, the world had been made stable and united by the Han.'

The final passage of the *Qin Shi Huang Ben Ji* clearly states that the goal of the rebels was to restore the feudality of the Warring States period, and the possibility cannot be dismissed that the rebels included members of the aristocracies that had not submitted to Qin Shi Huangdi.

This group of gray clay vases exemplifies the types of containers placed in the grave goods of the sacrificial pits and graves of accompaniment in the area of the Funerary Garden of Mount Li. They are designed to hold liquids and are generally stamped with a seal identifying the place of manufacture on the upper or lower part of the vessell. (Lintong, Terracotta Army Museum)

Nobles may well have been among the 'bandits' who lived in hiding, often mentioned in Qin documents to which Sima Qian had access. The allusion to the feudal system is also evident in the title chosen by Xiang Yu, formed by the concept of king (*wang*) and leader (*ba*), which evoked the political climate of the Spring and Autumn and Warring States periods.

The final passage also states that, with the destruction of Xianyang, something terrible and unprecedented occurred: the entire city was destroyed, including the ancestral temples and all the members of the Qin household. This means that nobody could ever more make sacrifices to the forefathers of the clan; this was an unheard of abomination that not even the terrible King Zheng, the future Qin Shi Huangdi, had dared to unleash on the households he defeated and subjected.

As a result of this bloodbath and devastation, what happened to the last resting place of the hated First Emperor of the Qin dynasty in the Mount Li Funerary Garden? It has been pointed out that many of the excavated structures show traces of a fire. A passage from the section 'River Wei' in the *Shui Jing Zhu* (Commentary on the Classic of the Waters) reminds us that the mysterious tomb of the First August Sovereign may not hide any more treasures as Xiang Yu went to the Lishan Lingyuan, approached the tomb, and … '… opened it. Three hundred thousand people in thirty days were unable to remove all the treasures. Thieves and robbers came from east of the Tongguan gate to melt down the sarcophagi to make copper. Shepherds who had been herding their sheep in that place set fire to it and the fire lasted ninety days without going out.'

Thieves and robbers came from the east but the majestic terracotta army that faced that direction was unable to stop them as it was not their duty to fight off an enemy made of flesh and blood. Then, around the 5th century AD, the tomb was pillaged again.

THE EMPEROR'S FORTUNE

We have mentioned several times that the passages in Sima Qian's *Shi Ji* that denigrate the person of Qin Shi Huangdi and his family are insertions by others that do not reflect on the moral integrity of the great historian. Yet it cannot be denied that Confucian historiography – commencing with Jia Yi (201-169 BC), author of the essay *The Sins of the Qin*, and continued by Sima Qian – has always been extremely negative in its appraisal of the First August Sovereign and his achievements, to the extent of transforming him into an antihero. The Confucians never forgave Qin Shi Huangdi for having had the opportunity to restore the Zhou feudal system and the moral supremacy of the Son of Heaven, not so much in its historical form as in the ethical expression elucidated by Confucius, but having instead rejected this possibility in favor of, as Derk Bodde has recently written, "… a transformation of the face of China so great both quantitatively and qualitatively that it deserves the name 'revolution' even though it was imposed from the top and not forced from below. This, rather than the transfer of political power brought about by the anti-Qin peasant rebellion, was the true revolution of ancient China. Indeed, it was China's only revolution until the present century."

On the other hand, the successive Han dynasty continued the centralized Qin model and, in particular, the organization of the state administration. This was both Confucian and Legalist and controlled centrally from above, but it was free to adapt itself to suit local circumstances. This centralized but flexible model was developed further under the Han and continued to adapt to historical and political events for another 1,700 years until the early 20th century.

Whilst it is true that a dim view started to be taken of the figure of Qin Shi Huangdi during the period of the Han dynasty, it is also true that the attitude of the Han emperors towards this awkward personality were always respectful, at least from a ritual point of view.

Indeed, we know that in 195 BC, 15 years after the death of Qin Shi Huangdi, Liu Bang, i.e., Gao Zu, the first emperor of the Han dynasty, ruled that 20 families should reside in the area of the Mount Li Funerary Garden to continue to perform the rites in honor of the deceased. Indirect evidence of this assignment was provided by the publication in 2004 of the details of excavations performed in 1986 that unearthed two graves from the Han period situated between the two large enclosures, near the southwest corner of the inner one, not far from the Pits of the Menagerie. The second of these graves contained the remains of an individual placed inside a double sarcophagus, a symbol of high rank, but accompanied by a handful of grave goods, including a gray clay "cocoon" vase typical of the Qin period. The first of the graves also housed a double sarcophagus and featured a richer collection of grave goods, revealing that the deceased occupant was a *shi*, a high-ranking functionary. Both the burial methods and the type of grave goods indicate that the two graves can be dated to the early decades of the Han dynasty. Although, we have no way of knowing if the two occupants belonged to the families ordered by Liu Bang to serve in the Funerary Garden, their presence and the fact that they were no ordinary graves appears to indicate that the location was not abandoned by the new dynasty.

Although Qin Shi Huangdi was never forgotten, it was only thanks to President Mao that the First August Sovereign returned to the center of attention of historians. It was in 1958, just after the One Hundred Flowers Campaign that had been devised to animate the political and cultural debate within the Chinese Communist Party. Dozens of biographies and essays were produced on the First August Sovereign during the 1970s, making him one of the best known figures in ancient Chinese history, however, all this fame would never have grown to such proportions without the coincidental discovery of the Terracotta Army.

In a country of avid readers far removed from consumerism, such as 1970s China, and in which that powerful means of mass communication, television, was still pretty much absent, political propaganda was communicated through daily papers, essays, political journals and graphical art Individual episodes and figures from ancient Chinese history, and the Warring States, Qin and Han periods in particular, were recounted in short illustrated stories in which the progressive spirit of the Legalist heroes tended to be praised at the expense of the reactionary spirit of the Confucians, usually presented as "champions" of the (in many ways mythical) state of slavery who invariably ended up being humiliated or beaten. The style of the generally black and white illustrations in these "educational" works aimed mainly at the young was chiefly based on formal models of Chinese-style Social Realism, which also reigned in the films of the time and were seen in historical epics as well as the Peking Opera and popular theater. However, the illustrators had a certain degree of originality, particularly those able to marry tradition with modernity and reinvent a vision of ancient China through new interpretations of historical iconography, in particular the clay tiles with stamped decorations used in the Han period to line tombs that formed one of the earliest examples of landscape art in China.

With the death of Mao Zedong in 1976, Qin Shi Huangdi did not return to the attic of history. Indeed, the discovery of the Terracotta Army was attracting the attention of the entire world to his tomb. The discovery and immediate transformation of Pit I into a museum exerted an irresistible appeal on the international tourist industry, which began to turn to the newly opened China during the early 1980s. The three pits of the Terracotta Army were proclaimed the "Eighth Wonder of the World" and the "greatest archaeological discovery of the twentieth century." All political leaders who visited China went to pay homage

to the findings, which rapidly became a means for expanding scientific knowledge of ancient China and an unprecedented opportunity for the economic development of the entire Xi'an region.

It must be said that the administrators of the Cultural Heritage of the Province of Shaanxi (well supported by Beijing) have successfully exploited the possibilities for cultural, social and economic growth offered by their exceptional and unique resource, one of the most important examples of the ancient history of the Chinese people.

Quite justifiably, on December 11, 1987 the Lishan Lingyuan was inscribed in the list of world monuments protected by UNESCO, thus becoming part of the world's cultural heritage.

Since the discovery, the emperor's fame and that of his mute and patiently aligned soldiers have merged and captured the collective imagination. Even the detective of the impossible, Martin Mystère, has encountered the terracotta soldiers in two episodes — *Intrigue in Beijing* and *The Terracotta Army*, written by S. Deidda and A. Castelli — in which an evil and mysterious woman named Li Voxian succeeds in animating and leading them in a fight to the death that risks setting East against West. Whereas the Army has inspired comics, the emperor has been the subject of films and soap operas that have kept the Chinese public glued to their TV sets for weeks. One such film was *The Emperor and the Assassin* by the famous Chinese director Chen Kaige. The 1999 work had superb settings and localization, particularly the costumes designed by Mo Xiaomin. The plot followed Sima Qian's account almost faithfully and was constructed around the personal feelings of the August Sovereign, interpreted by Li Xuejian with great passion. The narration made three key points: the first centered on the emperor's unfortunate origins and analyzed the relationship between the young man and his supposed father, Lü Buwei, portrayed by Chen Kaige himself; the

second focused on the personal drama between Qin Shi Huangdi and his mother during her affair with Lao Ai; and the third played on the emperor's relationship with death, symbolized by the episode of his attempted assassination by a hitman from Yan in accordance with the account related by Sima Qian. The interplay of contrasting emotions shown by Qin Shi Huangdi in these three relationships is interwoven with an aspect of his personality of which Sima Qian does not speak: love, in particular his love for a woman from Zhao, played splendidly by Gong Li. Qin Shi Huangdi met her as a girl when he was still the young Ying Zheng, the son of a peace hostage. In his depiction of the emperor's rule, Chen Kaige clearly emphasizes what for many made the First August Sovereign a great leader, i.e., his fulfillment of the design of power and unity developed by the dukes and kings of Qin who had preceded him. But this aspiration, according to the director Chen Kaige, unleashed the emperor's obsession — expressed by the voice that is heard only by Ying Zheng, "Remember your ancestors' dream to unite China" — which was to overwhelm him, preventing him from being a son, lover, friend or a just ruler.

Equally poetic, but perhaps with a more fascinating taste for mental hyperbole than that expressed by the Chinese film director, is the reflection by Jorge Luis Borges on the First August Sovereign, dating back to well before the discovery of the Terracotta Army and contained in the short essay *La Muralla y los Libros* (The Wall and the Books, 1950) which opens his collection *Otras Inquisiciones* (Other Inquisitions). In this essay, which the author refers to simply as a "note," Borges thoroughly examines the contradiction (as apparent in Sima Qian's account) between the appalling burning of the history books on the one hand and the cyclopic construction of the Great Wall on the other. Borges claims a metaphor is hidden in these two acts:

"…Perhaps Shih Huang Ti condemned

those who adored the past to a work as vast as the past and just as pointless. …

…The massive wall, that now, as always, looks over lands that will never see its shadows, is itself the shadow of a Caesar who ordered the most reverent of nations to burn its past; it is probable that this idea affects us by itself, regardless of the conjectures it conjures up…"

In any case, the idea of grandiosity that Qin Shi Huangdi's work expressed in its fulfillment of his ancestors' dream is, with the help of his silent army, a statement of a magical vision, and the same is true of his last resting place. It was not only a tomb, a funerary monument or mausoleum, the place in which the First August Sovereign of the Qin dynasty wished to be buried, nor was it just a manifestation of power intended as a warning to his contemporaries and as a memory for those who came after. Perhaps it was and is all these things together, but it is above all a magical universe.

Sima Qian wrote that in the last years of the emperor's reign, the mind of the ruler was tormented by the foolish and arrogant notion of reaching the Islands of the Immortals so that he might receive the elixir of immortality. This is a theory that a science such as archaeology would have great difficulty ever verifying, but is there any sense in attempting to do so if the answer is already there before our eyes? I actually believe that the answer is affirmative, that the emissaries of the First August Sovereign reached the Islands of the Immortals and were given the elixir, but on one condition: Qin Shi Huang could have immortality but only in exchange for his personal glory. And the emperor made his choice.

One day the tomb will be excavated and a small, unopened ampoule will be found in a corner, among the burnt treasures beneath a pile of ash. The smile of the emperor will hang in the air: just before his death he understood that the only real immortality is to survive in human memory, and thus it has been.

<hr />

276-277 The eerie silence of the pit ready to be sealed for eternity: this may be how the Emperor saw his soldiers arrayed in close ranks, silent warriors who seem ready to return to life at a prearranged signal. It is impossible not to feel the mystery and magnificence of a work that has defied the centuries to immortalize the memory of its creator, the First August Sovereign of a short-lived dynasty that nonetheless managed to achieve an everlasting project: the unification of the Warring States and the creation of a new nation, China.

THE PHOTOGRAPHER'S CHALLENGE

I have been photographing works of art, paintings, statues, jewelry, and both lesser-known and world-famous archaeological sites for many years. I have seen dawn break over Lake Nasser from the Temple of Ramesses and the last rays of the sun set ablaze the stones of Leptis Magna during extenuating, but rewarding, photo shoots. After spending time in Egypt, I thought I had reached the height of the experience of total fusion of self with subject, that sublime sensation of being attuned to the object being photographed, which enables the picture to come to life. Then I received the telephone call that was to take me Lintong in China. My task was to photograph the Terracotta Army. Once again I had to immerse myself in the centuries, but this time it was different, with another culture and other forms and sensations. I was accompanied by Guido, my assistant, and when we reached the site — following a grueling journey and a two-week wait at customs with 23 cases of photographic material and over 1,750 pounds of equipment — we were full of expectations. We were presented with an enormous hangar, large enough to house two jumbo jets. We looked around, perplexed, seeking something bearing a resemblance to the mental images of the mysterious army. However, once inside, the spectacle took our breath away: a chasm in the earth opens up around a multitude of soldiers, as if it had swallowed them, just as they are, arranged in parallel rows. The power of the sight stems from its realistic depiction, for the statues live, arouse fear and inspire veneration. I am accustomed to the power of images, but it is enormous here. We were intimidated at the sight of this huge army of 6,000 archers, foot soldiers and horsemen. I descended among them, carefully moving between the bodies, and was almost afraid that they might wake up and commence battle. They are imposing and each figure has its own personality. I scanned the faces for an angle that would enable me to capture the lines of the eyes, the motionless expression and the realistic imperfections. The formal canons of balance and symmetry, as construed by ancient art in both Cairo and Rome and to which my photographer's eyes are accustomed, do not exist here. Lintong represents a personal challenge for me, a way of rethinking light, distance, color and photography itself. The term "challenge" often comes to mind when I recall the relentless heat that we suffered in the excavated pits of the vast archaeological site to photograph the stone armor as it had been found: thousands of partially unearthed stone plates in 23-foot deep pits. The temperature was 122°F with a relative humidity of 100%, and the equipment was so hot that it could not be touched. The bronze chariots in the museum were enclosed by bulletproof sheets of glass measuring 16 feet by 13. At least ten especially shielded lights were necessary to penetrate the barrier. I captured thousands of images: hands clenched around invisible weapons, contracted bodies ready to leap to a silent command, the exquisitely worked harnesses and the meticulously reproduced personal objects. I witnessed the mystery of death in the ancient world, the attempt to preserve prestige and reinforce the memory. I am a photographer of works of art and I am accustomed to the task. However, this time the allure of Lintong was immense, and almost as great as its buried army.

278 *The face of this foot soldier bears witness to the art of the modeler who created it and skillfully used a wooden tool to harmonize the soft lines and curves of the eyebrows, nose and lips with the almost sharp angularity of the eyes, moustache and hair.*

279 *The photographer Araldo De Luca is shown (left) as he uses the optical bench, while his assistant (right) prepares the photography set with umbrellas and diffusers. The equipment was transported in 23 cases with a total weight of over 1,750 pounds.*

"Animalistic" style, a decorative and figurative style of the herder peoples of the steppe, which favors the depiction of animals, often moving or in mirror images.

A'fang, or E'pang, name of Qin Shi Huangdi's last imperial palace, unfinished at his death and located in the suburbs of modern-day Xi'an.

Ba, literally "Elder", but usually translated as "Leader", the term used to indicate the chief of the feudal alliances that were officially formed during the Spring and Autumn period to defend the Zhou king.

Banliang, a circular coin with square central hole worth "half a *liang*". A typical Qin coin from the late fourth century BC, which remained substantially unchanged up until the twentieth century.

Bu zhang, a sort of priest/augur, who was responsible for determining the right moment for a certain action by means of propitiatory sacrifices and divination.

Caldron or *fu* pot, any ceramic or bronze cooking vessel.

Chanbu, "spade coin", (or *kongshoubu*, "hollow head coin"), a type of bronze coin shaped like a miniature spade with two straight prongs (from which it takes its name), minted from the sixth century BC in the kingdom of the Eastern Zhou and the dukedom of Jin.

Chu, a powerful non-Hua Xia cultural and political entity and the cradle of a highly sophisticated civilization born from the fusion of different cultural elements in the middle Yangzi valley, but considered "barbarian" by the states of the Huanghe valley. In 706 BC one of its rulers adopted the title *Wang* (king), which was traditionally only used by the Zhou sovereigns.

Ding tripod, the most widespread ceramic or bronze vase with three solid feet. It was used to cook or serve food. Precise sumptuary regulations determined the number (always odd) of bronze tripod vases in the grave goods featured in the funeral rituals of the time of the Zhou dynasty.

The legendary "Nine Tripods" made of bronze were the symbol of Zhou regality.

Dou cup, a ceramic or bronze cup on a tall pedestal with a lid that was used to preserve, present and consume ritual foods, particularly during the Eastern Zhou period. The lid could be turned over and used as a bowl.

Feng, an enfeoffment ceremony during which the Zhou king (*wang*) granted a fortified city and its territory (*guo*), including its urban (*guoren*) and rural (*yeren*) population, preferably to a member of his own clan.

Ge halberd, a short bronze blade, possibly developed from a Neolithic stone prototype, which was secured to the tip of a long wooden shaft and used to spear and strike adversaries.

Gui bowl, a hemispherical vase with ring feet, often featuring two handles. As a ritual bronze vase, this kind of vessel was used to hold and serve the food eaten during ritual banquets. Along with *ding* tripods, it was used as a mark of status in the grave goods of the Zhou nobility.

Hangtu, a building technique consisting of the creation of layers of earth that were mallet-tamped until concrete hard. It was known as early as the Neolithic age and is still used in several rural regions of China.

Hann, the smallest of the three states (Wei, Zhao and Hann) that formed following the breakup of the dukedom of Jin. The double "n" at the end of the name is not actually an exact transcription of the Chinese, but was adopted to distinguish Hann from Han, the name adopted by the dynasty that followed that of the Qin.

He pitcher, generally any container with feet and a cylindrical spout used for pouring its liquid contents. In the case of ritual bronzes, the term refers to a type of pitcher with four feet and a cover that was used to heat spirits.

Hu bottle, the term denotes function rather than form and refers to any container – ceramic or bronze – with a mouth narrower than its body, used to contain or transport liquids.

Hun, the most ethereal component of the soul (also known as *hun* spirit), which leaves the perishable body at the moment of death on a dangerous journey towards the world of the spirits.

Mingqi, "spirit goods", in the broadest sense "substitute objects", used to denote all kinds of copies of real things, men or animals expressly manufactured to be placed in the grave goods that accompanied the deceased.

Nao bell, similar in shape to the *zhong* but fitted with a handle that enabled it to be secured on a wooden support, mouth upwards. The *nao* was also played as a percussion instrument.

Pan basin, a ritual bronze vase used to wash other vessels or for ablutions during ritual ceremonies. In the grave goods of the Spring and Autumn period, it is associated with *ding* tripods and other vases for ablutions and indicates the hierarchical level of the deceased in the Zhou aristocratic system.

Po, the heaviest component of the soul (also known as the *po* spirit), which resided in the tomb with the deceased until the body had completely decomposed.

Shang Di, the supreme spiritual power in the religion of the time of the Shang dynasty. Some scholars claim that it can be identified with the spirit of the first ancestor of the Shang royal clan.

Shi, originally members of the warrior class, although during the Spring and Autumn period the term came to denote the members of the lower branches of the noble houses educated in the "Six Arts" (rites, music, archery, war chariot driving, calligraphy and mathematics) Many of the great philosophers of the Spring and Autumn and Warring States periods, including Confucius, belonged to this social class.

Tai Fu, an upper-middle level in the hierarchy of court functionaries during the time of the Western dynasty.

Tian, literally "Heaven", the highest deity from the Zhou period onward.

Tianming, "Decree of Heaven" or "Heavenly Mandate", i.e. the will of Heaven in the case of the bestowal of the responsibilities of highest government on worthy and deserving people.

Tianxia, literally "everything under Heaven", indicating the civilized world.

Tianzi, literally "Son of Heaven", a title of the emperor.

Wey, an important fief in the northeastern area of Henan province that was established at the beginning of the Zhou dynasty. The transcription with a final "y" was adopted to distinguish it from Wei, one of the three states that formed following the breakup of Jin.

Yao keng, a small pit for sacrificial victims at the far end of the burial chamber in royal and princely tombs of the Shang dynasty and, less frequently, the successive Zhou dynasty. It contained either a dog or a soldier, or both.

Yi, a ewer, a ritual bronze vase used from the middle of the Western Zhou period for the purification of the officiant's hands during ritual ceremonies.

Yu basin, smaller than the *pan*, which it sometimes replaces in the grave goods of the aristocracy of the Qin dukedom.

Zhong bell, a very popular bronze musical instrument in the aristocratic circles of the Western Zhou dynasty. This trapezoidal-shaped percussion instrument had an accessory that enabled it to be suspended. One or more rows of *zhong* of varying sizes, pitch and tone were generally hung on racks in groups known as carillons. However, special very large bells (called *te zhong* and *bo zhong*) were used individually.

Zhongguo, Middle Kingdom, or *Zhonghua*, Central Flower, one of the most ancient terms used by the Chinese to define their country, which has resisted until the present (e.g. *Zhonghua Renmin Gongheguo* – People's Republic of China).

BIBLIOGRAPHY OF TEXTS
ROBERTO CIARLA

Bodde, Derk, *China's First Unifier: A study of the Ch'in dynasty as seen in the life of Li Ssu (280?-208 B.C.)* (Leiden: Brill, 1938)

Bodde, Derk, "The state and empire of Ch'in", in D. Twitchett and M. Loewe (eds.), *The Cambridge History of Ancient China. The Ch'in and Han Empires 221 B.C. - A.D. 220*, Vol. I (Cambridge: Cambridge University Press, 1986) 20-102

Borges, Jorge Luis, *Altre Inquisizioni*, foreword by Francesco Tentori Montalto (Milan: Feltrinelli, 1996)

Chang, Kwang-chih. *Shang Civilization* (New Haven and London: Yale University Press, 1980)

Chang, Kwang-chih, *The Archaeology of Ancient China*, 4th edn. (New Haven and London: Yale University Press, 1986)

(The) Ch'in Dynasty Pit Archaeological Team, "Excavation of the Ch'in Dynasty Pit Containing Pottery Figures of Warriors and Horses at Ling-T'ung, Shenxi Province", trans. Albert E. Dien, *Chinese Studies in Archaeology*, Summer 1979, I (I), 8-55

Ciarla, Roberto, "La Cina nella prima età del bronzo (2100-1100 a.C.)", in *Atlante di Archeologia* (Turin: Garzanti-Utet, 1994), 158-159

Ciarla, Roberto, "La Cina nell'epoca Zhou (1100-221 a.C.)", in *Atlante di Archeologia* (Turin: Garzanti-Utet, 1994), 160-161

Ciarla, Roberto, "La Cina nel periodo Qin e Han", in *Atlante di Archeologia* (Turin: Garzanti-Utet, 1994), 162-163

Ciarla, Roberto (ed.), *Cina 220 A.C. I guerrieri di Xi'an* (Milan: Editoriale Segesta, 1994)

Ciarla, Roberto, "Dalle prime società agricole alle società complesse: Estremo Oriente", in *Il Mondo dell'Archeologia*, Vol. I (Rome: Istituto dell'Enciclopedia Italiana, 2002), 567-573

Ciarla, Roberto, "L'Archeologia dell'Estremo Oriente: Cina", in *Il Mondo dell'Archeologia*, Vol. I (Rome: Istituto dell'Enciclopedia Italiana, 2002), 68-72

Sun Tzu, *The Art of War*, trans. Alessandro Corneli, (Naples: Guida Editori, 1988)

Cotterell, Arthur, *Ch'in Shih-Huang-Ti Primo Imperatore della Cina: l'emozionante scoperta della sua tomba* (Milan: Rusconi, 1981)

de Bary, Wm. Theodore and Irene Bloom, *Sources of Chinese Tradition. From Earliest Times to 1600*, Vol. I (New York: Columbia University Press, 1999)

Duyvendak, J.J.L., (eds.) *Book of the Lord of Shang*, trans. Alessandro Passi (Milan: Adelphi Edizioni, 1989)

Falkenhausen, Lothar von, "The Waning of the Bronze Age", in M. Loewe and E. L. Shaughnessy (eds.), *The Cambridge History of Ancient China from the Origins of Civilization to 221 B.C.*, (Cambridge: Cambridge University Press, 1999), 486-497

Han Wei, *Lüelun Shaanxi Chunqiu Zhangguo Qin mu* (On the Qin Graves of the Spring and Autumn and Warring States Periods in Shaanxi Province) (Kao Gu yu Wen Wu, 1981) I: 83-93

Hearn, Maxwell K., "The Terracotta Army of the First Emperor of Qin (221-206 B.C.)", in Wen Fong (ed.), *The Great Bronze Age of China: an exhibition from the People's Republic of China* (New York: The Metropolitan Museum of Art, 1980), 351-373

Hsun, Cho-yun and Linduff, Katheryn M., *Western Chou Civilization* (New Haven and London: Yale University Press, 1988)

Legge, James, *The Chinese Classics* (Oxford, 1893, rpt. in five volumes Hong Kong, 1960)

Li Xueqin, *Eastern Zhou and Qin Civilizations* (New Haven and London: Yale University Press, 1985)

Lewis, Mark Edward, *Writing and Authority in Early China* (Albany: State University of New York Press, 1999)

Macdonald, Fiona, and James, John, *Nella Cina di Ch'in Shi Huang il Grande Imperatore* (Florence: Giunti Marzocco, 1989)

Meng Jianmin, Zhang Lin, *Awakened, Qin's Terracotta Army* (Xi'an: Shaanxi Travel & Tourism Press, 2001)

Sima Qian, *Records of the Grand Historian: Qin Dynasty*, trans. Burton Watson (Hong Kong and New York: Columbia University Press, 1993)

Sima Qian, *Shi Ji*, Vol. I-X (Beijing: Zhonghua Shuju, 1982)

Thatcher, Melvin P., "Central Government of the State of Ch'in in the Spring and Autumn Period", *Journal of Oriental Studies* 23, (I) 1985: 29-53

Wang Xueli, *Qin du Xianyang* (The Qin Capital of Xianyang) (Xi'an: Shaanxi Renmin Chubanshe, 1985)

Wang Xueli (ed.), *Qin wuzhi wenhua shi* (The History of Qin Dynasty Material Culture) (Xi'an: San Qin Chubanshe, 1994)

Wang Xueli (ed.), *Qin yong zhuanti yanjiu* (Special Studies on Qin Terracotta Figures) (Xi'an: San Qin Chubanshe, 1994)

Wheatley, Paul, *The Pivot of the Four Quarters. A Preliminary Enquiry into the Origins and Character of the Ancient Chinese City* (Edinburgh: University Press, 1971)

Xianyangshi Wenwu-Kaogu Yanjiusuo, *Taerpo Qin mu* (The Qin Tombs of Taerpo) (Xi'an: San Qin Chubanshe, 1998)

Yang Kuan, *Zhangguo shi* (History of the Warring States) (Shanghai: Renmin Chubanshe, 1980)

Ye Xiaoyan, *Qin mu chutan* (Discussions on the Qin Graves) (Kao Gu, 1982), I: 65-73

Yunmeng Shuihudi Qin Mu (Qin Graves at Shuihudi near Yunmeng) (Beijing: Wenwu Chubanshe, 1981)

BIBLIOGRAPHY OF TEXTS
LIONELLO LANCIOTTI

Cheng, A., *Storia del pensiero cinese* (Turin: Einaudi, 1997)

Confucian School: Lippiello, Tiziana (ed.), *Confucio, I dialoghi* (Turin: Einaudi, 2003)

Dubs, H.H., *Hsuntze, the Moulder of Ancient Confucianism* (London: Probsthain, 1927)

Graham, Angus C., *La ricerca del Tao. Il dibattito filosofico nella Cina classica* (Vicenza: Neri Pozza, 1999)

Graham, Angus C., *Later Mohist Logic* (Hong Kong: S.O.A.S, 1978)

Han Fei Tzu, *Works*, trans. W.K. Liao, 2 vols. (London: Probsthain, 1959)

Lanciotti, Lionello, *Confucio: la vita e l'insegnamento* (Rome: Ubaldini, 1997)

Legalist school: *The Book of Lord Shang. A classic of the Chinese School of Law*, trans. J.J.L. Duyvendak (London: Probsthain, 1928)

Minor schools: Andreini, Attilio, *Il pensiero di Yang Zhu* (Trieste: Edizioni Università, 2000)

Mohist school: *Mo-Tzu, Basic Writings*, trans. Burton Watson (New York and London: Columbia U.P., 1963)

Mo Ti, *Solidarität und allgemeine Menschenliebe übersetzt von H. Schmidt-Glintzer* (Dusseldorf: Diederischs, 1975)

Mo Ti gegen den Krieg, *übersetzt von H. Schmidt-Glintzer* (Dusseldorf: Diederichs, 1975)

Scarpari, Maurizio, *La concezione della natura umana e il problema del male* (Venice: Cafoscarina, 1997)

Taoist School: Andreini, Attilio (ed.), *Laozi, Genesi del "Daodejing"* (Turin: Einaudi, 2004)

The Book of Lieh-tzu: a new translation, trans. A.C. Graham (London: John Murray, 1960)

The complete works of Chuang Tzu, trans. Burton Watson (New York and London: Columbia U.P., 1968)

Vandermeersch, Léon, *La formation du Légisme* (Paris: E.F.E.O., 1965)

BIBLIOGRAPHY OF TEXTS MAURIZIO SCARPARI

Hulsewè, A.F.P., *Remnants of Han Law* (Leiden: Brill, 1955)

Hulsewè, A.F.P., *Remnants of Ch'in Law: An Annotated Translation of the Ch'in Legal Administrative Rules of the 3rd Century B.C. Discovered in Yün-meng Prefecture, Hu-pei Province, in 1975* (Leiden: Brill, 1985)

Lewis, Mark Edward, *Writing and Authority in Early China* (Albany: State University of New York Press, 1999)

Scarpari, Maurizio, "Le leggi penali del principe di Lü", Annali di Ca' Foscari, 15, 3 (1976) 123-132

Scarpari, Maurizio, "Riscrivere la storia e la cultura della Cina antica: credenze religiose, correnti di pensiero e società alla luce delle recenti scoperte archeologiche", in Lionello Lanciotti (ed.), *Conoscere la Cina* (Turin: Fondazione Giovanni Agnelli, 2000), 113-126

Scarpari, Maurizio, *Antica Cina, la Civiltà Cinese dalle origini alla dinastia Tang* (Vercelli: White Star, 2000)

Shaughnessey, Edward L. (ed.), *New Sources of Early Chinese History: An Introduction to the Reading of Inscriptions and Manuscripts* (Berkeley: The Society for the Study of Early China and The Institute of East Asian Studies, 1997)

Shuihudi Qinmu zhujian (Beijing: Wenwu chubanshe, 1978)

Skosey, Laura A., "The Legal System and Legal Tradition of the Western Zhou (ca. 1045-771 B.C.E.)" (Chicago: PhD dissertation, 1996)

Twitchett, Dennis, and Loewe, Michael (eds.), *The Cambridge History of Ancient China: The Ch'in and Han Empires (221- B.C.-A.D. 220)*, Vol. I (Cambridge: Cambridge University Press, 1986)

Yates, R.D.S. and K.C.D. McLeod, "Forms of Ch'in Law: An Annotated Translation of the Feng-chen shi", in *Harvard Journal of Asiatic Studies*, 41 (1981)

Yates, R.D.S., "Some Notes on Ch'in Law. A Review Article of Remnants of Ch'in Law, by A.F.P.Hulsewè", in *Early China*, 11-12 (1985-1987)

Yunmeng Shuihudi Qin Mu (Beijing: Wenwu Chubanshe, 1981)

BIBLIOGRAPHY OF TEXTS ALEXANDRA WETZEL

Bayerisches Landesamt für Denkmalpflege, Museum of the Terracotta Warriors and Horses (ed.), Annual Reports 1999 and 2000, Part I: "Research reports and documentations" (Munich: Bayerisches Landesamt für Denkmalpflege, 2001)

Bayerisches Landesamt für Denkmalpflege, Museum of the Terracotta Warriors and Horses (ed.), Annual Reports 1999 and 2000, Part II: "Interim reports and travel reports" (Munich: Bayerisches Landesamt für Denkmalpflege, 2001)

Blänsdorf, Catharina, Emmerling, Erwin, Petzet, Michael (eds.), *The Terracotta Army of the First Chinese Emperor Qin Shi Huang* (Munich: Arbeitshefte des Bayerischen Landesamtes für Denkmalpflege, Vol. 83, 2001)

Terracotta Army Museum (ed.), *Qin Shihuang bingmuyong bowuguan* (The Terracotta Army Museum of Qin Shi Huang), (Beijing: Wenwu chubanshe, 1999)

Terracotta Army Museum (ed.), *Qin Shihuang ling tong che ma xiufu baogao* (Report on the Restoration of the Bronze Horses and Chariots of Qin Shi Huang's Burial Mound), (Beijing: Wenwu chubanshe, 1998)

Terracotta Army Museum, Research Center of Shaanxi Province (ed.), *Qin Shihuang ling tong che ma xiufu baogao* (Report on the excavation of the bronze horses and chariots of Qin Shi Huang's burial mound), (Beijing: Wenwu chubanshe, 1998)

Terracotta Army Museum, Research Center of Shaanxi Province (ed.), *Qin Shihuangdi ling yuan kaogu baogao* (Archaeological report on the necropolis of the Emperor Qin Shi Huang), (Beijing: Kexue chubanshe, 2000)

Scheder, Siegfried, *The Stone Armour from the Burial Complex of Qin Shi Huang. Pilot Study Report in Collaboration with the Museum of the Terracotta Warriors and Horses in Lintong* (Munich: Bayerisches Landesamt für Denkmalpflege, 2001)

Wenwu tiandi (weekly magazine), "Qin yong Qin ling Qin Shihuang zhuanhao" (Special issue on the figures, burial mound and emperor of the Qin dynasty), (Beijing, October 2002)

Yongyi, Wu, Tinghao, Zhang, Petzet, Michael, Emmerling, Erwin and Blänsdorf, Catharina (eds.), "The Polychromy of Antique Sculptures and the Terracotta Army of the First Chinese Emperor. Studies on Materials, Painting Techniques and Conservation", Report of the International Conference of Xi'an, China, March 1999 (Munich: Arbeitshefte des Bayerischen Landesamtes für Denkmalpflege, Vol. III, 2001)

PHOTO CREDITS

page 79 top Asian Art & Archaeology, Inc./Corbis/Contrasto

page 79 bottom Cultural Relics Publishing House, Beijing

Pagg 82-83 Panorama Stock

page 84 Panorama Stock

page 85 Panorama Stock

page 86 top and bottom Panorama Stock

page 87 left and right Panorama Stock

page 89 Panorama Stock

page 92 Panorama Stock

page 94 Bibliothèque nationale de France

page 95 Panorama Stock

page 96 Panorama Stock

page 97 Panorama Stock

page 98 Angelo Colombo/ Archivio White Star

page 99 Panorama Stock

page 100 left Panorama Stock

page 100 right Thierry Ollivier/Photo RMN

page 101 Panorama Stock

page 102 Panorama Stock

page 103 Panorama Stock

page 104 Panorama Stock

page 105 Panorama Stock

page 106 Panorama Stock

page 107 left and right Panorama Stock

page 110 Archivio Scala

page 111 Panorama Stock

pages 112-113 The Bridgeman Art Library/Archivio Alinari

page 114 Charles & Josette Lenars/Corbis/Contrasto

page 115 Mary Evans Picture Library

page 117 in alto Cultural Relics Publishing House, Beijing

page 120 and 121 Taisei Corporation

page 130 Bibliothèque Nationale Paris/The Art Archive

pages 134-135 Angelo Colombo/Archivio White Star

page 136 and 137 Taisei Corporation

page 145 Cultural Relics Publishing House, Beijing

page 163 Cultural Relics Publishing House, Beijing

page 164 left, center and right Cultural Relics Publishing House, Beijing

pages 170-171 Cultural Relics Publishing House, Beijing

page 172 left and right Cultural Relics Publishing House, Beijing

page 173 Cultural Relics Publishing House, Beijing

page 174 Cultural Relics Publishing House, Beijing

page 175 left and right Cultural Relics Publishing House, Beijing

page 178 and 179 Cultural Relics Publishing House, Beijing

page 180 bottom Cultural Relics Publishing House, Beijing

page 182 left and right Cultural Relics Publishing House, Beijing

page 182-183 Cultural Relics Publishing House, Beijing

page 183 Cultural Relics Publishing House, Beijing

pages 190-191 Elisabetta Ferrero/Archivio White Star

page 208 left Cultural Relics Publishing House, Beijing

page 208 right Roberto Ciarla

page 209 Cultural Relics Publishing House, Beijing

page 216 Roberto Ciarla

pages 220-221 bottom Cultural Relics Publishing House, Beijing

page 223 right Cultural Relics Publishing House, Beijing

page 236 center right China Photographic Publishing House

page 248 Photoservice Electa/AKG

page 249 Bayerisches Denkmalamt, München (Germany)

page 256 left and right Bayerisches Denkmalamt, München (Germany)

page 257 Bayerisches Denkmalamt, München (Germany)

page 259 Imagine China/Contrasto

page 263 Bayerisches Denkmalamt, München (Germany)

page 267 center Bayerisches Denkmalamt, München (Germany)

page 271 left Cultural Relics Publishing House, Beijing

ACKNOWLEDGMENTS

The Publisher would like to thank, for the precious cooperation to the realization of this book:

Zhang Tinhao, Director, General Shanxi Provincial Administration of Culture Heritage
Wang Limei, Director, The Millennium World Art Museum
Wu Yongqi, Director, The Museum of Qin Terra-cotta Warriors and Horses
Zhan Changfa, Director, Sino-Italian Cooperation Training Center of Conservation and Restoration for Cultural Heritage

The Publisher would also like to thank:
Catharina Blänsdorf, Bayerisches Denkmalamt, Munich
Giudo Paradisi photography assistant;
Alessandra Morelli

The Editor would like to thank Lionello Lanciotti, Maurizio Scarpari and Alexandra Wetzel, who enthusiastically agreed to work on this book, offering their time, patience and in-depth knowledge of the subject.